PENGUIN BOOKS
A GUIDE TO TUSCANY

James Bentley is an experienced travel writer whose books include: *The Loire*, *Life and Food in the Dordogne*, *Secrets of Mount Sinai*, *Oberammergau and the Passion Play*, *West Germany and Berlin* and *The Languedoc*. His *Guide to the Dordogne* (Penguin 1986) led the *Evening Standard* to write: 'France with a Bentley – it's the only way to travel.'

A Guide to Tuscany

JAMES BENTLEY

PENGUIN BOOKS

Penguin Books Ltd, 27 Wrights Lane, London w8 5TZ (Publishing and Editorial)
and Harmondsworth, Middlesex, England (Distribution and Warehouse)
Viking Penguin Inc., 40 West 23rd Street, New York, New York 10010, USA
Penguin Books Australia Ltd, Ringwood, Victoria, Australia
Penguin Books Canada Ltd, 2801 John Street, Markham, Ontario, Canada L3R 1B4
Penguin Books (NZ) Ltd, 182–190 Wairau Road, Auckland 10, New Zealand

First published by Viking 1987
Published in Penguin Books 1988

Copyright © James Bentley, 1987
All rights reserved

Made and printed in Great Britain by
Richard Clay Ltd, Bungay, Suffolk
Filmset in Monophoto Sabon

Contents

List of Illustrations

Photographs by courtesy of the Italian State Tourist Office (ENIT), London.

Preface

Tuscany is ancient. My book begins with the Etruscans, who created their great civilization there many centuries before Christ, the men (as D. H. Lawrence pictured them) 'naked, darkly ruddy-coloured from the sun and wind, with strong, insouciant bodies', the women 'wearing the loose, becoming smock of white or blue linen'; and somebody, surely, 'singing, because the Etruscans had a passion for music, and an inner carelessness'.

This book is also about a superb countryside: 'the little pointed green hills; and the white oxen and the poplars and cypresses and the sculptured shaped infinitely musical, flushed green land from here to Abbazia', which so entranced Virginia Woolf. It is about the British who have warmed to Tuscany. It is about the artists, architects and writers who have enriched life in what must be the finest group of exquisite towns and cities in the whole world.

It is also about Tuscan wine and cooking which (as Elizabeth Romer observed in her enchanting book *The Tuscan Year*), by making use of the freshest ingredients of superior quality unadorned with anything to mask the intrinsic excellence of the basic food, expresses perfectly the character of the Tuscans themselves: 'nothing more than our old virtue of *simplicitas* – recognizing things for what they really are'.

In writing this book I have been extremely grateful for the help of Signora Giovanna Burnet, Miss Joanna Doherty of the Italian Wine Centre, Mrs Audrey Bentley (of course), Signor Italo Somariello of the Italian State Tourist Board, the Revd Neil Handley, Mr Michael Alcock, the staff of Slough Reference Library and British Airways.

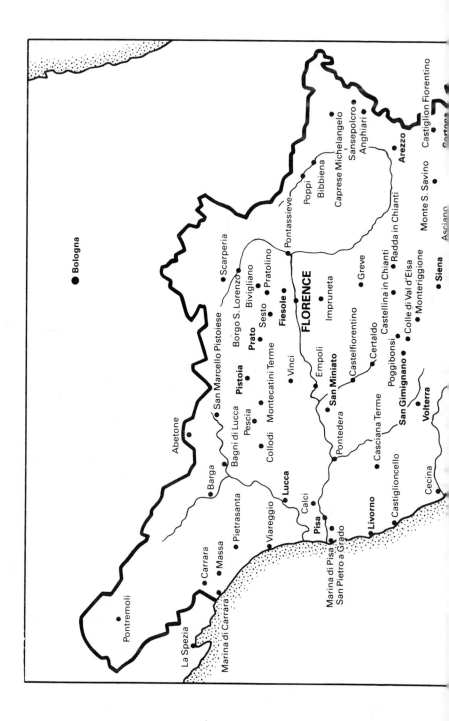

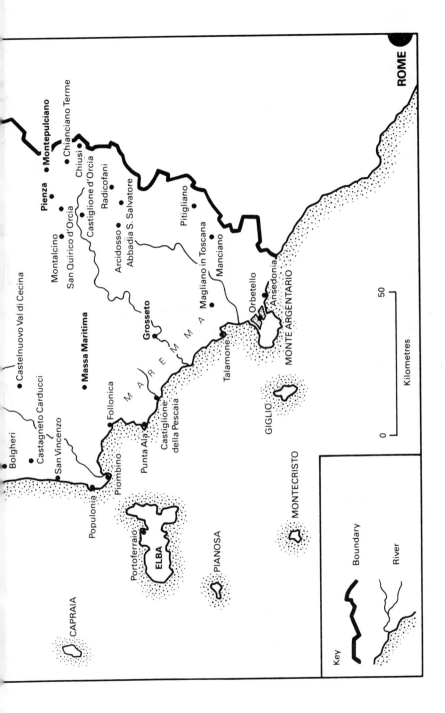

I

From the Etruscans to the Renaissance

In the city of Chiusi in the sixth century before Christ lived the legendary Etruscan king Lars Porsena. When Tarquinius Superbus was expelled from Rome, he took refuge here, and to avenge him Lars Porsena, at the head of a huge army, advanced on Rome, where he planned to establish a Tuscan king. In spite of the famous defence of the Tiber by Horatius, Lars Porsena did reach the Janiculum and even managed to forbid the Romans to manufacture any more iron weapons.

Pliny tells us more about Lars Porsena: that the king hewed for himself a tomb out of the stone at Chiusi, three hundred feet long and sixty feet high, and there he lies, his body protected by a labyrinth so complex that only by marking the route with a length of string could anyone entering hope to find the way out again. As yet no one has discovered this tomb, but you can visit others at Chiusi. The finest is the so-called Tomb of the Ape (Tomba della Scimmia) dating from the early fifth century BC. You descend twenty-seven Etruscan steps into the excavated tufa as far as the original door of the tomb. The first burial chamber is no more than 2.7 m (9 ft) in height, but it is almost entirely covered with animated wall-paintings: the heads of gorgons on the ceiling; on the walls athletes, dancers and a she-ape tied to a tree (hence the name of this tomb). In the next chamber are paintings of naked youths exercising, and this in turn leads to other chambers with benches for cinerary urns. In the national Etruscan museum (situated on the Piazza della Cattedrale at Chiusi, and where you find a guide to take you round the tombs), amongst many fine Etruscan urns and sarcophagi is an alabaster urn from the Tomba della Scimmia, carved with a portrait of Lars Sentinates Caesar.

At Vetulonia near Piombino you can visit other Etruscan tombs that more closely approach the dimensions reported by Pliny for the tomb of Lars Porsena. The charming hill-top village of Vetulonia (not far from the modern seaside resort of Follónica) was actually built on a great Etruscan necropolis. Nearly all the best objects excavated here have gone to the Archaeological Museum of Florence, but the tombs themselves, dating from the seventh century B C, are remarkable. The finest, the Tumulo della Pietrera, some 3 km out of the village, is domed, and is 4.9 m (16 ft) wide and 11 m (36 ft) high. From here it is not far to Populonia, where splendid tombs, some with domes, some small, individual graves, some used by more than one family, were uncovered in a beautiful state of preservation in 1908. One of the excavated tombs at Populonia takes the form of a perfect small stone temple, while another is a huge round affair.

Scholars cannot agree precisely where the remarkable people who built these tombs came from. Some scholars allege that they were indigenous to Italy. Others argue that they came here from Asia Minor some time after the Trojan War. The evidence usually advanced is artistic: in the seventh century B C, for instance, Etruscan art displays powerful oriental aspects. But this evidence is far from conclusive, for any study of the many thousands of beautiful works the Etruscans left behind over six centuries reveals how skilled they were at adopting influences from elsewhere and making them their own.

Wherever they came from, the Etruscans dominated the whole of modern Tuscany and much more of Italy by the mid seventh century B C. South and east of the Tiber they faced strong opposition from the Umbrians and the Picenes. To the north they were unconquerable. They established their city of Felsina where Bologna is now; they pushed eastwards as far as Rimini and Ravenna; they reached Volterra and far beyond to the cities of Galli and Paeti north of the River Po. Then they felt strong enough to push south, reaching Salerno and Pompeii. Only when they attacked the Greeks at Cumae in 524 B C were the Etruscans defeated in battle and their advance checked. They none the less had established a thriving economy and agriculture, and their twelve greatest cities had set themselves up in a powerful confederation. Etruria was at the height of its power around 500 B C. Not till the third century B C did the Etruscans finally come under the burgeoning sway of Rome.

To the Romans they brought their own particular learning. In the words of the Emperor Claudius (reported by Tacitus), 'it frequently happened that when the state fell on evil days, the Etruscan sooth-sayers were summoned to Rome and ceremonies were revived and thereafter faithfully observed. The leading citizens of Etruria were the depositories of this religious learning and, either of their own accord or at the request of the Roman Senate, passed it on to their descendants.' So prized was this religious learning that Cornelius Labeo in the second century AD wrote a commentary on it in fifteen volumes.

The Etruscans themselves have left us over 10,000 inscriptions, some of them written with one line reading left to right and the next right to left. Probably deriving from the Chalcidian Greek alphabet, Etruscan fathered other Italic alphabets including the Latin that finally replaced it (though the language continued to be spoken well into the Christian era). As yet, unfortunately, no one today can read Etruscan. In 1985 the University of Perugia set up a four-year project to break the code by establishing a database of a hundred thousand Etruscan words, about 80 per cent of which are still meaningless to us.

Perugia already possesses one largely deciphered Etruscan 'document', namely the famous 'Cippus' – a series of third-century property deeds inscribed on a stone. Soon material from a yet more remarkable Etruscan document will be fed into its computer. This is the only Etruscan book known to us: a linen text discovered by a Croatian explorer in the mid nineteenth century. A group of Etruscan merchants travelling in Egypt in the first century BC are thought to have lost it. About fifty years later an Egyptian cut it into strips and wrapped them round the mummy of a fifteen-year-old girl. The Croatian discovery of this mummy nearly two thousand years later brought the book to Zagreb, where it lay virtually unknown until 1984, when it was taken for restoration to Berne in Switzerland.

This one book, now half-deciphered, is, fascinatingly, a priests' manual of instruction. It sets out the Etruscan religious year, giving instructions for sacrifices and offerings of wine and milk in connection with the earth god, the sea god and the god of the rising sun. We know from other sources that the Etruscans longed for some reassurance about the future. They specialized in divination by examining animals' livers. Cicero records the legend that their skill in this matter derived from a miraculous revelation from a certain Tages, who 'had the appearance of a child but the wisdom of an old man'. He appeared to a startled Etruscan who was ploughing near Tarquinia. The ploughman soon gathered many others to hear what the child-sage had to say. 'Tages then spoke on many subjects as the crowd listened,' wrote Cicero, 'and they collected and wrote down all he said. And what in fact he spoke of was the science of divination from the entrails of animals.'

Fear of the future and the attempt to dissolve this fear by means of religion was strongly allied in Etruscan religion (and its related art) with fear of death and the hope for a life after it. That death inspired enormous terror is vividly apparent, for instance, on a tufa urn in the Museo Guarnacci in Volterra. Dating from the early first century BC, the urn depicts a cloaked man returning from the grave to visit his wife, who lies in bed (perhaps seriously ill), while two terrified figures to the right of the bed flee. Another urn from the same museum, this time made of alabaster a hundred years earlier than the tufa urn, depicts a man about to leave for the next world, along with his already dead parents. To take him away a messenger has arrived on horseback, leading a riderless steed.

The gladiatorial combats painted on the walls of Etruscan tombs are not simply entertaining pictures of athletes; they also have a deep significance for the life to come of those buried there, especially if the combat leads to death. A fourth-century Christian writer named Arnobius tells us that the Etruscan Books of the Dead commend the shedding of the blood of animals to placate the deities of the underworld and thus release the dead, who then (says Arnobius) were believed to have become divine themselves.

Since the followers of Bacchus believed in life after death, Bacchic cults became increasingly popular in Etruria from the fourth century BC onwards. As a result, Bacchic processions, Dionysian rites and dancers carrying Bacchic wands add merrier elements to the illustrations on Etruscan funeral urns and sarcophagi.

Many of the sarcophagi are splendid. Usually an effigy of the deceased is sculpted on the lid and often the reliefs depict scenes from classical mythology. The reliefs on the so-called Sarcophagus of the Magnate at Tarquinia (in the Museo Nazionale Tarquiniense, housed in the former Palazzo Vitelleschi) illustrate a battle between the Greeks and the Amazons. A relief on a second-century-BC alabaster urn in the Museo Guarnacci, Volterra, depicts Capaneus hurtling down from the walls of Thebes. Classical mythology clearly fascinated the Etruscans and invades some of their most sombre tombs. A mid-sixth-century-BC fresco in the Tomb of the Bulls, Tarquinia, shows Achilles about to ambush and kill Troilus, the son of Priam. It is hard to know what relationship was conceived between this scene and the Etruscan corpses that once lay here. Even more puzzling is the connection between death and the realistic, almost erotic depiction of love-making in the frieze above (though some ingenious scholars have suggested that generation and rebirth might have gone hand in hand in Etruscan religious thought).

Perhaps the fact that most of our Etruscan treasures come from tombs lends an unduly morbid air to much Etruscan art. In fact the Etruscan culture produced an extraordinary variety of artistic treasure. The marble quarries of Carrara were not properly opened up until the first century BC, and the Etruscans in consequence had to use for their art such materials as local stone, terracotta, bronze and (in the region of Volterra) alabaster. Out of these they fashioned vases, soldiers, groups of women conversing, statues of orators and gods, curious elongated statuettes, reliefs of bizarre demons, scenes of revellers and satyrs. They could create the most tender images. In the Museo Archeologico Mecenate at Arezzo are two sculpted lovers, only 14 cm (5½ in) high, dating from the fifth century BC. Of these the writer Laura Huxley has observed: '"Eroticism" can transform a human being into a brutal beast or a godlike creature . . . What a relief to see the amorous nobility of the Etruscan lovers, the depth of their unending ecstasy!' The Etruscans, she recalls, were conquerors and gamblers, traders, warriors and artists whose language we still cannot decipher. 'It is our good fortune that the record of that civilization has come to us in magnificent frescos, potteries, carvings. From this one we can assume the Etruscans loved beautifully.'

It is all too easy to read into the exquisite and sometimes alien remains of Etruscan civilization exactly what one wishes. To the British novelist and poet D. H. Lawrence, wandering about the tombs of Etruria, Etruscan works of art spoke of a people of tremendous vitality. Far from finding the Etruscans morbidly obsessed with death and the fearful hope of a future life, he believed that their civilization represented his own ideal of a free and natural existence, in touch with primordial forces. 'Fragments of people at banquets, limbs that dance without dancers, birds that fly into nowhere, lions whose devouring heads are devoured away!' he exclaimed. 'Once it was all bright and dancing; the delight of the underworld; honouring the dead with wine, and flutes playing for a dance, and limbs whirling and pressing. And it was deep and sincere honour rendered to the dead and to the mysteries. It is contrary to our ideas, but the ancients had their own philosophy for it.' Lawrence sensed the vitality of their religion. 'They know the gods in their very fingertips,' he wrote. 'The wonderful fragments of limbs and bodies that dance on in a field of obliteration still know the gods, and make it evident to us.'

Their extremely aggressive statuettes of warriors also make it evident, to me at any rate, what a warlike race they were. Macaulay's poem 'Horatius' has as its hero a Roman, not the ranks of Lars Porsena invading the city of Rome. Even so Macaulay perfectly catches in his verse the gleaming vigour that we can still sense in the military figurines of the Etruscans:

> Meanwhile the Tuscan army,
>   Right glorious to behold,
> Came flashing back the noonday light,
> Rank behind rank, like surges bright
>   Of a broad sea of gold.
> Four hundred trumpets sounded
>   A peal of warlike glee,
> As that great host, with measured tread,
> And spears advanced, and ensigns spread,
> Rolled slowly towards the bridge's head,
>   Where stood the dauntless Three.

In the end the military might of Rome crushed the Etruscans. In the Roman civil war of the eighties BC many Etruscans fought on the side of Gaius Marius, who lost. At the end of the struggles the only resistance against the victor, Sulla, was to be found in Etruria. It took him two years to starve out Volterra. Then Sulla made himself dictator and began mercilessly to stamp out those who had defied him. Great Etruscan families were outlawed and their property seized, with a reward for anyone who should kill them. Great Etruscan cities, such as Chiusi and Arezzo, were savagely pillaged. Any city that had opposed Sulla lost its Roman citizenship. He sent troops to execute his Etruscan foes and he let his own veterans colonize their land. After his death these terrible reprisals eased. Cicero in particular did much to bring back the Etruscans into good favour at Rome. But they were a broken nation.

> Were they then vicious, the slender, tender-footed,
> Long-nosed men of Etruria?
> Or was their way only evasive and different, dark, like
> cypress-trees in a wind?

asked D. H. Lawrence.

> They are dead, with all their vices,
> And all that is left
> Is the shadowy monomania of some cypresses
> And tombs.
>
> What would I not give
> To bring back the rare and orchid-like
> Evil-yclept Etruscan? . . .
>
> For oh, I know, in the dust where we have buried
> The silenced races and all their abominations,
> We have buried so much of the delicate magic of life.

Lawrence returned to the theme. 'Because a fool kills a nightingale with a stone, is he therefore greater than the nightingale? Because the Roman took the life out of the Etruscan, was he therefore greater than the Etruscan? Not he! Rome fell, and the Roman phenomenon with it. Italy today is far more Etruscan in its pulse than Roman: and will always be so.'

Even so the Romans made their mark on Tuscany. Volterra, for example, possesses a splendid Etruscan gateway and Etruscan walls whose circumference was three times that of her medieval ramparts. But the city also boasts magnificent Roman baths with a mosaic pavement and an equally fine Roman theatre. At Fiesole 8 km outside Florence you can see Etruscan and Roman achievements side by side. Here the Roman amphitheatre, constructed in 80 BC to seat 3,000 spectators, is still used for plays. Close by are the Roman baths, built in the first century B C and enlarged by the Emperor Hadrian. Between these baths and a Roman temple that was excavated in 1918 you can see the old Etruscan gateway and wall. And lower down are the remains of an Etruscan temple built two centuries before the Roman one.

Other extensive excavated Roman remains well worth visiting are at Ansedonia on the Tuscan coast just south of Orbetello. Ansedonia was once the Roman city of Cosa, founded nearly three hundred years before Christ. Here the Romans chose a site with a lovely view over the Busano lagoon. They surrounded their city with walls, boasting no fewer than eighteen towers that still stand largely intact. The way through the Porta Romana leads to the forum, close to where a citizen's house has been excavated and partly restored. Once this city had two temples as well as the acropolis that is rewarding to climb up to, for itself and for its view out to sea towards the island of Giannutri. This is in truth an area rich in Roman remains. Not far away at Sette Finestre recent excavations have brought to light a villa built in the first century B C. Here are Roman wall-paintings of the second and third centuries A D. Here too you can see mosaic floors and a Roman farm containing presses for olives and grapes.

Fifty or so kilometres north (by way of Grosseto) at Roselle lies another splendid Roman site on an Etruscan base. Ancient Roselle is now mostly a romantic ruin, though nearly two miles of its Roman–Etruscan walls (which, as you can easily make out, were once pierced by six gates) are intact. Inside the walls you can visit the Roman forum, the baths, houses and streets, with more being excavated each year.

The Romans built roads for Etruria, which became the seventh region of Italy under the Empire. They built their villas on Monte Argenario and on Elba. They colonized the last enthusiastically, founding towns where now have grown Portoferraio, Capoliveri and Marciana. From Elba they took granite to build the Pantheon in Rome and iron ore for their legions' swords. The Ligurian city of Pisa had become a Roman colony in 180 B C and was developed as an important naval base. (Augustus Caesar named the city 'Colonia Julia Pisana'.) And Julius Caesar founded Florence at the easiest spot to cross the Arno. For the next two centuries this Roman city so flourished that it grew huge, dwarfing the neighbouring city of Fiesole which the Etruscans had founded in the fifth century B C.

Lucca, a town that came to overshadow Florence for centuries after the decline of Rome, was also significant for Julius Caesar. Here in 56 BC he, Pompey and Crassus set up the first triumvirate. The rectangular Roman walls of Lucca, which once stood 8–9 m (26–29 ft) high and were made from great blocks of limestone, have disappeared – save for one charming remnant, preserved *inside* the early-fourteenth-century church of Santa Maria della Rosa because part of the little building is supported by it. As well as partly keeping its Roman street plan, Lucca also retains another particularly delightful Roman feature: the Piazza Amfiteatro. Although houses were built here in the middle ages on the site of the old Roman amphitheatre, the Piazza, set out in its present form in 1830 without destroying two rows of fifty-four Roman arches, perfectly preserves its ancient elliptical shape.

If legend is to be countenanced, Siena was founded as a result of Roman rivalries – as the symbol of that city, a she-wolf, suckling Romulus and Remus, indicates. Apparently Ascius and Senius, the sons of Remus, were obliged to flee from Rome to escape the wrath of their uncle Romulus. They called the spot where they stopped to make sacrifices to Diana and Apollo 'Castelsenio' (still the name of a district of Siena), around which the present city gradually developed. Two alternative legends connected with this episode account for Siena's city colours: black and white. Either Senius rode a white horse and Ascius a black one; or else the smoke from Diana's altar rose white and the smoke from Apollo's black.

Much of Tuscany soon became Christian. Just outside Pisa stands the lovely church of San Pietro a Grado where St Peter may well have landed on his journey from Antioch to Rome. Lucca claims to have been the first Tuscan city to accept the new faith, converted by St Peter's disciple Paulinus. Volterra was the birthplace of St Linus, the second Bishop of Rome. The first evangelist of Siena was Ansano Anicio, of the noble Roman Anicii family, who died a martyr under Diocletian in AD 303.

The Roman Empire declined and fell, and Tuscany became prey to the barbarians. Lucca managed to withstand a long siege by the Byzantines but fell to the Goths. Under Totila the Goths savaged Florence in 552, in spite of her new Byzantine walls. Finally the Lombards gained control of the whole region, basing their rule on Lucca. These invaders, the least civilized yet seen in Italy, succumbed to Christianity. They were goldsmiths and some of their works of art survive in Tuscany. The Bargello, Florence, for instance, contains a striking copper frontal made in 600. In Pisa, tombs and two Lombardic sarcophagi were discovered near the cathedral and are now housed in the San Matteo Museum.

Lombardic rule in Tuscany was replaced in 774 A D by that of the Franks under Charlemagne. Lucca remained the centre of power, and when the Franks in the early ninth century made the region a margravate the first margrave established himself there. Tuscan churches began to flourish again. The Benedictines founded a splendid monastery at Abbadia San Salvatore, and their church – though rebuilt – retains its marvellous and huge eighth-century crypt.

When the margravate of Tuscany became one of the greatest in the Empire, its rulers continued to endow new religious foundations, many of which remain to this day. In 978, for instance, Willa, the widow of margrave Uberto, founded the first religious house inside the walls of Florence, a Benedictine monastery whose church – much rebuilt – is now the Badia Fiorentina in the Via dei Proconsulo. In his turn Willa's son Ugo became margrave (Dante called him *il gran barone*), and on his death was buried in the Badia, in a tomb still to be seen there in the left transept.

Naturally Lucca and its region thrived (though its greatest and most creative architectural period was yet to come, when the margraves were gone and the city had become a free commune). Its eleventh-century bishop, Anselmo da Baggio, became Pope Alexander II and rebuilt the cathedral in 1060 (coming back as pope ten years later to consecrate it). Outside the city the group of spas known as Bagni di Lucca prospered for the first time. (They prosper still.) In 1027 the margravate was conferred on the Canossa family. The daughter of the first of these new margraves, the Countess Matilda, who assumed power in Tuscany in 1076, died in 1115 leaving her lands to the pope – to the eternal anger of the emperors. The margravate of Tuscany was beginning to break up. In the struggle between papacy and emperor the great cities began to free themselves from subjection to either. Yet the emperors long insisted on their rights in Tuscany, continuing to appoint powerful representatives to try to protect their interests there. And they continued to build around Lucca. Barga, for instance, a hill-town dominating the valley of the River Serchio half a dozen kilometres north-west of Bagni di Lucca, was fortified in 1186 by Frederick Barbarossa and – to the surprise of the twentieth-century tourist – given an unexpectedly remarkable romanesque cathedral.

By now another Tuscan city was beginning to benefit architecturally from these imperial representatives, for the eleventh-century margraves decided to transfer their seat from Lucca to the city of San Miniato, half-way between Florence and Pisa. The Lombards had brought St Miniato's body here in the eighth century, and in 783 a new church had been built to honour and house them (to be rebuilt later). In 1046 Countess Matilda was born in San Miniato in what is now called the Torre di Matilde, one of two on the Rocca which Barbarossa was to rebuild. (It has fallen into ruins again, but the towers remain.)

Not all was strife in eleventh-century Tuscany. Men and women still felt the peaceful call of the cloister. One of these was a remarkable saint named Romuald, who at the age of twenty was so horrified that his father had killed a relative in a quarrel about property that he retired from the world to the monastery of Sant'Apollinare in Classe, near Ravenna, to try to expiate the crime. He stayed there only three years, before becoming the disciple of an austere hermit named Marinus, who lived near Venice. Romuald's rejection of the world had not dulled his social conscience or his courage. He and Marinus, helped by the Abbot of Cuxa, persuaded a doge of Venice, who had gained his position by acquiescing in a murder, to repent and resign. The former doge then joined Romuald and Marinus in a new hermitage at Cuxa.

Ten years later Romuald returned to Italy. To his joy, his father had repented of the murder and was himself contemplating living as a monk. The emperor appointed the saint abbot of Sant'Apollinare in Classe, but he resigned after two years to take up once again the more austere life of a hermit. Next he decided to try to convert the Magyars of Hungary, but ill health made him return to his native land. His last great achievements were to establish two new monastic foundations in Tuscany, both dedicated to bringing a new austerity to the Benedictine order, both in exquisite locations and endowed with fascinating buildings, both certainly worth visiting today. The first was at Vallombrosa, 15 km south-east of Pontassieve in the forests of the Pratomango hills. As a plaque records,

John Milton stayed here in 1638, for even that stern Protestant was impressed by Vallombrosa.

In 1023 St Romuald established another community of hermits at Camaldoli, high in the Apennines due west of Vallombrosa. His original hospice is still here, among later fascinating buildings (such as the monastery's sixteenth-century pharmacy). And 300 m higher up the mountains you can visit the spartan cells of the hermitage where Romuald and his fellow reformers chose to live. (There are, happily, many tourist facilities for such of us as possess neither his religious nor his physical stamina.)

Other Tuscans, religious as well as secular, were more warlike. The quarrel between emperor and papacy was developing into that notorious struggle between Guelph (the papal side) and Ghibelline (the imperial supporters) that savagely divided communities and cities. As well as suffering the frightful vicissitudes of this quarrel (which almost bankrupted the city when the pope turned against her), Siena had to cope with her own secular–ecclesiastical strife. As the city reached the apogee of her feudal life, the bishops gained an ascendance soon to be much resented by the three secular consuls who claimed to represent the people. Eventually the consuls won; in 1147 Bishop Raniera was forced out of Siena; the rule of the Commune was decisively established. Yet even now peace had not come to the city. Nobles strove for supremacy over rich merchants; the rich strove against the democrats. Siena cherished territorial ambitions and was galled to lose control of Montalcino, Montepulciano and Poggibonsi in 1235. As a Ghibelline stronghold she was at odds with Guelph Florence – who defeated Siena at the battle of Monteriggione in 1255, was obliged to concede a partial victory at Monteaperti in 1260, and won again at Colle Val d'Elsa in 1269. So treacherous were these battles that Dante's *Inferno* considered as a valid occasion for revenge the battle at Monteaperti, when a treacherous Florentine named Bocca degli Abbati had sheared away the hand of the city's standard-bearer.

And still these people were creating marvellous buildings. The church of Sant'Agostino, Siena, was begun in 1258 (to be rebuilt centuries later). The dome of her cathedral and the apse which was later demolished were built between 1259 and 1264. As these great Tuscan cities attempted to shore up their republican experiments by appointing what they called a '*podestà*' (often a foreigner) to oversee

law and order, each built a great Palazzo del Podestà: Siena's –
undoubtedly one of Tuscany's finest Gothic palaces – between 1297
and 1310; that at Florence (now the Bargello) forty years earlier; that
at San Gimignano begun in 1288. These often battlemented *palazzi*
frequently bear on their facades the coats of arms of each successive
podestà. A Palazzo del Podestà in these years of experimental
government clearly needed complementing by some sort of public
town-hall. So in Florence Arnolfo di Cambio was commissioned in
1299 to build a Palazzo del Popolo, which then – as political power
changed hands – became known successively as the Palazzo dei Signori,
the Palazzo Ducale and finally the Palazzo Vecchio when the city's
Medici rulers left it to live in the Pitti Palace.

Similarly the citizens of Siena built their beautiful Palazzo Pubblico,
with its street-level arcade, between 1297 and 1310 (adding the slender
tower in the 1340s). Siena's experiments in government in these years
produced even more startling and rapid changes than those at Florence.
From 1271 to 1280 a group of Guelph captains ruled the city; from 1280
to 1286 power was in the hands of fifteen governors and defensors; and
from 1287 to 1355 the city was run by a council of nine priors and
defensors. Inside the Palazzo Pubblico you can today visit the debating
chamber from which these nine governed (the 'Sala dei Nove', sometimes called the Room of Peace, or Sala della Pace). On its walls is a
famous cycle of frescos, painted by Ambrogio Lorenzetti in 1338. His
theme – significantly enough – was *Good and Evil Government*.

The fresco gives a unique insight into the political desires of anxious
men and women in late-fourteenth-century Tuscany. In the centre
'Good Government' is represented not, as one would expect, by a
symbol of republicanism but by one single figure, wearing the black
and white colours of Siena. This, however, is no overweening lord,
but a symbolic representative of all those dedicated to justice. As the
inscription underneath declares, 'Wherever this sacred virtue reigns, it
unites many souls, and once united they constitute the Common Good
which rules over them.' This is the ideal Siena, as we gather from her
coat of arms, which he carries, and from the she-wolf and her charges
at his feet. Symbolic representations of justice, of concord and of
peace (reclining on a cushion), of the six great virtues and of faith,
hope and charity are also depicted here, reverenced by twenty-four
Sienese elders.

To the right of this complex scene is illustrated the beneficent effect of good government. In the foreground merchants trade, girls dance, holding each others' hands, a wedding party sets off in procession. Here is portrayed the prosperous city, its squares and shops and narrow streets, its workshops and palaces, its bustling citizens. In the distance the countryside also prospers as citizens hunt, trade, grow crops, work metals, practise medicine, make music and – once again – dance. In between the countryside and the city a naked figure represents safety and carries a scroll proclaiming, 'Let all free men go their way without fear, and let everyone without fear work and sow, while this lady rules over such a community. She has taken away all the power of the wicked.'

Ambrogio Lorenzetti's frescos depicting bad government are much more decayed and less easy to decipher, but you can easily make out soldiers ravaging the land. Justice has been bound. Fear has supplanted safety. And to symbolize contemporary political evil, the coat of arms of France – at that time the chief supporter of Siena's Guelph opponents – has been painted over the whole scene.

In truth, the citizens of Siena scarcely needed any symbolic representation of bad government: the Council of Nine failed to provide it. The Emperor Charles IV occupied the city in 1355. For a time the Visconti of Milan took over. Insurrection and strife throughout the fifteenth century led to the dictatorship from 1502 to 1512 of the merchant Pandolfo Petrucci. After his death the divided city was even attacked by an army sent by Pope Clement VIII, though the papal troops were defeated by the Sienese in 1526. Finally in 1555 the city surrendered to the forces of the Emperor Charles V.

However much these Tuscan city states might seek the freedom to conduct their own affairs, many of them – above all Florence – also strongly desired to dominate the affairs of their neighbours. Florence annexed Fiesole with particular savagery in 1125. Others behaved scarcely less brutally. Cortona sacked Arezzo in 1258. Lucca remained all-powerful in western Tuscany between 1316 and 1328, when her fortunes were directed by the brilliant Castruccio Castracani degli Antelminelli. Soon, however, Pisa dominated this city, until in 1399 she managed to buy her independence from Charles IV (at a cost of a hundred thousand florins). So greatly did the people of Lucca hate the memory of their oppression by Pisa that after this liberation they demolished the fortress which Castruccio Castracani had built in the Piazza Grande (to designs by Giotto), because the Pisans had ruled from it. In its place Lucca built a new Palazzo Pubblico. After 1369 the city managed to remain free until Napoleon gave her as a principality to his sister. When Napoleon fell, Lucca became a duchy belonging to the Bourbons.

Other Tuscan cities lost their independence far earlier, as Florence – increasingly dominated by the Medici – extended her sway, conquering Pistoia, Arezzo, Pisa (weakened by the defeat of her navy by the Genoese in 1284), Livorno and finally Siena, sold to Florence in 1557 by Philip of Spain.

The Medici had become Dukes of Florence in 1530. Now Cosimo de' Medici set his coat of arms on the facade of the once proud Palazzo Pubblico at Siena. And in 1569 the triumph of Florence was sealed when Duke Cosimo was created Grand Duke of Tuscany.

The Medici were international bankers who moved into politics. Giovanni di Bicci de' Medici, who founded the bank in 1397, became public arbiter of Florence in 1421. His son Cosimo the Elder represented the family bank at the Council of Constance and then at the papal court, where by a brilliant stroke he secured from Pius II a monopoly of the Tolfa alum mines (which were essential for Florentine textiles) and became one of the richest men in the world. Many hated him. In 1431 he was indicted of 'having attempted to make himself higher than others', imprisoned in a dungeon in the Palazzo Vecchio, and almost murdered (by poisoning) before being allowed to escape into exile. Four years after Cosimo's indictment, the Medici achieved political power in Florence (by fixing the elections) and he returned in triumph, exiling his enemies in their turn. His wealth now made him secure. Cosimo paid the Sforzas of Milan to provide him with a small army. Instead of following the traditional custom of drawing lots for members of the Senate, he simply appointed them himself.

Yet, surprisingly, the man who had thus so flagrantly made himself virtual dictator of Florence, while publicly appearing to have preserved its constitution, was in many respects and by many accounts an admirable person. He erected a hospital in Jerusalem for poor and sick pilgrims. Machiavelli's history of Florence says that he 'surpassed all others in magnificence and generosity', recounting that after Cosimo's death his son Piero found to his alarm that there was scarcely any needy person in the city to whom his father had not lent considerable sums. Another less flattering contemporary, the Florentine bookseller Vespasiano da Bisticci, tells us that Cosimo spent so much on the arts and on charity because 'he knew his money had not been over-well acquired'.

What no one could deny was Machiavelli's contention that Cosimo loved to enhance the city he ruled with new and splendid buildings:

for in Florence are the convents and churches of San Marco and San Lorenzo and the monastery of Santa Verdiana: in the mountains of Fiesole the church and abbey of San Girolamo; and in the Mugello he not only restored but rebuilt from its foundation a monastery of the Priors Minor.

To these sacred edifices are to be added his private dwellings: one in Florence, of extent and elegance adapted to so great a citizen; and four others, situated at Careggi, Fiesole, Cafaggiolo and Trebbio.

Florence was not, of course, without great public buildings before Cosimo came to power. He had, after all, been imprisoned in one of them, the Palazzo Vecchio, which the seven priors from the city guilds who ruled Florence in the late thirteenth century had built for themselves. All but its famous tower was complete by 1314. Even older was the medieval fortress which became the Palazzo del Podestà in 1261 and later the police headquarters (or *bargello*), from which it takes its present name.

The city's earliest religious masterpiece – at least among those that had survived to the fifteenth century – was its beautiful romanesque Baptistery, built between the mid eleventh century and the early twelfth century and incorporating structures that may well have been five hundred years older. Its octagonal shape, inspired by the Pantheon in Rome and the palatine chapel at Aachen, became the pattern for many later renaissance churches. Its decoration inside and outside deployed the bands of coloured marble already brilliantly used by the architects of Pisa and Lucca.

Andrea Pisano had come from Pisa in the 1330s to design and cast the great bronze doors to the south of this Baptistery, illustrating scenes from the life of John the Baptist. (The marvellous bronze doors to the north and east are by the Florentine sculptor and goldsmith Lorenzo Ghiberti, who had won a competition to make them in the early fifteenth century. These are the doors, particularly the east one with scenes from the Old Testament, that Michelangelo described as 'worthy of paradise'.)

Andrea Pisano stayed on in Florence to design at least part of the cathedral bell-tower, even though it is always dubbed '*il campanile di Giotto*', for Giotti was the master of the cathedral works.

Cosimo would also know the church of Santi Apostoli, nestling – then as now – among medieval houses, though without the renaissance porch it boasts today. Built in the tenth century, the church nowadays reveals its age by sinking lower down than the pavement of the Borgo Santi Apostoli in which it stands, as well as by its green marble columns, two of which had once belonged to nearby Roman baths.

A far more famous church already stood imposingly on its hill in Florence: San Miniato al Monte, first built as a shrine over the tomb of a Christian martyred in AD 303, and then rebuilt, mostly in the first half of the eleventh century, as the abbey church of a Cluniac monastery. Again the church is carried on pillars some of which were re-used from an older building. Its crypt, almost as old as the church of Santi Apostoli, dates from the eleventh century. Its exquisite green and white marble facade was begun around 1090. When the nave was paved in 1207, the monks commissioned a superb marble intarsia decorated with the twelve signs of the zodiac and the symbols of the four Evangelists. And in the same century they incorporated into the facade a mosaic, with a glittering background of gold, depicting Christ flanked by their martyred patron St Minias and by the Blessed Virgin Mary.

A third church, which no longer exists in its ancient form because the Medici themselves decided to rebuild it, was at the time of Cosimo the oldest church in the city. San Lorenzo (lying today behind the Palazzo Medici-Riccardi) had been built in AD 393 at the command of no less a person than St Ambrose of Milan, and for three hundred years served as Florence's first cathedral.

The monastic orders had enriched (and continued to enrich) the religious architecture of Florence. The abbey church of the Dominicans was Santa Maria Novella. They had begun building it in 1246 on the site of a tenth-century oratory. Two humble friars designed the nave, and as the building of Santa Maria Novella progressed, Florentine gothic was created, its first example one of its greatest. Gothic now affected another monastic church – Santa Trinità, which the Vallombrosians had built in the late eleventh century and rebuilt two hundred years later. Under the inspiration of Santa Maria Novella, the monks now employed Neri di Fioravanti to gothicize their own church.

Neri di Fioravanti was one of the two architects charged with overall supervision of by far the most important and original Florentine building of the thirteenth century, Orsanmichele. To the mind of a Christian banker such as Cosimo de' Medici, this must later have seemed a perfect blend of business and religion, for it was designed to serve both as a church and a granary. Its site was a grain market built by Arnolfo di Cambio at the end of the thirteenth century and burned down in 1304. It cost a great deal of money – eight thousand gold pieces for its construction, as well as the donations from the prosperous city guilds, who filled the niches outside with statues to the glory of God, and to their own glory.

Orsanmichele also embodied the civic pride of the city fathers who had taken control of Florence after the expulsion of the Duke of Athens in 1343. Architecturally it is quite unusual: built like a cube, with three huge Gothic windows along each side and two more in the upper storey.

Inside – among many superb works of art – is an unquestioned masterpiece: a Gothic tabernacle built by Andrea Orcagna between 1349 and 1359 to house a miracle-working image of the Virgin Mary (the Madonna delle Grazie, later destroyed by fire and replaced by one painted by Bernardo Daddi). Orcagna decorated his tabernacle with reliefs and enamels, with mosaics of gold and lapis lazuli.

Thus Florence already offered a rich civic leader such as Cosimo not only examples of superb architecture but also the notion that these could both honour God and his saints and at the same time testify to his own munificence. By the time he took power, other new Florentine churches were ready for consecration (in particular the Franciscans' Santa Croce). But what above all excited the whole city was the fact that its new cathedral was nearing completion.

The people of Florence had determined on a new one in the thirteenth century and appointed Arnolfo di Cambio as its architect. When he died in 1302, Giotto took over, though he directed his energies chiefly to the cathedral bell-tower. Amongst the many later architects who worked on the new cathedral were men of the calibre of Giovanni d'Ambrogio and Orcagna himself. By the early fifteenth century the one great task ahead was to design a cupola to crown this lovely new building. And this, as everyone acknowledged, would be technically enormously difficult.

The man who was to achieve this stupendous feat was Filippo Brunelleschi, a protégé of Cosimo de' Medici, and the first – perhaps the greatest – renaissance architect.

2

Brick, Marble, Bronze and Stone

'The day before yesterday, as I was descending upon Florence from the high ridges of the Apennines, my heart was leaping wildly within me,' recorded the French novelist Stendhal. 'What utterly childish excitement! At long last, at a sudden bend in the road, my gaze plunged downward into the heart of the plain, and there, in the far distance, like some sparkling dark mass, I could distinguish the sombre pile of the cathedral of *Santa Maria del Fiore* with its famous Dome, the masterpiece of Brunelleschi.'

Since the years 1420 to 1436 when Brunelleschi raised his cupola over the octagonal drum of Florence cathedral, its outline has dominated and symbolized the city. Yet, as the artist, author and architect Giorgio Vasari recalled, when he first put forward his proposals to the leading citizens of Florence, they dismissed him as an ass. Indeed, he grew so heated when they doubted his plans that the more he explained them, the more sceptical his audience became. 'Several times he was ordered to leave, but he absolutely refused until in the end the ushers bodily carried him away, leaving everyone there convinced he was deranged.' Even later, after he had persuaded the Florentines that he could succeed and had actually finished building the dome, he was forced to submit to another public competition before they were convinced that he was capable of crowning the whole with a lantern.

Filippo Brunelleschi was born in Florence in 1377 and trained as a goldsmith and sculptor before taking up architecture at the age of forty. A masterpiece of his earlier career is the silver altar he made for Pistoia cathedral at the turn of the century. He was brilliant enough to tie with Ghiberti in the competition for designing the new bronze doors of the Baptistery in Florence but was not willing to collaborate in a joint work. Instead he and the Florentine sculptor Donatello went to Rome together to study antique sculpture. They spent so long watching excavations, measuring ruins and examining medallions that people thought they were searching for treasure. What Brunelleschi was trying, successfully, to formulate were the laws of linear perspective. 'He was scarcely concerned with how he ate, drank, lived or dressed,' observed the contemporary chronicler Gianozzo Manetti, 'provided he could satisfy himself with these things to see and measure.' Eventually no piece of architecture Brunelleschi created would lack an overall design in which every element responded to another spatially, through measurable relationships. This was the skill which above all helped him to solve the problem set by the unfinished cathedral of Florence.

The meeting that threw Brunelleschi out took place in 1420 in the office of works attached to Santa Maria del Fiore. Architects had been brought at great expense from France, Germany, England and Spain to offer their opinions on the possibility of building a dome. Many thought the only possible solution lay in raising a central pier to keep it up. Some, Vasari claims, wanted to shore it up with earth into which had been mixed a number of coins, so that when the work was finished greedy citizens looking for the coins would remove the earth for nothing. Brunelleschi alone insisted that the work could be carried out without either earth or huge arches to support the cupola.

'If the method I have worked out is used, what is needed is a double dome, with one vault inside and the other outside, so that a man can walk upright between them,' he said. 'Over the corners of the angles of each of the eight sides the whole fabric must be bound together by dovetailing the stones. The sides must be bound by ties of oak. We shall need to take care over the lights, the stairways, and the conduits to take away the rainwater. As for internal scaffolding, as many of you seem to have forgotten, that will be needed for such tricky matters as mosaics.'

Filippo Brunelleschi began to crown the great dome with its lantern only a few months before his death in 1446 and the work had to be completed by others. By the time his fellow goldsmith and sculptor Andrea Verrocchio had placed the bronze ball and cross at the top of his lantern, the architect lay in his grave, under a simple slab in the south aisle of Santa Maria del Fiore, the only Florentine ever to be honoured by burial in the cathedral. His adopted son Andrea Buggiano took a deathmask to make the architect's bust in the tondo above the grave.

Brunelleschi's genius at creating beautifully proportioned spaces came into its own when he was commissioned to design and build a Foundlings' Hospital in Florence. This Spedale degli Innocenti – still an orphanage five and a half centuries later – stands in the Piazza Santissima Annunziata, which Brunelleschi made into the most elegant square in the whole city, respecting in his design the church of the Annunziata at one end, and leaving it to later renaissance architects to enhance the square still more by means of fine colonnades.

Their colonnades are all inspired by the exquisite colonnade of Corinthian arches Brunelleschi created for his Foundlings' Hospital, based on the classical models he had measured in Rome. As a totally charming culmination of Brunelleschi's work, Andrea della Robbia in 1487 added the delightful blue and white medallions of babies in swaddling clothes to the spandrels of each arch. (There's an art gallery in the Hospital with some outstanding works of art. Among its delights are Botticelli's *Madonna with an Angel*, matched by two other paintings on the same theme by Andrea del Sarto and Filippino Lippi, and an *Adoration of the Magi* by Domenico Ghirlandaio in which the artist has painted himself as the second figure to the right of the Virgin Mary.)

Brunelleschi loved to experiment with spaces. You can see this again by taking a short walk south from the Foundlings' Hospital down the Via di Fibbia and across the Viale degli Alfani to the former church (now a lecture hall) of Santa Maria degli Angeli. Not surprisingly, the Florentines have never much regarded this as a sacred building and generally refer to it as 'Il Castellacio', since it does far more resemble a castle. Brunelleschi had just made another visit to Rome when this commission came, and he decided to model the church on the Temple of Minerva Medica which he had seen there. The decision was revolutionary. Designed on the outside with sixteen sides and inside as an octagon with eight chapels around the centre space, Santa Maria degli Angeli, alas, was never finished. It would have been the first centrally planned church in renaissance Italy.

Fortunately Brunelleschi's monastic church of Santo Spirito, on the south bank of the River Arno, designed in 1435, was completed, though only long after the architect's death. Here his brilliant spatial sense has created a wonderfully tranquil interior, composed of cubes, half-cubes and double-cubes. The transept – three cubes, corresponding to the four cubes of the nave – is linked to the nave by a continuous arcade of Brunelleschi's favourite Corinthian columns. A stroke of genius was to continue the side aisles around the entire building (save for the west end), hollowing the outer walls of each of the thirty-eight chapels with deep niches, so that the whole seems to undulate in a quite remarkable fashion. Brunelleschi deliberately reduced the decorative features inside Santo Spirito to a minimum, so as to emphasize above all the play of its architecture. (He was not of course responsible for the baroque high altar which, though in many ways a treat, goes against the grain of his own vision.)

The Pazzi Chapel he designed for the cloister of Santa Croce in 1429 is equally remarkable in terms of space and perspective. He planned the square in front in a proportion of one to three; the proportions of the main church are two to three; and the chancel is a perfect square. Once again Brunelleschi used Corinthian columns, both inside and on the facade. He built a delicate vaulted dome for this chapel, with little apertures to light up the interior and show to their best advantage Luca della Robbia's terracotta roundels of Evangelists and Apostles.

But my favourite of the churches Brunelleschi designed for Florence is the one commissioned by Cosimo de' Medici: San Lorenzo (my favourite even though, to our great loss, the facade designed for it by no less a genius than Michelangelo was never completed). Because Brunelleschi was at this time almost unknown as an architect, his first commission at San Lorenzo (by Cosimo's father) was to build only the sacristy. He created a splendid dome (designed, as the architect put it, 'with crests and sails', i.e., with the roof stretched like a canvas over its ribs) surmounting a perfect cube. He proudly painted the walls white, to emphasize its grey stone architectural structure. Then he was commissioned to build the church.

The serenity of the church of San Lorenzo derives totally from

Brunelleschi's brilliant use of geometric space. San Lorenzo's columned basilica is based on the Italian Byzantine churches of the fifth and sixth centuries, with a flat wooden roof. As we expect, the columns are Corinthian in style. And he added a lovely dome, a feature Brunelleschi excelled at – and one not found in his Byzantine prototype. Not long after Brunelleschi's death Donatello, ageing himself, designed two marvellous bronze pulpits for the church, courteously mirroring its classical architecture by carving classical motifs around the upper panels. He also decorated the sacristy Brunelleschi designed for San Lorenzo, a building whose gentle greys and white point up its own geometric perfection.

Cosimo de' Medici chose to be buried here, as did many of his successors in the dynasty. He lies under the dome, with a simple (and arrogant) inscription: *Pater Patriae* ('Father of his Country').

A few yards east of the church of San Lorenzo is the *palazzo* that Cosimo built in Florence, the one which Machiavelli described as being 'of extent and elegance adapted to so great a citizen'. Known today as the Palazzo Medici-Riccardi (because it was bought by the Riccardi family in 1659), its architect was Michelozzo di Bartolommeo, who had trained under Ghiberti and then worked with Donatello. He designed massive round arches for the rusticated ground floor, giving way to far more graceful ones on the next and to yet gentler arches on the third storey, all topped by a renaissance cornice. Inside the columned courtyard the Medici arms and reproductions of antique cameos fill the roundels. From here steps lead up to a small, magical chapel. Here in 1459 and 1460 Benozzo Gozzoli painted his famous fresco of the long, winding journey of the Magi, who are processing towards the altarpiece of the Virgin and Child. Gozzoli has done a portrait of himself in the procession (signed on his hat), and leading the worshippers is Lorenzo de' Medici.

Michelozzo's Palazzo Medici-Riccardi was so admired that it became the model for all the later fifteenth-century Florentine palaces. They in their turn continued to break away more and more from traditional medieval designs. In 1446 the multi-gifted Leone Battista Alberti – athlete, musician, playwright, scientist, mathematician and painter as well as architect – designed the Palazzo Rucellai for the rich merchant Giovanni Rucellai. Completed by Alberti's friend and collaborator Bernardo Rossellino, this palace for the first time in Tuscany introduced into its facade classical orders of architecture.

Not to be outdone, another rich Florentine family, the Pazzi, banking rivals of the Medici, commissioned in the 1460s the Palazzo Quaratesi in the Via del Proconsolo. It stands on a rusticated lower wall that (probably) Brunelleschi designed for an earlier building. A decade later this family's rivalry with the Medici reached so savage a peak that they murdered Giuliano de' Medici in Florence cathedral and wounded his brother Lorenzo il Magnifico. Supporters of the Medici trapped Francesco de' Pazzi in this palace, and hanged him and his fellow conspirators from a window of the Palazzo Vecchio.

The lovely Palazzo Antinori (in the Piazza Antinori) also dates from the 1460s, with its charming renaissance well in the courtyard, and a homely washbasin set in an alcove. And in 1489 work was started on the most magnificent of the Florentine palaces, the Palazzo Strozzi. Building took nearly fifty years. The massive stone walls, the splendid wrought-iron lanterns, the colonnaded interior, the cornice which the architect Simone del Pollaiuolo (who was known as Cronaca) modelled on an antique fragment, all make their contribution to an overwhelmingly majestic building. And the inspirer of its spacious symmetry is ultimately Brunelleschi, the man who, as Vasari declared, 'was sent by heaven to invest architecture with new forms, after it had wandered astray for many centuries'.

Behind all these buildings lay the wealth of great merchants and bankers, above all the wealth which Cosimo de' Medici needed to spend on good works in order to salve an uneasy conscience. When Pope Eugenius IV urged him to rebuild the Dominican convent of San Marco, Cosimo spent over forty thousand florins on the task and in addition provided the monks with a superb library. But he was not slow at paying for great secular buildings for his own comfort and display, as the Palazzo Medici-Riccardi demonstrates.

So do the lovely villas the Medici created. From Roman times a villa had meant a country estate, which in the middle ages was conceived as a setting – inevitably with a garden – in which a man of culture could be at ease with his books, his thoughts, his congenial friends. Georgina Masson has spelled out the importance of Cosimo de' Medici in adapting this concept for a new age:

Already at the end of the fourteenth century the poet Petrarch, at Arquà in the Euganean Hills, had anticipated the humanist ideal of a country villa as a retreat for a man of letters. But it was to the patriarch of the Medici, Cosimo il Vecchio, and his villas at Careggi, that the Italian renaissance conception of the villa really owed its origin. It is interesting to note that Careggi was an old castellated house converted about 1434 for use as a villa in the Renaissance sense, with loggias and gardens adorned with statuary and exotic plants and, as such, it was the prototype of many castles converted into Renaissance villas, especially in the environs of Rome. The Medici villa at Fiesole, which shares with Careggi the honour of having been the cradle of the humanist movement, was built about 1450 expressly as a villa, and its hillside site and hanging terraced gardens were to exercise a tremendous influence upon Italian garden design.

Giovanni di Bicci de' Medici had bought the old house at Careggi in 1417. His son engaged Michelozzo to transform it, but the architect was wise enough to keep most of the old building intact externally, sensitively adding to it instead of changing it. Here as we shall see the Medici set up a Platonic academy of learned men, dedicated to the new (and old) humanism.

At Fiesole the architect of the Villa Medici, with its lovely garden, was also Michelozzo. Twenty-five kilometres or so from Florence on the Bologna road he built for Cosimo the Villa Cafaggiolo and also converted the nearby castle of Trebbio into a fourth Medici villa. Both lie in a beautiful part of the Mugello valley, Il Trebbio situated on a hill with superb views. More than any other Tuscan villa, its grounds preserve their original layout – a classic Tuscan renaissance garden. One feature that has happily survived is its vine pergola, flanking one entire side of the garden, its columns made from fine red, semicircular bricks, topped with capitals carved to represent foliage.

Small wonder, then, that Arthur Young, visiting Florence in December 1789, noted first what was – to him – the antiquity of its buildings, everything 'of three or four hundred years standing', and secondly that the whole city seemed dominated by the extraordinary legacy of the Medici:

There is hardly a street that has not some monument, some decoration, that bears the stamp of that splendid and magnificent family. How commerce could enrich it sufficiently to leave such prodigious remains, is a question not a little curious; for I may venture, without apprehension, to assert, that all the collected magnificence of the House of Bourbon, governing for eight hundred years twenty millions of people, is trivial, when compared with what the Medici family have left, for the admiration of succeeding ages, sovereigns only of the little mountainous region of Tuscany, and with not more than a million subjects.

Another Englishman visiting Florence in the eighteenth century recorded a different impression. Edward Gibbon, passing through the city on his way to Rome, perceived for the first time that sculpture might be superior to draughtsmanship (or, as he put it, 'that the chissel may dispute the pre-eminence of the pencil').

Both men were right. More: their views can be seen to converge in a marble portrait bust by Mino da Fiesole, now in the Museo Nazionale, Florence. Sculpted in 1453, it is the first portrait bust to have been made since Roman times. The marble beautifully simulates the rich clothing warn by its subject. He was Piero de' Medici, son and heir of Cosimo de' Medici the elder.

In Florence the truth is that no one need visit its museums – splendid though their contents are – for an enthralling insight into Tuscan sculpture of the renaissance and later. You need walk only as far as the Loggia dei Lanzi.

The Loggia dei Lanzi in Florence, which was built between 1376 and 1382 to designs by Orcagna, takes its present name from the Swiss lancers that Cosimo I hired to stand on guard here. For two hundred years it has exhibited the most exciting open-air display of sculpture in the world. When I first went to Florence a masterpiece by the greatest sculptor of the fifteenth century, Donatello, stood here, but his bronze *Judith and Holofernes* has now, to my regret, been moved to the Sala d'Udienza on the second floor of the Palazzo Vecchio, for – it is alleged – its better preservation.

Donatello was born in Florence in 1386, trained in the cathedral workshops sculpting marble, and studied in the studio of Ghiberti learning how to work in bronze. He lived in Padua for ten years before returning home to live in Florence till his death at the age of eighty in 1466. His *Judith and Holofernes* is a work of the artist's late maturity, almost the last statue he made, commissioned by the Medici for the garden of their palace and only placed in the Loggia dei Lanzi when they were expelled from Florence in 1495. As Giorgio Vasari noted, Donatello 'was so satisfied with the work that he wished to place his name on it – which he had not done elsewhere – as can be seen in the words *"Donatello opus".*' And indeed you can see these words (or nearly these words: in fact OPVS. DONATELLI. FLOR.) on the cushion between Holofernes's hands.

In its day *Judith and Holofernes* was revolutionary. In the words of John Pope-Hennessy, 'Faced with the commission for the statue, Donatello might well have represented Judith holding a severed head. Instead he chose what no other sculptor in the fifteenth century would have attempted, an active pose, and showed Judith in arrested motion with sword raised, and Holofernes . . . in front of her.' Holofernes's head is savagely twisted. Judith stands on one of his wrists. His seemingly already dead legs hang down behind ('the effects of wine and sleep and death revealed in his limbs', as Vasari put it, 'which because he has lost his senses are represented as cold and drooping').

There's much more by Donatello in Florence. In the Museo Nazionale in the Bargello is his exquisite, sensuous bronze of David, an Old Testament subject inspired in Donatello's case by a classical model (though Vasari observed that 'the figure is so natural, lifelike and soft that to artists it seems impossible that it was not modelled from a living body'). The nude youth, a sword in his right hand, the other resting on his thigh, stands almost languidly on the head of the Goliath he has just slain. (The same museum houses a splendid *David* by Andrea del Verrocchio, created around 1470, adopting exactly the same pose as Donatello's statue.)

In the Baptistery at Florence used to stand an altogether different statue by Donatello, *St Mary Magdalen.* (Today, for safety, it is in the nearby Museo dell'Opera del Duomo.) Carved out of wood, the saint appears emaciated through fasting and great abstinence. Her sunken eyes yearn for her Lord, her mouth half open, the veins on her neck bulging.

To seek more masterpieces by this astonishingly gifted man, go to the church of San Lorenzo, where he made two free-standing bronze pulpits, with scenes from the passion and resurrection of Christ. Look out his *Annunciation* in Santa Croce, with a kneeling angel and a

standing, hesitant, reticent Virgin Mary. Find his St George and the
Dragon beneath the tabernacle of the Arte dei Corazzai on the north
side of Orsanmichele, and his marble St Mark in the same church.
And if you thirst for more, enjoy the brilliant group of statues now in
the cathedral museum.

Yet of the statues in the Loggia dei Lanzi my own favourite is not
Donatello's *Judith and Holofernes*, awe-inspiring though it undoubtedly is, but Benvenuto Cellini's sadistic *Perseus with the Head of
Medusa*. Cellini was born in this city in 1500 and trained as a
goldsmith. He spent much time in Rome, Venice and France (at the
court of Francis I). In 1545 he returned to Florence and visited Cosimo
I at his villa at Poggio a Caiano. Cosimo asked Cellini to produce a
Perseus for the great square. To train himself for the task Cellini
made an exceedingly handsome bronze bust of his patron, sculpted
(as he said in a letter to Cosimo) 'in accordance with the noble fashion
of the ancients'. You can see it today in the Museo Nazionale of
Florence.

Then he began work on what was to prove his greatest achievement.
'I very gladly set myself the task and in a few weeks had finished my
model in yellow wax, which was about a cubit high, very delicately
finished in all its details,' Cellini recorded. (You can see this model
too at Florence in the Museo Nazionale.)

The bleeding dead head of Medusa, held aloft by Perseus, was the
first part of the statue to be cast by Cellini. 'The first cast I took in my
furnace succeeded in the superlative degree,' he rejoiced, 'and was so
clean that my friends thought I should not need to retouch it.' Perseus
was a different affair. Even Cosimo I told the sculptor that to cast so
ambitious a bronze was impossible. The anxiety made Cellini ill.
To make matters worse, his studio accidentally caught fire. The
enterprise was completed successfully only when, as the statue was
being fired, the sculptor threw into the furnace all his pewter plates
and vessels.

Two other statues in the Loggia dei Lanzi are outstanding masterpieces, both of them by Jean Boulogne, who was born at Douai in
1529 and is now known as Giambologna. The first is his *Rape of the
Sabines*. (In fact, he cared little as to its title, telling the Duke of
Parma that 'the figures can be interpreted as the rape of Helen, or
even as that of Proserpine, or as the rape of one of the Sabine women'.

It is said that Giambologna's friend Raffaello Borghini, and not the sculptor himself, finally decided on the latter title for the group.) Three figures, a vanquished man, a terrified woman, and the victor who carries her off, are extraordinarily animated. Yet they seem almost static compared with Giambologna's *Hercules and the Centaur* near by, which was completed in 1599. To a commission of the Grand Duke Ferdinand I, Giambologna sculpted Hercules in the very act of slaying the centaur, whose neck is twisted back, whose despairing legs are bent under himself.

The Loggia dei Lanzi lies to the south side of the Piazza della Signoria, for which Giambologna (again commissioned by Ferdinand I) created the superb equestrian statue of the great Cosimo I. Of the three reliefs at the base of this statue (depicting Cosimo's coronation as Grand Duke, his triumph over Siena, and his acceptance by the Senate as Duke of Tuscany), the last is by Giambologna. On the west end is the inscription in Latin:

> To Cosimo Medici, first Grand Duke of Tuscany
> God-fearing, fortunate, unconquered, just and merciful,
> promoter of holy war and peace in Tuscany: Ferdinand,
> his son and third Grand Duke, erected this to his
> excellent prince and father.

Giambologna's work is elsewhere in Florence too. In San Marco is a bronze tomb of St Antoninus, as well as an animated angel, both in the Salviati chapel, for which Giambologna also designed the crucifix. There is a lovely Apollo by him in the Palazzo Vecchio, and a Bacchus at the corner of the Via Guicciardini and the Borgo San Jacopo. And for the Boboli Gardens Giambologna created the fountain of Oceanus, making the basin out of a huge block of granite quarried on Elba, and carving statues representing the Nile, the Ganges and the Euphrates, topping the lot with Neptune himself.

Neptune also appears in the Piazza della Signoria, dominating the gigantic fountain by Bartolommeo Ammannati and his followers. Neptune has three marble tritons between his legs and rides in a seashell pulled by four horses. Bronze putti, cornucopias, two male sea gods, and the female figures of Thetis and Doris decorate the basin of the fountain, with eight satyrs sitting at the sides. And water spouts everywhere.

Yet all this wonderful statuary fails to match what is now only a copy (made in 1905, for the original is now on the Accademia) of Michelangelo's famous *David* in the Piazza della Signoria.

The statue was commissioned by the city itself in 1501, to symbolize the victory of republicanism over tyranny (for had not the young David overcome the tyrant Goliath?). In Florence in those days was a huge, coveted block of marble which Simone da Fiesole had attempted to carve and bungled. At one time the city fathers had contemplated giving it to Leonardo da Vinci. Michelangelo took it for his *David*. He did the work in secret; and when it was revealed the Florentines immediately dubbed it 'the Giant'. From that moment too his contemporaries called Michelangelo 'divine'.

He had been born in 1475 in the little hill-town of Caprese near Arezzo, where his father was mayor. Soon the family came to Florence and lived in the neighbourhood of Santa Croce with the boy's uncle. Michelangelo joined the artists' school of Francesco da Urbino at Settignano and then became apprenticed to Domenico Ghirlandaio. Soon he was spotted by Lorenzo de' Medici and brought to study sculpture under Bertoldo di Giovanni in the Medici garden (where he also learned from such humanists as Politian and Marsilio Ficino). He was to visit Bologna and Rome (sometimes because the fortunes of the Medici were at a low ebb), where Pope Julius II became his patron and where he painted the ceiling of the Sistine chapel. When the Medici regained power in Florence, Michelangelo returned, living and working in the city more or less permanently till 1534 (when he went back to Rome, to stay there until he died).

Happily, then, we can find some of his profoundest works in Florence. Here too are his juvenilia – such as the *Madonna of the Stairs* and the *Battle of the Centaurs*, both in the Casa Buonarroti – imperfect perhaps and yet unmistakably the works of a genius. Then, in Rome, he carved one of his most controversial figures, the statue of Bacchus, now in the Bargello, Florence. Bacchus holds a bunch of grapes which a dreadfully debauched satyr, about seven years old, is slyly eating. Amongst the many who have criticized this statue was Shelley, who could not bear the thought that a god who never was drunk should have been portrayed by Michelangelo as lewd, inebriated and coarse. By contrast Vasari recognized in this work of art 'a marvellous blending of both sexes, combining the slenderness of a young man with the round fulness of a woman.' There is indeed a sexual oddness about Michelangelo's *Bacchus*; but there was a sexual oddness in Michelangelo himself – a homosexual whose religious beliefs led him to renounce any homosexual practice – and in *Bacchus* he created a stunningly ambivalent portrait of sinful indulgence.

He also created a superb *Pietà*, begun in Rome in 1550 (and now in the Museo dell'Opera del Duomo in Florence) – a statue I return to more than any other by this greatest of all sculptors. He planned it for his own tomb. The head of Nicodemus in the group is an idealized self-portrait. Yet it was finished only by chance, and not by Michelangelo. The sculptor had tired of the work; the marble was flawed; one of the elbows of the Madonna had broken away; and Michelangelo had been annoyed by the way his servant Urbino constantly urged him to finish the statue. Eventually he gave the broken piece of sculpture to his friend Francesco Bandini. Now Bandini had a friend named Tiberio Calcagni who was also a sculptor. Bandini begged Michelangelo to let Calcagni finish the work, and Michelangelo agreed.

Even now Michelangelo's *Pietà* remains unfinished. You can see where the Madonna's left hand is damaged, as are the left nipple and elbow of the Christ. The figure that kneels to the left of the Madonna is about to wash the corpse of Jesus (as Michelangelo wrote, an 'office which his mother could not undertake') and alas is dreadfully carved, doubtless by Calcagni. On the unfinished, unpolished figure of Nicodemus we can still see the swift first strokes of Michelangelo's powerful chisel. Yet everything remains perfectly clear – and deeply, deeply moving. As Vasari observed, the mother of Jesus, 'overcome by grief, failing in strength, cannot uphold him', so that Nicodemus stretches forward to help her and Christ himself 'sinks with his limbs hanging limp, in an attitude totally different not only from that of any other statue of Michelangelo, but from that of any other figure that was ever made'. As for Nicodemus, in the words of John Pope-Hennessy, he 'expresses the compassion not of one onlooker, but of mankind'.

More of these moving unfinished statues by Michelangelo, in which a human being struggles to be born out of the marble, can be seen in Florence. The Palazzo Vecchio houses his *Genius of Victory*, in which a slender youth triumphs over an older, bearded, vanquished, unfinished warrior. In the Museo Nazionale is the early unfinished *Pitti*

Madonna. And in the Accademia are the extraordinary unfinished statues of St Matthew and four beautiful slaves: *The Young Slave*, *The Awakening Slave*, *The Bearded Slave* and *The Atlas Slave*. To my mind all four are infinitely more impressive than the finished *Rebellious Slave* and *The Dying Slave* in the Louvre in Paris.

Michelangelo created another outstanding masterpiece in Florence: the Medici Chapel. In terms of architecture, it is not revolutionary. Michelangelo simply placed a fine cupola over a copy of Brunelleschi's sacristy. But he created here two superb tombs, one for the Duke of Urbino (Lorenzo de' Medici's son) and the other for the Duke of Nemours (Lorenzo's grandson). He created statues over the tombs that (as people objected) did not remotely resemble the two men – to which Michelangelo replied (anticipating that his work would last for millennia) that in two thousand years no one would remember what they looked like!

Underneath he placed his famous statues of *Dawn, Evening, Day* and *Night*. Underneath the tomb of the Duke of Urbino lie the female *Dawn* and the male *Evening*. Underneath the Duke of Nemours are the male *Day* and the female *Night*. There is a bitterness and a languor about these monumental statues, as if they lament the fate of mankind. None of them is totally finished. And in the same chapel is a *Madonna and Child*, the infant Jesus struggling on his mother's knee, the Virgin deeply contemplative and in repose.

On the statue of *Night* a Florentine poet, Giovanni di Carlo Strozzi, hung a poem in praise of the sculptor. Michelangelo replied:

> *La Notte, che tu vedi in si dolci atti*
> *dormir, fu da un Angelo scolpita*
> *in questo sasso, e, perchè dorme, ha vita;*
> *Destala, se non credi, e parleratti.*
> *Caro m'è'l sonno et più l'esser di sasso*
> *Mentre che'l danno et la vergogna dura;*
> *Non veder, non sentir m'è gran ventura*
> *Però non mi destar, deh, parla basso.*

> [Night, which you see sleeping here in so sweet an aspect,
> was sculpted by an Angel in this stone
> and, because she is sleeping, must be alive;
> If you disbelieve this, wake her and she will speak.

Sleep is precious to me, all the more so being stone,
all the more as long as ill-fortune and dishonour endure;
for me, neither to see nor to hear is great good fortune
so do not wake me, and speak quietly.]

Michelangelo's poetry here, as always, expresses his tormented self. It was a torment that made him fearsome – terrifying, said Pope Leo X. ('You frighten everybody, even the popes,' Sebastiano del Piombo dared write to him.) Altogether he wrote 343 quatrains, sonnets, madrigals and other poems, with no thought of publication, works which now give us a unique insight into his mind and soul. So charged are they with meaning that William Wordsworth, who decided to translate some of the sonnets in 1805, found the task indescribably difficult. 'I can translate,' he wrote, 'and have translated two books of Aristotle at the rate, nearly, of a hundred lines a day, but so much meaning has been put by Michelangelo into so little room, and that meaning sometimes so excellent in itself, that I found the difficulty of translating him insurmountable.'

Yet he managed to translate some poems, among them the most alarming and desperate:

For if of our affections none finds grace
In sight of heaven, then, wherefore hath God made
The world we inhabit.

Or again:

The crown of thorns, hands pierced upon the tree
The meek, benign, and lacerated face,
To a sincere repentance promise grace,
To the sad soul give hope of pardon free.

In late 1557 this tormented genius's body began finally to turn against him. 'Because of the stone I cannot urinate. My sickness in my side and back are so great that often I cannot climb the stairs. I am filled with pain,' he wrote. He sent his last letter on 28 December 1563, thanking a friend for a gift of 'twelve excellent and delicious *marzolini* cheeses. He promised that in future – since his hand was too gnarled to write properly – he would ask others to write on his behalf and simply sign the letters. Then he died. His body lies in Santa

Croce, Florence, in a fine tomb designed by Vasari. The tomb is surmounted, not as Michelangelo wished by his own *Pietà*, but by his bust and by statues representing those arts in which he supremely excelled: painting, sculpture and architecture. Only the muse of poetry is missing.

3

Lovers, Libertines,
Philosophers and Poets

'If we seek to analyse the charm which the Medicis of the fifteenth century, especially Cosimo the Elder and Lorenzo the Magnificent, exercised over Florence and over all their contemporaries, we shall find it lay less in their political capacity than in their leadership of the culture of the age.' So wrote Jacob Burckhardt in *The Civilization of the Renaissance in Italy*.

Burckhardt was referring above all to the group of writers and scholars that Cosimo and Lorenzo gathered around them in their country villas. These men were consciously seeking the meaning and purpose of life, in this world and the next. 'I desire nothing so much as to know the best road to happiness,' declared Cosimo the Elder. But their inspiration was not merely Christian. They also turned to the ancient philosophers, particularly Plato. At Villa Careggi the translator and philosopher Marsilio Ficino, the mystic and grammarian Pico della Mirandola and the classical scholar Politian founded the Platonic Academy. Each year on 17 November the members of this Academy celebrated Plato's birthday with a great banquet at the Medici villa. Cosimo's grandson, Lorenzo il Magnifico, who was tutored by Ficino, enthusiastically supported the Academy – all the more so because the man who had saved his life when the Pazzi family murdered his brother in Florence cathedral was Politian. It was a group of friends and scholars, under an enlightened patron, almost unique in history. In the words of Burckhardt, 'The famous band of scholars which surrounded Lorenzo was united together, and distinguished from all other circles of the kind, by their passion for a higher and idealistic philosophy', the revived philosophy of Platonism. This passion for an apparently abstruse system of thought fired many others in their turn.

Shortly before his death Cosimo wrote to one of the band, Marsilio Ficino, 'Yesterday I came to the villa at Careggi, not to cultivate my fields but to cultivate my soul. Come to us, Marsilio, as soon as possible, and bring with you Plato's *De summa bono*, for I suppose you have already translated it from the Greek into Latin, as you promised.' In fact the greatest translator of the age was Politian. He was also a poet and a philosopher. As well as producing some of the most exquisite Greek and Latin poetry of the age he even turned his inaugural philosophy lectures into Latin verse.

Only because this group of scholars consisted of exceedingly well-rounded men was their apparently abstract philosophizing so influential. As Burckhardt observed, the Platonic Academy was not solely a forum for talking about philosophy; it was especially 'a sacred refuge' for Italian poetry. And it was much more. Ficino, for instance, learned to play the lyre and applied his philosophy to architecture – the new architecture inaugurated by Brunelleschi and based, as Ficino put it, on 'the eternal truths' of geometry. Lorenzo's circle reckoned versatility as one of the great ideals of the ancient world. Every human activity (they believed), properly understood, contributed ultimately to a person's understanding of the whole scheme of things. Cicero's remark that he had been studying philosophy with the greatest devotion precisely when he seemed to be doing something else became a byword in Florence.

The new humanists were also able to absorb pre-Christian philosophy without qualms because they believed that Christianity had in fact triumphed, that the new humanism was not its pagan rival, but rather something which in many ways *foreshadowed* the Christian revelation. As they scoured the great libraries that were being set up by rich men such as Cosimo, they enthusiastically pored over Jewish, Arabic and Christian documents, as well as the writings of classical Greek and Rome. Cosimo methodically sought out ancient manuscripts, even sending his agents to the orient with permission of Sultan Mehmed II. He opened his library to the scholarly world. But it was crammed with Christian and Biblical texts as well as manuscripts from the non-Christian and pagan world. So anxious was Pico della Mirandola to read the Bible in its original tongue that in the late 1480s he set himself to add Hebrew and Aramaic to his other languages. In the minds of Cosimo and his Platonic friends enthusiasm for the ancients and for new learning involved no disloyalty to the Christian faith.

This helps to explain the paradox that an enormous boost towards the rebirth of pagan philosophy in Florence was actually given by an ecumenical Christian Council that met at Ferrara, Florence and Rome between 1439 and 1445. This great assembly is generally known as the Council of Florence – justly, for when the pope found that the cost of keeping the Council going had risen beyond his means, the Florentines paid for it.

The aim of the Council of Florence was to settle once and for all the numerous differences between the Eastern and Western church. The chief of these was the abstruse theological question whether the Holy Spirit proceeds from God the Father alone (as the Eastern church held) or also from God and the Son (as the West maintained). Other debated questions were the nature and existence of purgatory, the use of leavened or unleavened bread at the Eucharist, and the moment when the bread and wine of Holy Communion might be said to have become the body and blood of Christ. Behind all these questions lay the major one of the precise position and authority of the pope in relation to the rest of Christendom.

The Council was wrong in supposing that it had solved these questions and healed the East–West schism of the Christian church. Its unexpected bonus was to bring to Florence Greek Christians of extraordinary learning and fascination. At the age of fifty the banker Cosimo was to be found at the lectures of these Greek scholars. It was then he became a Platonist and set up the Platonic Academy at Careggi.

So the new humanism was in part inspired by Christianity. And yet there was a difference. It can be seen in the emphasis placed on what seemed to be the infinite possibilities open to human beings. At the Council of Florence a man named Paolo Toscanelli carefully questioned the visiting Greeks about the geography of their homelands. His subsequent speculations about the size of the Atlantic led Christopher Columbus to write to him for advice before setting out on his epoch-making voyage. Toscanelli sent him back a map of the Atlantic. A doctor by profession, Toscanelli exemplifies the new sense that the universe was here to be fully explored by men. (He was, for instance, the first person properly to work out the course of Halley's comet.)

Again, none of this presupposed a willingness to jettison Christianity. These new insights into what human beings might be capable of were still conceived as God-given. In the words of Pico della Mirandola, 'God the Father endowed man from birth with the seeds of every possibility and every life.' So the sculptors and painters of the age sought to express this view by presenting visions of the human form that were both realistic and ideal at the same time. Mino da Fiesole's bust of Piero de' Medici is a genuine portrait; a real man looks out from the marble face; but the portrait gives no hint that Piero suffered so drastically from gout that at times he could scarcely talk. Many men and some women of the age were assiduously cultivating and presenting to the world their own personalities, combining this with an ideal notion of the perfectly rounded human being they all strove to become. Some believed they were succeeding. Everyone, wrote the mid-fifteenth-century humanist Matteo Palmieri, should 'thank God that he has been permitted to be born in this new age, so crammed with hope and promise and rejoicing in a greater concourse of noble and gifted souls than the world saw in all the thousand years that went before'.

In fact seeds of this new age had been sown a century earlier, in the age of Petrarch, Dante and Boccaccio. The thirst for antiquity was already strong. In the words of Burckhardt, 'Petrarch, who lives in the memory of most people nowadays as a great Italian poet, owed his fame among his contemporaries far rather to the fact that he was a kind of living representative of antiquity, endeavouring by his voluminous historical and philosophical writings not to supplant but to make known the works of the ancients.' Similarly Boccaccio, now remembered almost solely for his *Decameron*, was in his own generation and for two centuries afterwards scarcely known north of the Alps save for his defence of the ancient and newly discovered humanism.

As the humanist Leonardo Bruni (who became chancellor of Florence) generously acknowledged, Petrarch 'showed the way for us by revealing how we might acquire learning'. Petrarch worked out a pattern of studies to open up the spirit of the classical antiquity. He insisted that the only true way to understand the ancients was through their own language. And in 1397, for the first time for seven hundred years, Greek was taught again in the West, when the University of

Florence invited the Greek scholar Manuel Chrysoloras to lecture there.

Oddly enough, Petrarch himself never learned Greek – partly, perhaps, out of idleness, and partly because he was personally convinced that the greatest of the ancients had been the Romans. He loved editing the works of Cicero. He, like Cosimo in the next century, assembled a superb library of ancient manuscripts. And of course he was one of the greatest lyric poets ever to have written, composing three hundred sonnets and songs to immortalize his love for his lost Laura:

> Chiare, fresche e dolci acque,
> ove le belle membra
> pose colei che sola a me par donna;
> gentil ramo, ove piacque
> (con sospir mi rimembra)
> a lei di fare al bel fianco colonna;
> erba e fior, che la gonna
> leggiadra ricoverse
> con l'angelico seno;
> aer sacro sereno,
> ov'Amor co'begli occhi il cor m'aperse:
> date udienzia insieme
> alle dolenti mie parole estreme.

> [Clear, fresh and sweet waters,
> where rested the lovely limbs
> of the only one who to me is woman;
> gentle tree, where she was pleased
> (how I remember it with sighing!)
> to make a column for her lovely flank;
> grass and flower, which her happy
> dress lightly covered
> along with her heavenly breast;
> holy and serene air,
> where, with those lovely eyes, Love pierced my heart:
> all of you listen
> to my final, sorrowing words.]

No doubt Petrarch picked up strains of courtly love from the troubadour traditions of Provence, where he spent much of his life.

But I also like to think he learned something about love-poetry from, of all people, his schoolmaster. If you go to Pistoia, look out the monument to this man on the south wall of the cathedral. His name was Cino, and the monument includes a relief showing him teaching. In his class sit both Petrarch and also Selvaggia de' Vergiolesi, the daughter of the military commander of Pistoia. To her Cino da Pistoia addressed exquisite, yearning love-poetry. One stanza, it seems to me, remarkably parallels the verse I have quoted from Petrarch:

> E' mi rimembra de la bianca parte
> che fa col verdebrun la bella taglia,
> la qual vestio Amore
> nel tempo che, guardando Vener Marte,
> con quell sua saetta che più taglia
> mi diè per mezzo il core:
> e quando l'aura move il bianco fiore,
> rimembro de begli occhi il dolce bianco
> per cui lo mio desir mai non fie stanco.

> [I remember the white part of the dress
> and the green that gave it its fine shape,
> the dress which Love wore when,
> as Mars and Venus watched,
> she struck me through the heart
> with the arrow that bites deepest:
> and when the breeze moves the white flower,
> I remember the sweet whites of her lovely eyes
> for which my desire shall never fail.]

The fashion for unattainable objects of romantic love was evidently catching in fourteenth-century Tuscany. Giovanni Boccaccio, like his friend Petrarch, conceived a passion for a girl who died too soon. When in 1374 the ageing Boccaccio learned that Petrarch had died, he composed a lament in which he very soon remembered that Petrarch in heaven had been reunited not only with his own Laura but also with Boccaccio's Fiammetta, 'she who first fired me with love'. Boccaccio's one consolation was that he soon would join them, as he did by dying the following year.

Dante too fell hopelessly and passionately in love. His ideal lady was in real life a girl called Beatrice Portinari. One extraordinary feature of this unrequited love is that Dante first saw and fell in love with her when Beatrice was only eight years old and he was nine. 'Her dress on that day was of a most noble colour,' he recalled: 'a subdued and excellent crimson, girdled and adorned in a fashion that perfectly suited her tender age. At that moment I truly say that the spirit of life, which dwells in the innermost chamber of the heart, began to tremble so violently that the least pulses of my body shook with it.' Nine years later he saw Beatrice again, dressed this time in white, walking with two older women. 'She turned her eyes towards the place where I most timidly stood, and in her indescribable courtesy saluted me so graciously that at that moment I seemed to see the heights of blessedness.'

In describing his emotions Dante made use of what are to us the curious physiological/psychological notions of his age; but the emotions ring familiarly enough. His heart told him, 'Behold a god stronger than myself, who is come to rule over me.' His brain declared, 'Now your beatitude has appeared to you.' And his liver exclaimed, 'O misery! how I shall henceforth be disturbed!'

Dante certainly sometimes spoke to Beatrice Portinari. To try to conceal his yearning for her, he pretended to be amorously involved with two other women. The result was that Beatrice cut him in the street. He soon resolved to renounce any hope of a physical union with her. Instead his response to this overwhelming love for Beatrice was to transmute it into an image of the divine love and a parable of heaven. At the moment he first saw her, he was conscious of being transported into such a state of grace as to feel total goodwill to the rest of mankind. And at the beginning of his *Paradiso* it is Beatrice who descends from heaven, with the words, 'Did you not know that your happiness lies here?'

Their second meeting had provoked in Dante a vision that included a presentiment of Beatrice's early death. She died on 8 June 1290, and he comforted himself with the certainty that she had instantly been carried 'to heaven on high, to that kingdom where the angels live in peace'. The poems in his *Vita nuova* perceive his lost love in absolute glory. Dante then determined that he should say no more about the woman who had clearly now become his muse until, as he put it, he could set down about her what had never before been written of any woman. The result, fifteen years later, was his *Divine Comedy*, which begins with the poet, in the midway of this our mortal life, lost in a gloomy forest. Unable to climb a mountain because of wild beasts who bar the way, Dante meets Virgil, who promises to show him both Hell and Purgatory, after which Beatrice will lead him into Paradise.

The poem Dante's *Divine Comedy* most closely resembles is Virgil's *Aeneid*, for Dante is repeating in the context of Christian imagery Aeneas' descent to Avernus. The poem is deeply allegorical. (The three beasts who prevent the poet ascending the mountain, a female leopard, a lion and a wolf, stand for lust, pride and avarice.) Throughout the *Comedy* the poet's own sufferings give an urgent passion to his search for paradise. Throughout, too, he alludes to and comments on contemporary events as well as episodes from Tuscany's turbulent past. Dante's *Divine Comedy* is a quest that leads through horror to happiness, just as (to use one of its own metaphors) the javelin of Achilles caused pain first and then the boon of health restored.

This remarkable poet, rhetorician, philosopher and statesman had been born in Florence in May 1265. His grandfather had been one of the city's moneylenders. His father pursued the same profession in Prato. His mother died when the future poet was still young, and Dante was brought up with an older sister, and stepbrothers and sisters from his father's second marriage.

From the Florentine poet Brunetto Latini he learned that to write great literature is 'how a man becomes eternal'. His greatest friend at this time was the poet Guido Cavalcanti, to whom he dedicated the *Vita nuova*. At this time Dante was betrothed to Gemma Donati, and among the sonnets he addressed to Cavalcanti is one explaining why he didn't like her. (After their marriage his life with Gemma was decidedly unhappy.) Dante also sent to Cavalcanti a sonnet containing an extraordinary vision of the torments of love:

> *Allegro mi sembrava Amor tenendo*
> *meo core in mano, e ne le braccia avea*
> *madonna involta in un drappo dormendo.*
> *Poi la svegliava, e d'esto core ardendo*
> *lei paventosa umilmente pascea:*
> *appresso gir lo ne videa piangendo.*

[Happy Love seemed to hold
my heart in his hand; and in his arms
my lady lay asleep, wrapped in her cloak.
Then he woke her, and humbly and in fear
she ate this burning heart:
and after this I watched him go away, weeping.]

Dante spent two and a half years after Beatrice's death studying the classics, especially Virgil and Ovid. But he was also a man of action. A year before she died he had risked his own life at the front of the cavalry, fighting on the side of the Guelphs against Ghibelline Arezzo. Now he became a Florentine politician, a member of the council which supposedly balanced the authority of the Podestà. He was elected to the Council of the Hundred, and sought here to limit the powers of the great magnates of the city. His standing was such that he was sent to San Gimignano to make there a famous speech urging the Guelph cities of Tuscany to common action and unity. In 1300 he served as one of the six priors of the Florentine guilds, during which time the leaders of the factions that were splitting the city were sent into exile. They included members of his own wife's family, and his former friend Cavalcanti, whose death was attributed to the unwholesome air of Sarzanza where he was forced to live.

Dante was making enemies. The city was in danger from the forces of Charles of Valois, the pope's ally and brother of the French king. Dante and his supporters desperately tried to find some compromise. He and three others left Florence at the end of October 1301, to try to negotiate with the pope. He never returned.

Charles of Valois took the city on 1 November. The following year Dante was savagely fined for alleged maladministration of public funds and ordered not to return to Tuscany within two years. He was to live in exile and considerable poverty for the rest of his life. In his *Divine Comedy* he bitterly described Florence as an 'evil stepmother'. And in a mellower, still unhappy mood, he wrote of her in his remarkable poem 'Three Women Have Come Round My Heart' as 'grieving and bewildered, like a hunted, weary person without any followers'.

In 1306, along with the rest of the exiles from Florence, Dante was expelled from Bologna. He longed for peace in Italy, and hoped that this might be brought by the Holy Roman Emperor. When he discovered that his own native city opposed the emperor, he denounced her, with the result that he was excluded from the general amnesty granted to her exiled citizens in 1311. Finally he reached Ravenna, living in the home of the poet Guido da Polenta. His children Pietro, Jacopo and Antonia joined him there. On the night of 13–14 September 1321 he died of malaria.

Dante's choice of the vernacular rather than Latin for his poetry makes his work a crucial turning-point in the history of Italian literature. Yet in countless respects – in, for instance, his use of allegory and his medieval psychology – he remains the supreme literary giant of the middle ages. It is his contemporary Giovanni Boccaccio, born eight years before Dante died, whose works presage the future course of Italian literature. As the nineteenth-century Italian critic Francesco de Sanctis put it, 'Dante brings one epoch to a close, Boccaccio opens up another.'

Boccaccio's father was a Florentine banker who wanted his son to follow in the family business. He took Giovanni to Naples, and when the young man showed no liking for banking, attempted to turn him into a lawyer. This calling, too, irked Boccaccio, who simply wished to live as a *savant* and man of letters.

He was by no means idle, amassing vast learning and at the same time loving the cultivated society around the court of the Angevin King Robert. He returned to Florence in 1341, seven years before the deadly bubonic plague which was the occasion for his most famous work, *The Decameron*.

The Decameron opens with a terrifying description of the plague. 'Large quantities of refuse were carried out of the city by officials specially appointed for the purpose, all sick persons were forbidden entry, and numerous instructions were issued for safeguarding the people's health, but all to no avail,' he recorded. As for the disease itself, 'its earliest symptom, in men and women alike, was the appearance of certain swellings in the groin or the armpit, some of which were egg-shaped whilst others were roughly the size of a common apple . . . From these two areas the swellings would spread, appearing at random all over the bodies of the victims. Then the symptoms would change into dark blotches and bruises on the arms, thighs and elsewhere, sometimes large and few in number, sometimes tiny and closely spaced. The doctors were as helpless as the many quacks that quickly set themselves up in practice to make money out of the misfortunes of the Florentines. Once the symptoms had appeared nearly every sufferer died within a few days.'

Boccaccio wrote as an eye-witness. The pestilence, he said, 'whenever those suffering from it mixed with people who were still unaffected, rushed upon these with the speed of a fire racing through dry or oily substances'. He recounted how he saw the rags of a pauper who had died of the disease thrown into the street, where they attracted the attention of two pigs. 'In their wonted fashion, the pigs first of all gave the rags a thorough mauling with their snouts, after which they took them between their teeth and shook them against their cheeks. And within a short time they began to writhe as though they had been poisoned, then they both dropped down to the ground, spreadeagled upon the rags that had brought about their undoing.'

On this melancholy basis of fact Boccaccio created his enchanting and famous book. He recounts how seven women met by chance on Tuesday morning in the virtually deserted church of Santa Maria Novella. They decided to escape from the plague to a country estate, taking with them three men. The names invented by Boccaccio for the men give a hint of what is to come: Pamphilio, which means, 'he who is all love'; Philostrato, which means 'he who is crushed by love'; and Dioneo, which means 'he who is given to Dionaea', i.e. the mother of the goddess of sensual love. As for his seven women, Boccaccio called the eldest Pampinea ('the energetic one'), and the other six Fiammetta ('little flame', the name of Boccaccio's lamented true love), Neiphile ('novice in love'), Emilia ('the flatterer'), Philomena ('lover of songs') and then two names hinting at the author's literary masters: Laura, and Elissa (another name for Virgil's passionate heroine Dido).

The ten escape from Florence. Out of the plague's reach, they play chess and draughts. They sing and dance. They stroll in the beautiful gardens. They write poetry. Pampinea proposes that each day they appoint one of their number either king or queen, and that each day every member of the group should tell a story. Sometimes the king or queen can decide to set the theme for the whole day, sometimes the storytellers can choose their own theme. So it came about that in ten days the group told each other one hundred tales.

Far more than the learned editions of Latin authors which Boccaccio made in the last years of his life when he was living at Certaldo, *The Decameron* has assured his fame. The first French translation was completed in 1414 (and Philip le Bon, Duke of Burgundy, commissioned two Flemish artists to create some justly celebrated miniatures illustrating the text). The British were more prudish. As Boccaccio's best British translator, G. H. McWilliam, has explained, 'Before the appearance of John Payne's magniloquent English version in 1886, Boccaccio's taste for the erotic and the profane had been consistently toned down in varying degrees.' This is, perhaps, scarcely surprising. At least fifteen out of the hundred tales are indubitably indecent and another forty or so come near it. In addition, Boccaccio derived much joy from portraying the religious as equally prone to fleshly sins as secular men and women. In a famous story told on the third day by Philostrato, a sturdy peasant named Masetto di Lamporecchio feigns dumbness, in order to get a job as a gardener for eight nuns and an abbess. The lustful nuns, and even the abbess herself, all sleep with him, convinced that he can never tell anyone about it. Unable to stand the pace Masetto eventually claims to have miraculously recovered his speech, and explains his plight to the nuns. They all believe the miracle, make Masetto steward of their nunnery, and share him out between themselves on a less arduous basis.

Again, on the seventh day Elissa tells the story of Friar Rinaldo who goes to bed with his godchild's mother. When her husband finds them together in the bedroom, they manage to persuade him that Rinaldo was charming away the baby's worms. Even where monks, nuns and the clergy in general are not portrayed as lustful, they often appear as unscrupulous tricksters. On the sixth day, for instance, Dioneo tells the story of Friar Cipolla, who promises to show one of the Angel Gabriel's feathers to a crowd of bumpkins. Finding that someone has substituted lumps of coal for the relic, the wily friar declares that these were coals left over after the roasting of St Lawrence.

The most celebratedly vulgar tale in Boccaccio's *Decameron* also comes from Dioneo and concerns Fr. Gianni, who persuades his neighbour Pietro that he can turn his beautiful young wife Gemmata into a mare, changing her back at night after she has done a useful day's work. Pietro readily agrees, since he has only a donkey to carry around the goods he buys and sells at the various fairs of Apulia. The one condition laid down by the priest is that no one should utter a word while he is working the spell, or else the whole enterprise will fail. Gemmata then removes all her clothes and stands on all fours like a mare. Fr. Gianni begins to fondle her head and face, declaring, 'This is a fine mare's head.' He continues by stroking her hair ('This is a fine mare's mane'), her arms and the rest of her body, to the delight of various onlookers and to Pietro's growing consternation. Only when the priest begins to insert the mare's tail does Pietro finally cry out, 'No, Fr. Gianni, no tail! I don't want a tail.' Dioneo's tale concludes: 'Now that it was no longer possible to turn the young woman into a mare because of the words that Pietro had uttered, she put on her clothes again, feeling all sad and forlorn. Meanwhile her husband prepared to return to his old trade, with no more than a donkey as usual: then he and Fr. Gianni went off to the fair at Bitonto together, and he never asked the same favour of him again.'

However profane or scatological Boccaccio's tales in *The Decameron*, nothing can hide his brilliance as a storyteller. Particularly charming are the passages of pseudo-moralizing he inserts from time to time at the beginning of a story. Philostrato, about to tell the tale of Peronella, who hid her lover in a tub when her husband unexpectedly returned home, begins by declaring to his seven women companions:

Adorable ladies, so numerous are the tricks that men, and husbands in particular, play upon you, that whenever any woman happens to play one on her husband, you should not only be glad to hear about it but you should also pass it on to as many people as you can, so that men will come to realize that women are just as clever as they are. All of which is bound to work out to your own advantage, for when a man knows that he has clever people to deal with, he will think twice before attempting to deceive them.

The whole book is so skilfully varied that one scarcely notices how cunningly this has been achieved. One of Boccaccio's prettiest devices for varying the pace of *The Decameron* is to introduce poems at the end of each day. So at the end of the second day, whose theme was those who suffer misfortunes and then are brought to a state of unexpected happiness, Pampinea sings:

> Come Love, the cause of all my joy,
> Of all my hope and happiness,
> Come let us sing together:

> Not of love's sighs and agony
> But only of its jocundness.

Everyone joins in the chorus. They sing some more, dance many dances and play several tunes. Then the queen decides it is time for them all to go to bed, so the ten retire to their respective rooms, carrying torches to light them on their way, and eagerly looking forward to their next day of revels and storytelling.

Part of Boccaccio's subtlety can be seen in the fact that his revellers themselves remain entirely chaste throughout their whole sojourn in the country. But after him the tradition of libertinage seems powerfully to have entered Tuscan literature. The notorious Pietro Aretino was born to a shoemaker and his wife in Arezzo in 1492. His more serious writings, bitingly attacking the powerful in dialogues and letters, his comedies and his tragedy *Orazia* are not so well appreciated as they merit, simply because his lewd sonnets (which he shamelessly entitled as such) scandalized many even in that tolerant age. His best comedy, *The Courtesan*, though still dabbling among the sexually corrupt, offers an unusually candid picture of the life of the early-sixteenth-century Italian lower orders.

Perhaps, however, some of his writings seemed dangerously close to the truth to be acceptable to many powerful hypocrites. He called himself the 'scourge of princes', and in his *I ragionamenti* published the alleged discussions of prostitutes dissecting the characters of their clients, many of them persons of considerable substance in the Rome of his day. In spite of his support of the successful papal candidature of Giulio de' Medici, Aretino was driven from Rome to spend the rest of his dissolute days much admired in Venice.

Peter Burke has interestingly compared the moral stance of Aretino's *I ragionamenti* to the political stance of Niccolò Machiavelli's notorious political discourse *The Prince*, published a decade earlier in 1513. *The Prince* despises any kind of faithfulness. As Peter Burke comments, 'Machiavelli's central value is not keeping faith (*mantenere la fede*): it is keeping in power (*mantenere lo stato*). To do this it is necessary to know how to deceive others and how to avoid being deceived oneself.'

I ragionamenti can be justly seen as 'the whore's Machiavelli'. One whore instructs another in the rules of their game:

Above all, study the ways of flattering and pretending . . . Men want to be deceived . . . They prefer feigned caresses to the real thing without the extras; never keep them short of kisses, glances, laughter, and talk . . . It is obvious that the problem is not making friends, it is keeping them.

It is in truth hard to say which man came to be more deplored: probably Machiavelli, since of the two men he was the profounder.

Niccolò Machiavelli (1469–1527) was born and died in Florence. His father was a lawyer who had gone bankrupt, and (as the son put it) 'I learned to go short, before I learned to enjoy.' Niccolò, deprived of the fine schooling available to his contemporaries, was – when not suffering under inadequate beaks – self-taught. His native brilliance led to an important appointment in the Florentine civil service when he was only twenty-nine. The post carried with it the opportunity for diplomatic missions abroad, and in 1500 Machiavelli spent five months at the French court. Florence, on his return, was in much peril and Machiavelli was prompt with suggestions as to how to deal with it. His first important work, *Methods of Dealing with the Rebels of the Valdichiana* trenchantly recommends swift and, if necessary, brutal action. Already in his thought are many traces of what people later regarded as extreme cynicism. He had watched and approved of the way Cesare Borgia executed some of his officers who had mutinied the previous year. He rejoiced, he said, at witnessing 'such a rare and memorable event'. Machiavelli judged that liquidation was one of the two ways to treat vanquished rebels. The other way was to offer them coldly calculated kindness. Once rebels have been put down, he asserted,'either kill them or shower them with benefits'.

Machiavelli's star was rising. When Piero Soderini became head of state in Florence, Machiavelli soon became his intimate counsellor. Believing that part of the weakness of Florence derived from defending herself with undisciplined mercenaries, he persuaded Soderini to raise a militia and virtually took charge of it himself. He was with this militia in 1509, when it forced Pisa to return to Florentine hegemony. He journeyed to Switzerland, Germany, Mantua and France in the service of the republic, always observing and assiduously analysing the weaknesses and strengths of each government with which he had to deal.

Then, in 1512, he fell from power, along with his patron Soderini.

The Medici, back in control of Florence, barred him from the Palazzo della Signoria. For a time they imprisoned and tortured him for allegedly conspiring against them. Desperately Machiavelli tried to ingratiate himself with the new masters of Florence, to no avail. Eventually the Medici did give him small tasks and favours. Sadly, when they fell from power again, their successors counted these against him, and once more the would-be courtier and statesman was cold-shouldered.

Yet, like Dante in his exiled poverty, Machiavelli used the time of his misfortune to write the book that made him famous. In Machiavelli's case, it also made him notorious. *The Prince*, which he hopefully dedicated to the Medici, is his sometimes bitter, often pessimistic plea for a ruler who would restore the fortunes of the city he loved.

Some have taken Machiavelli's book as a satire on tyrants by one whose basic instincts were always democratic. Some have suggested that he even hoped the hated Medici might follow his prescriptions – to their own ruin. For other readers it simply represents the pent-up bitterness of an ambitious failure. To my mind all these interpretations of Machiavelli's thinking seriously underestimate the subtlety of *The Prince*.

Certainly *The Prince* is a deeply pessimistic book, especially in its view of human nature. 'It may be said of men in general,' declared Machiavelli, 'that they are ungrateful, voluble, dissembling, anxious to avoid danger, and covetous of gain.' He lauds conventional virtues, only to point out that they can lead to one's ruin:

> How praiseworthy it is for a prince to keep good faith, and live with integrity rather than cunning. Still, the experience of our times shows that those princes who have done great things had little regard for good faith, using instead their cunning to confuse people and in the end to overcome those who have made loyalty the cornerstone of their lives.

Good and evil as they are commonly understood have no place in politics, Machiavelli held. Certainly a prince should pretend to possess and uphold the virtues praised by everyone else, without however supposing that these virtues will necessarily keep him in power, or keep the state prosperous. These aims, Machiavelli asserts, often require a prince to abandon conventional morality. 'It is well to seem merciful, faithful, humane, sincere, religious, and also to be so; but your mind must also be so disposed that when it is needful to be otherwise, you can change to the opposite qualities.'

He also spelled out what many knew in their bones but perhaps did not like to admit: that brute force keeps the state in peace. True, he combined the need for 'good arms' with the need for 'good laws'. But, he argued, any Florentine could convince himself of the vital need for a strong army to undergird the authority of the state and its ruler simply by considering the recent troubled history of his own city. In particular Machiavelli instanced the fate of Fra Girolamo Savonarola.

Savonarola on his appointment in 1491 as Prior of the Dominican Convent of San Marco in Florence had refused the customary homage to Lorenzo de' Medici, since he held that the honour had been given him by God and not the Florentine tyrant. Soon he was openly preaching against the evils of the Medici regime. The fact that he foretold the invasion of Charles VIII of France in 1494 gave him the status of a prophet in many people's eyes. He was also a brilliant preacher. A fellow-Dominican has left us a description of 'his glowing countenance, his fervent and reverent aspect, and his beautiful gestures which, as he preached, rapt the very soul of everyone who heard him, so that wonders and amazing appearances were seen by many, even while he was in the act of preaching'. People would rise in the middle of the night to secure places in the cathedral when Savonarola was to preach there, waiting outside in the cold before the doors were opened. Undoubtedly, too, his preaching for a time led to a reform in the morals of the Florentines. When carnival time came round, the customary feasting was replaced by a burning of nude statues, playing-boards, such vanities as looking-glasses, and what Girolamo Savonarola deemed to be heretical books.

But events soon turned against him. Savonarola personally welcomed Charles VIII into Florence and then was horrified when the French king threatened to sack the city. His attacks on what he perceived as papal corruption led to his excommunication. He in his turn demanded a general council to depose the pope. His enemies in the Signoria arrested, examined, and tortured him. As a letter they wrote to the pope admits, they weaned little from him: 'Notwithstanding a long and most careful interrogation, and with all the help of torture, we could scarcely extract anything out of him which he wished to conceal from us, although we laid open the innermost recesses of his mind.' In May 1498 it was decided that Savonarola should be burnt alive. In the museum of the Convent of San Marco a contemporary oil painting by an unknown artist depicts his death. Outside the Palazzo della Signoria a circular platform was erected, bearing a tall, solid piece of wood, with a crosspiece cut small so that the execution would not seem like some sort of crucifixion. Girolamo Savonarola and two other friars, their heads already shaven, were brought out fully robed. Then, as their captors solemnly affirmed that the three men were heretics, their robes were taken off one by one. They were hanged together, Fra Girolamo in the middle. The fire gradually consumed most of their bodies, their arms and legs dropping off one by one. Finally the last few ashes were carried to the Ponte Vecchio and flung in the River Arno.

The Florentine chronicler Francesco Guicciardini wrote that in Savonarola's life 'there was no trace of avarice, nor of luxury, neither weakness nor passion. His was the model of a religious life, charitable, pious, obedient to the monastic rule, not only the externals, but the very heart of piety.' Guicciardini adds, 'He achieved a holy and admirable work in his reforms of morals. There was never so much religion and virtue in Florence as in his day.' In short, the public and private life of Savonarola embodied all those virtues that Machiavelli thought a leader of the state needed to display. His problem was that his enemies possessed arms and he did not.

Machiavelli defined sinfulness in a fashion that would not have pleased Savonarola. Both men, as Machiavelli acknowledged, regarded the invasion of Charles VIII as a chastisement for the sins of the Italians. But Machiavelli meant by those sins the culpable errors of politicians. The Italians, he insisted, when it came to duelling were superior in strength, dexterity and intelligence to anyone. 'But when it comes to armies they make a poor show, which proceeds entirely from the weakness of their leaders.' Where Machiavelli shocks is when he also insists that a leader's errors might also derive from not following the opposite of conventional morality, such as, for example, *failing* to be cruel, where cruelty was necessary. Cesare Borgia, Machiavelli noted with approval, had been cruel, 'but his cruelty brought order to the Romagna, united it, and reduced it to peace and fealty'. Again, a statesman is often in error because he prefers peace to war, for, says Machiavelli, 'wars cannot be avoided, and to postpone them is to give others the advantage'.

In matters of sexual morality, Machiavelli undoubtedly did not approve of Savonarola's puritanism. Machiavelli was the amiable, though unfaithful, husband of Marietta Corsini, who bore him five children. And he wrote a superb, if immoral comedy, *Mandragola*, which Goldoni, though deploring its vulgarity, reckoned a splendid piece of theatre, Voltaire considered 'worth more than all the comedies of Aristophanes', and Macaulay judged 'superior to the best of Goldoni and inferior only to the best of Molière'. J. R. Hale, who made a translation of *Mandragola*, wrote: 'The plot is an ingenious and crude poetical joke of the sort familiar to generations of readers of Florentine *novelle*. Callimaco, a Florentine youth, is in love with Lucrezia, the young wife of Messer Nicià, a pompous old lawyer. She is virtuous and strictly guarded. How to seduce her? The play provides the answer.' Machiavelli's contemporaries loved it, and performed it first in 1520 before Pope Leo X.

Machiavelli's *Mandragola* is the authentic voice of Tuscan humanism at its least reverent, breathing the authentic spirit of the Florentine carnivals that Savonarola sought to suppress. A book of carnival songs by Lorenzo de' Medici and his friends (now displayed in the Museo Nazionale Centrale, Florence) has as its frontispiece a woodcut depicting Lorenzo leading a group of carnival singers through the streets, serenading young women leaning from their windows. Lorenzo and his friend Politian both wrote extremely merry songs for such occasions:

> *Donne e giovinetti amanti,*
> *viva Bacco e viva Amore!*
> *Ciascun suoni, balli e canti!*
> *Arda di dolcezza il core!*
> *Non fatica, non dolore!*
> *Quel c'ha esser, convien sia;*
> *Chi vuol esser lieto, sia;*
> *di doman non c'è certezza.*

> [Women and young lovers,
> Long live Bacchus and long live Love!
> Let everyone play, dance and sing!

Let your heart burn with sweetness!
Away with work and grieving!
Whatever will be, will be.
Whoever would be glad, let him be glad;
Nothing is certain of tomorrow.]

wrote Lorenzo. And the scholarly Politian wrote a song in praise of getting drunk:

Ognun gridi Bacco Bacco,
e pur cacci del vin giù:
poi con suoni farem fiacco.
Bevi tu, e tu, e tu.
I' non posso ballar più.
Ognun gridi eù, oè;
ognun segua, Bacco, te.
Bacco Bacco, eù, oè!

[Everyone cry Bacchus, Bacchus,
And drink more and more:
then with our noise we shall grow feebler.
You drink, and you, and you.
I can dance no longer.
Everyone cry 'Hey ho';
Everyone follow you, Bacchus.
Bacchus, Bacchus, hey ho!]

Christian humanism, especially in Florence at carnival time, had come much closer to some of its pagan sources.

4

Tuscany and the British

'Tuscany is especially flowery,' wrote D. H. Lawrence in 1926, 'being wetter than Sicily and more homely than the Roman hills.' To Lawrence the Tuscan countryside seemed wondrously varied. 'There are so many hills popping up, and they take no notice of one another. There are so many little deep valleys with streams that seem to go their own little way entirely, regardless of the river and sea. There are thousands, millions of utterly secluded little nooks, though the land has been under cultivation these thousands of years.'

Lawrence was a late – though by no means the last – example of a Briton falling in love with this entrancing part of Italy. He was also right about the extraordinary variety of countryside crammed into this one region. Tuscany comprises no fewer than nine provinces: Arezzo, Florence, Grosseto, Livorno, Lucca, Massa Carrara, Pisa, Pistoia and Siena. The Tuscans further divide their land. They call the lands around the upper reaches of the River Arno the Casentino. The Maremma embraces Monte Amiata and most of Grosseto. The Versilia is that part of the region running between the Apennines and the sea. Each has its own distinct history, its own distinct way of life, its own regional food, agriculture, folk memories and culture.

Admittedly British interest in Tuscany was initially almost entirely mercenary. King Edward I of England borrowed colossally from the Bardi and Peruzzi of Florence and then bankrupted them when he was unable to pay his debts. In the fifteenth century, to quote Pope Pius II, 'In our change-loving Italy, where nothing stands firm, and where no ancient dynasty exists, a servant can easily become a king.' His own career proved this to be so, since he had been born the eldest of eighteen children on a poor Sienese farm. Adventurers and warlords flourished in such a society, and none more than the English *condottiere* Sir John Hawkwood.

Hawkwood was born in Essex early in the fourteenth century and by 1359 was commanding a troop of pillaging mercenaries in Gascony. They threatened Avignon, at that time the seat of the papacy, and levied a considerable sum from Pope Innocent VI, before marching into Italy. Hawkwood's troops were dubbed the White Company, so splendid was their armour. Each 'lance' consisted of a knight and squire, mounted on chargers, and a page mounted on a palfrey. Soon the White Company numbered a formidable two thousand lances as well as another thousand foot-soldiers.

Sir John Hawkwood and his company fought for whoever would pay them. In July 1363 they were employed by the republic of Pisa, being paid ten thousand gold florins a month to attack and defeat Florence. Hawkwood led his troops to that city in an attempt to engage the Florentines in open battle. The Florentines wisely declined, and the White Company had to rest content with firing arrows over the city walls carrying messages such as 'Pisa sends this'. Eventually Hawkwood did manage to entice a Florentine general into battle and defeated his army. By April 1364 he was in command of the plain of Pistoia and had sacked Fiesole. But he failed to capture the city of Florence itself, retreating ignominiously. The Florentines now pressed their advantage, burning much of Livorno and camping menacingly at Cascina scarcely 10 km out of Pisa. Many of Hawkwood's mercenaries had seceded to the Florentines, and after another partial defeat he and the rulers of Pisa deemed it wise to sue for peace. The heavy price was a tribute of ten thousand gold florins for the next ten years.

For the next four years Sir John Hawkwood sold his services elsewhere in Italy. He ravaged the countryside, sometimes retreating to avoid defeat, sometimes victorious. To Pope Urban V, returning from Avignon, his company appeared so formidable that the pontiff declined to land at Livorno. The republic of Pisa was several times indebted to Hawkwood's army, and when the pope's German mercenaries captured him in 1369 he was immediately ransomed. This brief incarceration seems to have made Hawkwood even more pugnacious. He rallied his troops and forced the pope to flee. He then turned on the Florentines and savaged an army that was attempting to put down a revolt by the citizens of San Miniato. His troops attacked Reggio, but the Florentines managed to relieve the city.

The services of such a powerful commander were inevitably in much demand. Hawkwood was employed by Pope Gregory XI, though when the pope failed to pay him properly he turned against his master and simply exacted what he wished from the unfortunate Tuscan countryfolk. Florence, Arezzo, Lucca, Pisa and Siena were all forced to contribute to Hawkwood's coffers, and Florence, desperate that he should leave her alone, granted the English *condottiere* a pension of twelve hundred gold florins a year for the rest of his life.

Florence now increasingly relied on Hawkwood's services, though this did not prevent his fighting anywhere else that seemed profitable. By 1390 he was commander-in-chief of the Florentine forces. His later years were spent in Florence, and there he died after a brief illness in March 1394. As we shall see, the city honoured him with a superb monument in its cathedral.

He was a witty man. He disliked the clergy wishing him peace, since peace, he said, would ruin him. His nickname, appropriately, was '*acuto*', the sharp one. No doubt the memory of Sir John Hawkwood two centuries later led the English pedant Roger Ascham to report the insolent proverb *Inglese italianato è un diabolo incarnato*.

Ascham also regarded renaissance Italy as utterly devoted to Circe, the goddess whose magical arts could turn men into wild beasts. His fellow-countrymen, he wrote, 'being mules and horses before they went [to Tuscany], returned very swine and asses home again'.

The reputation of the Tuscans at this time was further blackened by their association with the notorious political philosophy of Machiavelli. Of course Englishmen were ready to behave if necessary with as much Machiavellian cunning as the man who invented Machiavellianism. Henry VIII's suave minister Cromwell had a copy of Machiavelli's treatise *The Prince* in his library, and his own political career was certainly Machiavellian enough, even if it ended on the scaffold. Sir Walter Ralegh did Machiavelli the singular honour of plagiarizing him without acknowledgement.

Then a new note appears in the seventeenth century. Francis Bacon conceded that a debt was owed to Machiavelli. The Florentine philosopher had shown that 'It is not possible to join the wisdom of the serpent to the innocence of the dove, if we do not know all the characteristics of the serpent – his meanness, his dragging his belly, his slipperiness, his inconstancy, his poison.' Without this knowledge, Bacon argued, 'virtue is vulnerable and defenceless'. The eighteenth-century historians continued Machiavelli's defence. David Hume held that though Machiavelli considered poisoning, assassination and perjury to be legitimate weapons of politics, he personally had displayed a keen indignation against vice and a warm approbation of virtue. And in 1827 Thomas Babington Macaulay attempted to draw a more complex picture of the Tuscan political philosopher than any had done hitherto: 'The whole man,' he wrote, 'seems to be an enigma, a grotesque assemblage of incongruous qualities, selfishness and generosity, cruelty and benevolence, craft and simplicity, abject villainy and romantic heroism.'

By this time the British had long contributed far more positively to Tuscany than had Sir John Hawkwood. Elizabeth I's favourite, Sir Robert Dudley, went to Florence and became a Catholic. Ferdinand I, Duke of Tuscany, impressed by Dudley's reputation as a naval engineer, commissioned him to build the great mole at Livorno and to administer that port. Ferdinand II engaged him to drain the marshes between Pisa and Livorno, and granted him a pension when Dudley successfully accomplished the work. Today you can see some of Dudley's navigational devices in the museum of the history of science in Florence.

Livorno in the twentieth century displays a number of those regrettably ugly commercial characteristics that afflict every great port (though it boasts some entirely pleasing features too). In Dudley's time it was entrancing: 'the neatest, cleanest and pleasantest place that I have seene, their houses painted without side in stories, landskipps, etc., with various Coulors, making a very delightful shewe', as Dudley's contemporary Peter Mundy reported.

Englishmen were increasingly reporting to their fellow-countrymen the astute ways of the Tuscans and the charms of their land. In 1617 Fynes Moryson published his *Itinerary* through the region. He noted, for instance, the wit of the Florentines. When they meet a man about dinner-time, he reported, they ask him has he dined. If he says yes, they then give the impression that had he not, they would have invited him to eat with them. If he says no, they reply, 'Go, Sir, for it is high time to dine.' Tuscans have retained this extremely diverting wit. They possess 'a crusted charm', wrote Norman Douglas in our own century, a 'hard and glittering sanity', a kind of 'ageless enamel' in their temperament.

A quarter of a century after Fynes Moryson visited Tuscany, John Evelyn followed in his footsteps. He was enchanted. At Siena he reported that 'the Air is incomparable'. Joseph Addison marked Evelyn's footsteps, admiring the gothic masterpieces of Siena in spite of his own classical taste: 'When a man sees the prodigious pains and expence that our forefathers have been at in these barbarous buildings, one cannot but fancy to himself what miracles of architecture they would have left us, had they only been instructed in the right way.'

British visitors to Tuscany, schooled in the stern rubrics of classicism, were becoming increasingly censorious. Tobias Smollett visited Tuscany in 1765 and hated it. His published account made people wonder how he ever got back alive. Sterne met him there and called him a 'Choleric Philistine', a 'Smelfungus'. Smollett's account of Siena is typical of the rest of his unfavourable report. He found himself 'indifferently lodged in a house that stunk like a privy'. He 'fared wretchedly at supper'. At Buonconvento the next day he refused to give money to the ostler who, 'in revenge, put two young unbroken stone-horses in the traces next to the coach, which became so unruly that, before we had gone a quarter of a mile, they and the postilion were rolling in the dust'.

Smollett professed distaste even for the pretty Tuscan ladies. 'For my part,' he averred, 'I would rather be condemned for life to the galleys than exercise the office of *cisibeo*, exposed to the intolerable caprices and dangerous resentment of an Italian virago.' Occasionally he would offer some curmudgeonly praise of one of Tuscany's superlative cities. Pisa, he admitted, was 'a fine old city, that strikes you with the same veneration you would feel at the sight of an ancient temple, which bears the marks of decay, without being absolutely dilapidated'.

Smollett visited Tuscany again in 1769, a dying man, attracted to this region because the dry air of Lucca and Pisa was accounted extremely healthy. He and his wife took a villa two miles out of Livorno. There he wrote the bulk of his masterpiece *Humphrey Clinker*, and became, in his own words, 'so dry and emaciated that I may pass for an Egyptian mummy without any other preparation than some pitch and painted linen'. He died aged fifty-one on 17 September 1771, exclaiming to his wife, 'All is well, my dear.' As his Italian doctor observed, he died as he had lived, *'temperamento molto collercio, ma riflessivo'*.

In consequence, perhaps, of its quondam English administrator, Sir Robert Dudley (though he had turned Catholic), and certainly because of the liberal disposition which characterized the citizens of this great port in the eighteenth century, Livorno boasts one of the first Protestant cemeteries in the whole of Tuscany. 'Perhaps the most entrancing sight in Leghorn [Livorno] is the English burying-ground,' Henry Matthews reported in 1820. In the 1770s this was the only spot in Tuscany that could offer a grave to Tobias Smollett. He was buried there in a tomb whose inscription wrongly incises the dates of his life. On the banks of the Leven his cousin erected in his honour a Tuscan column.

Equally censorious was William Beckford, who travelled to Italy in the 1780s, though the charm of the Tuscan countryside did begin to mellow him slightly. On the craggy road from Bologna to Florence, bereft as it seemed of trees, cornfields, even people, he observed, 'I would defy even a Scottish highlander to find means of subsistence in so rude a soil.' As he neared Tuscany the climate improved: 'we saw groves and villages in the dips of hills, and met a string of mules and horses laden with fruit'. He bought figs and peaches from the caravan, and then was entranced by the poplars and cypress groves of Florence. 'I felt, upon entering this world of refinement, as if I could have taken up my abode in it for ever.' He looked at Florence cathedral and justly observed that the architect seemed to have turned his building inside-out, 'nothing in art being more ornamented than the exterior, and few churches so simple within'.

Censoriousness soon returned. The hills around the Arno, covered with 'the hoary olive', seemed to him in a withering decrepit state which reminded him of an old woman dressed in grey. So bizarre seemed the Camposanto at Pisa that he walked round and round the cloisters fifty times, 'discovering at every time some odd novelty'. The environs of Lucca delighted him by their beauty, though he judged the city itself to be uniquely ugly: 'Narrow streets and dismal alleys, wide gutters and cracked pavements, everybody in black.' But his chief scorn was reserved for Siena. The cathedral he described as 'a masterpiece of ridiculous taste and elaborate absurdity. The font, encrusted with alabaster, is worked into a million of fretted arches and puzzling ornaments. There are statues without number and *rilievos* without end of meaning.' Inside he confessed that he 'hardly knew which was the nave, or which was the cross aisle, of this singular edifice, so perfect is the confusion of its parts'. Nicola Pisano's superb pulpit totally defeated Beckford's aesthetic sensibility. 'Near the high altar stands the strangest of pulpits, supported by polished pillars of granite, rising from lions' backs, which serve as pedestals,' he noted. 'In every corner of the place some glittering chapel or other offends and astonishes you.' He never seems to have noticed the lovely shell-like central piazza of this marvellous city.

Happily, other Englishmen were by now developing a renewed appreciation of Tuscan art and life – so many, that Sir Horace Mann, minister plenipotentiary to the ducal court in Florence, grew alarmed that his hospitality might be abused. 'If I could afford it, I really would take a villa near Florence,' he wrote, 'but I am afraid of its becoming a cheesecake house for all the English.' A welcome guest at Palazzo Manetti where he lived in Florence (no. 23 Via Santo Spirito) was Horace Walpole, visiting Italy with the poet Gray. Walpole, like Beckford, found the workmanship and taste of the cathedral at Siena beyond his powers of appreciation. He described the whole place as 'old, and very smug, with very few inhabitants'. But, he wrote, 'You cannot imagine how pretty the country is between this [city] and Florence; millions of little hills planted with trees, and tipped with villas or convents.' The countryside was not, however, geared to tourists. At Radicofani he found himself in a lone inn upon a black mountain by the side of an old fortress: 'no curtains or windows, only shutters! no testers to the beds! no earthly thing to eat but some eggs and a few little fishes!' This particular inn had not improved a hundred years later when Dickens stayed there.

As with many British tourists who visit Tuscany out of season, Walpole was surprised by the Italian weather. (I myself once arrived at San Gimignano on a February afternoon in such a blinding snowstorm that it was impossible to drive.) 'In Italy,' he wrote, 'they seem to have found out how hot their climate is, but not how cold.' He reported that to keep warm the men hung little earthen pans of coals upon their wrists and the women carried portable stoves under their petticoats. In November the river flooded.

The jewellers on the Old Bridge removed their commodities, and in two hours after the bridge was cracked. The torrent broke down the quays, and drowned several coach horses, which are kept here in stables under ground. We were moated into our house all day, which is near the Arno, and had the miserable spectacle of the ruins that were washed along with the hurricane. There was a cart with two oxen not quite dead, and four men in it drowned: but what was ridiculous, there came tiding along a fat hay-cock, with a hen and her eggs, and a cat. The torrent is considerably abated; but we expect terrible news from the country, especially from Pisa, which stands so much lower and nearer the sea. There is a stone here, which when the water overflows, Pisa is entirely flooded. The water rose two ells yesterday above that stone.

The Arno is still capable of flooding, and did so disastrously in 1966.

Soon, as Dr Johnson put it, a person who had not visited Italy was conscious of an inferiority. David Garrick went to Florence and was, he confessed, 'astonish'd at the profusion of fine things'. And Byron called Florence the Etrurian Athens.

> There, too, the Goddess loves in stone, and fills
> The air around with beauty,

he wrote. In the church of Santa Croce he mused on the great Florentine writers of the past, on 'starry Galileo' and on Machiavelli:

> In Santa Croce's holy precincts lie
> Ashes which make it holier, dust which is
> Even in itself an immortality.

His fellow-poet Samuel Rogers declared that of all the fairest cities of the earth, none was so fair as Florence, where (he noted) the past contends with the present and each in turn has the mastery.

William Hazlitt by contrast judged that in Florence the past had overcome the present. 'Florence is like a town that has survived itself,' he wrote in 1826. 'It is distinguished by the remains of early and rude grandeur; it is left where it was three hundred years ago.' (Hazlitt was, so to speak, something of a throwback to the age of Beckford. He described Michelangelo's *David* as 'like an awkward overgrown actor at one of our minor theatres, without his clothes: the head is too big for the body, and it has a helpless expression of distress'.)

English connoisseurs now began to collect Tuscan works of art. The Revd John Sandford deemed it wiser to live in Florence from 1815 to 1837 because of his liaison with a divorcee (whom he subsequently married). He bought an *Annunciation* by Filippo Lippi that had been commissioned for the cathedral of Pistoia and a *Madonna Adoring the Child Jesus* by Luca della Robbia. Another clerical connoisseur, the Revd John Fuller Russell, began to buy Sienese old masters, including an *Adoration of the Magi* by Andrea Vanni, as well as three panels of a polyptych painted in the early fourteenth century by Simone Martini. A third, the Revd Frederick Heathcote Sutton, bought the celebrated *Madonna and Child* by Masaccio that now hangs in the National Gallery, London.

In 1818 Shelley and Mary Godwin took refuge in Italy. At Florence two years later she gave birth to their one surviving child, whom they called Percy after his father and Florence after the city of his birth. Florence appealed to the poet:

. . . the most beautiful city I ever saw. It is surrounded with cultivated hills & from the bridge which crosses the broad channel of the Arno, the view is the most animated and elegant I ever saw. You see three or four bridges – one apparently supported by Corinthian pillars, & the white sails of the boats relieved by the deep green of the forest which comes to the waters edge, & the sloping hills covered with bright villas on every side. Domes and steeples rise on all sides, & the cleanliness is remarkably great.

He loved the hills of olive and vine south of the river, and the chestnut woods and the blue and misty pine forests on the slopes of the Apennines. A young English girl named Sophia Stacey came to stay for a while and charmed the poet before leaving for Rome. About this liaison he wrote his revealing poem 'I Fear Thy Kisses, Gentle Maiden'.

Shelley was frequently ill and would visit Pisa to consult the noted Italian doctor Andrea Vacca Berlinghieri, who told him to give up pills and move to the countryside. So he and Mary rented a house in the chestnut forests near Bagni di Lucca. Mary wrote her novel *Castrucci* about the warlord who ran Lucca in the early fourteenth century. They all rode horses in the woods. Shelley would sit naked by a stream, reading. They also made friends in Livorno, which the poet disliked, though he wrote his ode 'To a Skylark' there.

Then they moved to Pisa. Initially Shelley found Pisa far less congenial than Florence: 'a large and disagreeable city, almost without inhabitants'. Its deserted streets and sombre aspect reminded him of the precinct of Oxford and Cambridge during the vacation, but he set up here a celebrated circle of writers and savants, including among them Byron. He and Mary took rooms in Pisa on the left bank of the Arno, and soon the city began to charm him. When Byron suggested that Venice was more beautiful, Shelley pointed to the old fortress of the city (now, alas, much destroyed by the Second World War) as the sun was sinking. 'Stand on the marble bridge,' he said, 'cast your eye if you are not dazzled on its river glowing as with fire, then follow the graceful curve of the palaces on the Lung' Arno till the arch is naved by the massy dungeon tower, forming in dark relief, and tell me if anything can surpass a sunset at Pisa.'

Shelley and some of his friends now conceived a passion for boating, and in April 1822 the family moved to San Terenzo on the Gulf of La Spezia in order to spend summer by the sea. At the end of June Leigh Hunt and his family arrived at Genoa, and Shelley, anxious to meet them, sailed there on 1 July in his yacht the *Don Juan*. Seven days later he and two companions sailed back. The *Don Juan* sank with all sails up ten miles out to sea from Viareggio.

After ten days the three bodies were washed ashore. In Shelley's pocket was a copy of Keats's poems, which Hunt had lent him. Mary wished to bury Shelley in Rome, near the body of their child, but the quarantine laws forbade it. Instead Shelley's friend Edward John Trelawny first buried the corpses in quicklime and then built a furnace on the beach near the mouth of the River Serchio. In the presence of the local militia, some fishermen, Byron and Leigh Hunt, Shelley was cremated, with offerings of salt, oil, wine and frankincense. Trelawny threw on the pyre the copy of Keats's poems. Byron turned away and swam three miles out to the yacht *Bolivar* and three miles back. Then Trelawny raked out Shelley's heart and gave it to him. Byron gave it to Leigh Hunt. Leigh Hunt gave it to Mary. The poet's ashes were gathered together and transported in the *Bolivar* to Rome, to be buried there in the Protestant cemetery under a stone engraved with

Leigh Hunt's words '*Cor cordium*' and Trelawny's quotation from Shakespeare:

> Nothing of him that doth fade,
> But doth suffer a sea-change
> Into something rich and strange.

For the Romantic poets Tuscany was now sacred. Wordsworth went there in 1837 with Henry Crabb Robinson. They visited the old monastic sanctuaries of Camaldoli and Vallombrosa, Wordsworth impassioned to write a poem on the life and character of St Francis and desperately searching for a copy of Cardinal Buonaventura's biography of the saint. Instead he composed a poem against what he perceived as the tyranny of papal government and then, in 1842, published his poetic *Memorials of a Tour in Italy*. In Florence he had been inspired by the thought of exiled Dante:

> pensive and alone,
> Nor giving heed to aught that passed the while,
> I stood, and gazed upon a marble stone,
> The laurelled Dante's favourite seat. A throne,
> In just esteem, it rivals; though no style
> Be there of decoration to beguile
> The mind, depressed by thought of greatness flown.
> As a true man, who long had served the lyre,
> I gazed with earnestness, and dared no more.
> But in his breast the mighty Poet bore
> A Patriot's heart, warm with undying fire.
> Bold with the thought, in reverence I sat down
> And, for a moment, filled that empty throne.

The Tennysons visited Tuscany when Mrs Tennyson was convalescing from the birth of their stillborn child. On the way they came upon Browning in the Louvre, who suggested that they would infinitely prefer Bagni di Lucca to Lake Como. He was wrong. The couple spent most of the time sitting in a darkened room, veiled against flies and mosquitoes. Distrusting Italian food, they subsisted on peaches and bits of rough, roasted meat. After three weeks they moved to Florence, which they enjoyed much better. Emily Tennyson believed that most Italians were about to forsake Catholicism for the Protestant faith. Alfred feared she would be distressed by the civil strife in Italy at that time. After ten days they set off home. Some said Tennyson left Florence early because he could not find his favourite tobacco there.

Two years later the memory of their visit to Tuscany had metamorphosized itself in Alfred's mind into an idyll:

> O love, what hours were thine and mine,
> In lands of palm and southern pine;
> In lands of palm, of orange blossom,
> Of olive, aloe, and maize and vine.

Inevitably Dickens visited and reported on Tuscany. His recently published *American Notes* had been much criticized, and this time the novelist was determined to present a mellower face to his readers. At Carrara he described the savage treatment of the oxen who dragged the heavy cartloads of marble along the bed of a stream tumbling down the mountainside. Their driver was

the very Devil of true despotism. He had a great rod in his hand, with an iron point; and when they could plough and force their way through the loose bed of the torrent no longer, and came to a stop, he poked it into their bodies, beat it on their heads, screwed it round and round in their nostrils, got them on a yard or two, in the madness of intense pain; repeated all these persuasions, with increased intensity of purpose, when they stopped again; got them on once more; forced and goaded them to an abrupter point of the descent; and when their writhing and smarting, and the weight behind them, bore them plunging down the precipice in a cloud of scattered water, whirled his rod above his head, and gave a great whoop and hallo, as if he had achieved something, and had no idea that they might shake him off, and blindly mash his brains upon the road, in the noon-tide of his triumph.

Later that afternoon Dickens stood in a great workshop in Carrara, filled with beautiful marble statues, and mused that many virtues spring up in miserable ground and many good things have their birth in sorrow and distress. So Dickens blandly suggested, there is an unseen divinity that shapes marble, even though it might also involve some cruelty to animals.

Dickens warmed to the great Tuscan cities: Siena, with its piazza and 'a great broken-nosed fountain in it'; Florence, 'stern and sombre', full of 'Prodigious palaces, constructed for defence, with small distrustful windows heavily barred'; Pisa, which he judged the seventh wonder of the world because of its tower and at least the second or third because of its beggars. He adored 'the whole sweet valley of the Arno'. After leaving Florence he travelled through cheerful Tuscany, he said, with a bright remembrance of it that made 'Italy the fairer for its recollection'.

But for most British, Florence recalls the Brownings. Robert did not in fact respond to Tuscany with anything like Elizabeth's fervour. 'My liking for Italy was always a selfish one,' he told Isa Blagden in 1866. 'I felt alone with my own soul there.' They eloped there partly for the sake of her health in 1846, and immediately she grew better. Even her dog Flush liked Pisa, she reported, 'going out every day and speaking Italian to the little dogs'. After their arrival in Florence she described her life as 'pure magic'.

> The city lies along the ample vale,
> Cathedral, tower and palace, piazza and street,
> The river trailing like a silver cord
> Through all.

At Pisa, she declared, 'we say, "How beautiful!" here we say nothing; it is enough if we can breathe'.

At Florence Elizabeth wrote her 'Casa Guidi Windows' (initially called 'A Meditation on Tuscany') and her 'Pleas before Congress'. There her son was born. The countryside entranced her:

> I found a house at Florence on the hill
> Of Bellosguardo. 'Tis a tower which keeps
> A post of double observation o'er
> The valley of the Arno (holding as a hand
> The outspread city) straight towards Fiesole
> And Mount Morello and the setting sun,
> The Vallombrosan mountains opposite,
> Which sunrise fills as full as crystal cups
> Turned red to the brim because their wine is red.
> No sun could die nor yet be born unseen
> By dwellers at my villa.

Nathaniel Hawthorne and his mother visited the Brownings in Florence in 1858. 'Mrs Browning met us at the door of the drawing-room and greeted us most kindly,' he recalled; 'a pale little woman, scarcely bodied at all; at any rate, only substantial enough to put her slender fingers to be grasped and to speak with a shrill, yet sweet, tenuity of voice. Really, I do not see how Browning can suppose that he has an earthly wife, any more than an earthly child; both are of the elfin-breed, and will away from him, some day when he least thinks of it.' Two years later Elizabeth was dead. In 1861 Robert left Florence for good. Over the fifteenth-century Casa Guidi where they lived (no. 8 Piazza San Felice) a plaque records:

> *Qui scrisse e more*
> *ELISABETTA BARRET BROWNING*
> *che in cuore di donna conciliava*
> *scienza di dotto e spirito di poeta*
> *e fece del suo verso aureo anello*
> *fra Italia e Inghilterra*
> *pone questa memoria*
> *Firenze grata*

> [Here wrote and died
> Elizabeth Barrett Browning
> who in her woman's heart blended
> learning and the spirit of poetry
> and made of her verse a ring of gold
> joining together Italy and England.
> This memorial was placed here
> by grateful Florence
> 1861]

While the Brownings were living in Italy John Ruskin was making those extraordinarily fruitful visits to Tuscany that were, as a result of his subsequent writings, to rehabilitate completely the art and architecture of the region in the eyes of the British. In 1845 he was exploring its medieval sculpture with a growing delight, sketching and making assiduous notes. Of course he was quirky and prejudiced. At Florence, he later recalled, 'the Newgate-like palaces were rightly hateful to me; the old shop and market-streets rightly pleasant; the inside of the Duomo a horror, the outside a Chinese puzzle'. But he adored Lucca; and he had an acute feeling for textures, so that, for instance (as he observed in *The Seven Lamps of Architecture*), 'The transparent

alabasters of San Miniato . . . are more warmly filled, and more brilliantly touched, by every return of morning and evening rays; while
the hues of our cathedrals have died like the iris out of the cloud.'

The British once again were appreciating some of the riches Tuscany
offered. 'It was for this country I was predestined,' wrote Matthew
Arnold in 1865, 'for I found everything just as I expected.' For
Swinburne Siena was a lady, the 'loveliest of my loves'.

In 1902 was published a masterpiece of travel writing: Hilaire
Belloc's *The Path to Rome*. As he descended the Apennines into
Tuscany he described 'the noise of falling waters upon every side,
where the Serchio sprang from twenty sources on the southern slope,
and leapt down between mosses, and quarrelled, and overcame great
smooth dark rocks in busy falls'. For a long time he gazed at the hills
of Carrara, shaped as if to exalt man with unexpected and fantastic
shapes, and to expand his dull life with permanent surprise. The name
given here to the valley of the River Serchio, the Garfagna, sounded to
him 'like the clashing of cymbals'. As for Lucca, it was, said Belloc,
'the neatest, the regularest, the exactest, the most fly-in-amber little
town in the world, with its uncrowded streets, its absurd fortifications,
and its contented silent houses – all like a family at ease and at rest
under its high sun'.

The following year appeared E. M. Forster's *Where Angels Fear to
Tread*, in which the city of Monteriano is in fact the Tuscan town of
San Gimignano. The humanist Forster was prepared to approve even
of the city's patron St Fina (who he calls in his novel St Deodata), a
saint so holy that she ate nothing and died at the age of fifteen, which,
the novelist observed, 'shows how much is within the reach of any
schoolgirl'.

Forster's Italy was the antidote to all the stuffiness he perceived in
his own country. 'There is something majestic in the bad taste of
Italy,' he asserted in *Where Angels Fear to Tread*; 'it is not the bad
taste of a country which knows no better; it has not the nervous
vulgarity of England, or the blinded vulgarity of Germany. It observes
beauty, and chooses to pass it by. But it attains to beauty's confi-
dence.'

A Room with a View, which he published five years later, is even
more besotted with the virtues of Tuscany. When its heroine finds
herself in Santa Croce, Florence, without a Baedeker, she is initially

nonplussed. Of course it had been frescoed by Giotto, but where? Of course Ruskin had praised some of its sepulchral slabs, but which? 'Then the pernicious charm of Italy worked on her,' wrote Forster, 'and instead of acquiring information, she began to be happy.'

Twentieth-century Tuscany did not escape Italian fascism, and in the Second World War the English-speaking world found itself bombing and destroying much that it had previously cherished. Eric Linklater's account of the campaign in Italy points some ironies. French colonial soldiers, for instance, took San Gimignano. 'If the visitor to San Gimignano shudders to read a plaque commemorating its capture by Moroccan infantry – while he has been recalling Dante's embassy from Florence – he may be reconciled a little to history's violent incongruity by remembering that the state of Venice once employed a distinguished soldier of the same race and colour. Othello too was a Moor.' If, as Linklater judged, the viciousness of that campaign was 'no more than evidence of humanity's failure to be sensible, and of the slenderness of its claim to be civilized', at least no one made the attempt to cross the River Arno by force near Florence – thus avoiding making a battlefield of that city.

The campaign in Italy cost fifty-nine thousand dead. The poet Gavin Ewart, serving as an officer in the Royal Artillery, brooded about one of them near La Spezia in April 1945:

> With grey arm twisted over a green face
> The dust of passing trucks swirls over him,
> Lying in the roadside in his proper place,
> For he has crossed the ultimate far rim
> That hides us from the valley of the dead.
> He lies like used equipment thrown aside,
> Of which our swift advance can take no heed,
> Roses, triumphal cars – but this one died.
>
> Once war memorials, pitiful attempt
> In some vague way regretfully to atone
> For those lost futures that the dead had dreamt,
> Covered the land with their lamenting stone –
> But in our hearts we bear a heavier load:
> The bodies of the dead beside the road.

War memorials do have their uses. In Tuscany I often drive to look at the rows of white crosses in the American Military Cemetery (in the valley of the River Greve, on the N2 just south of Florence). Here are buried the remains of 4,402 American servicemen who died in this war, their names beautifully inscribed on a memorial wall. On a headstone are recorded another 209 names: those of Americans who gave their lives in the service of their country and who lie in unknown graves. Maps and plans of the war against Germany and Japan are laid out in mosaic on another wall, as well as a mosaic illustrating the Italian campaign. A cenotaph proclaims: 'Freedom from fear and oppression is ours only in the measure that men who value freedom are ready to sustain its possession and defend it.' Two collects are inscribed on the east wall of the chapel:

O God who art the author of peace and lover of concord, defend us thy humble servants in all assaults of our enemies, that we surely trusting in thy defence may not fear the power of any adversaries;

and

O Lord support us all the day long until the shadows lengthen and the evening comes and the fever of life is over and our work is done. Then in thy mercy grant us a holy rest and peace at the last.

The Second World War ended with a divided world, with Tito of Yugoslavia already threatening Italian territory by force. As Eric Linklater commented, the allies 'had won their laurels, but they must wear their wreaths about a steel helmet, and drink their wine with a rifle between their knees'.

Yet to come to Italy in the Second World War had been welcome to many. Gwenyth Hughes, serving with the Second New Zealand Division, came here from the Middle East and wrote:

> I had not seen the earth so tender green
> For two long dusty years:
> Only I knew nostalgia too keen
> Where sands of Egypt stretched
> In utter desolation to the line
> Of merging sand and sky.

Tuscany was welcoming, even in wartime. Tuscany is yet more welcoming in peacetime.

Horace Walpole found it so during the carnival of 1740. 'I have done nothing but slip out of my domino into bed, and out of bed into my domino,' he exulted. 'The end of Carnival is frantic bacchanalian; all the morn one makes parties in masque to the shops and coffee-houses, and all the evening to the operas and balls. *Then have I danced, good Gods! How I have danced!*'

Walpole found the courtesy and complete lack of censoriousness shown by the Tuscans utterly refreshing. 'Here they do not catch at those little dirty opportunities of saying any ill-natured thing they know of you, do not abuse you because they may, or talk gross bawdy to a woman of quality.'

A hundred years later Elizabeth Barrett Browning discovered the same charm. You can discover the Tuscans today, equally charming, gay and innocent.

5

The Allure of Florence

Florence in my imagination is a dream city, like Rose Macaulay's ancient Trebizond, 'shining towers and domes shimmering on a far horizon'. Oddly enough, even those who have lived there a long time have often wondered whether the beauties they saw existed as a marvellous fantasy, not as reality. 'Florence is beautiful, as I said before, and must say again and again, most beautiful,' wrote Elizabeth Barrett Browning in a letter of 1847:

> The river rushes through the midst of its palaces like a crystal arrow, and it is hard to tell, when you see all by the clear sunset, whether those churches, and houses, and windows, and bridges, and people walking, in the water or out of the water, are the real walls and windows, and bridges, and people, and churches.

What is odder is that this vision persists, even at the height of the tourist season, when to say that the city is full is an enormous understatement.

I first went to Florence one March at the age of seventeen. I arrived by train late at night and went to bed. In the morning the klaxons of bus and taxi-drivers woke me. They sounded delicious. After breakfast I walked along the Via Cavour in the morning sunshine, past the Palazzo Medici-Riccardi, and then down the Via Martelli to the cathedral square. I shall never forget turning the corner and seeing both cathedral and Baptistery, the former's walls encased in white marble from Carrara, green from Prato and red from the Maremma, the latter simply green and white. Contrary to what aesthetes might say, it was undoubtedly the facade of the cathedral that most entranced me. I am certain that in those days I did not know that the original facade, which had reached only a third of its projected height, was demolished in the second half of the sixteenth century and that the present one, designed by Emilio de Fabris, was built between 1871 and 1887. Nor did I know then that the great bronze doors were created and placed here even later, between 1899 and 1903. I know these things now and still do not care. Indeed I think the creators of these doors – G. Cassioli, who designed the one on the right in 1899, and A. Passagli, who spent the years 1897 to 1903 making the one on the left – deserve far more credit than they are usually given.

The porches of Florence cathedral are magnificent. The Porta dei Canonici near the bell-tower bears lovely fourteenth-century sculpture by Lorenzo d'Ambrogio and Piero di Tedesco. A few years later Giovanni d'Ambrogio supervised the carving of the Porta della Mandorla on the north side. The statues of the gable depicting the Assumption of the Virgin date from the early fifteenth century, and the late-fifteenth-century mosaic of the Annunciation in the lunette is by the brilliant Ghirlandaio brothers.

Fortunately I had been out of bed almost at the crack of dawn. In those days I did not know that every day at noon Florence cathedral closes for two and a half hours – as does most of Florence. (Museums may not, but beware that they do not simply stay open till two o'clock in the afternoon, and then close for the rest of the day.) Naturally I had done a good deal of homework and particularly wanted to see inside the monument painted by Paolo Uccello to the memory of the English *condottiere* Sir John Hawkwood.

It disappointed me. After the bright sunshine outside, the interior of Florence cathedral can seem momentarily gloomy, even dull. These days I like Uccello's monument much better. It needs setting in its historical context for a proper appreciation. The Italian renaissance had simply not quite solved the problem of creating equestrian statues. Two existed from antiquity: one at Pavia and the famous statue of Marcus Aurelius in Rome. However much they tried, the Italians of renaissance Tuscany failed to match them. Successful equestrian monuments in wood, stucco and cement had been created. By their very nature, they soon crumbled into dust. The first successful bronze equestrian monument was in fact cast in Ferrara only eight years after Uccello was commissioned to paint the memorial to Hawkwood. Incredible though it may seem, this Ferrara monument was demolished in 1796. The earliest ones that survive are Donatello's Gattamelata monument in Padua, followed closely by Verrocchio's Colleoni monument in Venice. So in 1436 it was deemed best to commission Uccello to paint a fresco of the dead mercenary. Uccello was already noted for his uncanny gifts with perspective. And he had spent his early career working on the mosaics of San Marco, Venice, where the bronze horses over the entrance to the cathedral were a daily inspiration. In the words of John Pope-Hennessy, 'When he came to plan the Hawkwood fresco, his memory of these great bronze castings was still fresh, and round his painted horse there blows, for the first time in portrayals of the kind, the life-giving breath of the antique.'

The very excellence of the proportions can make you forget that you are inside the world's fourth largest cathedral. So spare and uncluttered is the interior that you almost must search for its treasures. Here, for example, in the third chapel of the central apse is a superb bronze urn by Ghiberti, containing the bones of St Zenobius. The bust of Giotto (with its epitaph by Politian) was made in 1490 by Benedetto da Maiano and is to be found in the first bay of the south aisle. Find in the south aisle the tomb and bust of Brunelleschi, who created the great dome surmounting the cathedral. Over the door of the old sacristy (between the central and south apses) is Luca della Robbia's glazed terracotta sculpture of the Ascension. There is more fine work by Della Robbia in the new sacristy, as well as his terracotta of the Resurrection over the door. Florence cathedral gave Della Robbia some fine commissions at this time, for he was also employed to work with Michelozzo in creating the bronze doors to this sacristy.

If you are intrigued by what existed here before this superb building, you can visit the excavations of the old cathedral underneath. Here are a romanesque crypt, tombs and the remains of old Roman buildings. But, as if to intrude even into the past, four huge pillars from the present nave thrust down into the excavations.

When I first went to Florence the finest work of art in the cathedral was the unfinished *Pietà* that Michelangelo intended for his own tomb. Now you must go to see it in the Museo dell'Opera del Duomo (no. 9 Piazza del Duomo). As with all Michelangelo's work, no one word sums up its subject. Here we are looking not really at a Pietà so much as at an indescribably moving combination of the Deposition and a Lamentation over the dead Christ. As we have seen, Michelangelo began the work in 1547, and having become frustrated because of flaws in the marble first apparently mutilated parts of the work before allowing his assistant Tiberio Calcagni to finish it.

No assistant – scarcely any other sculptor – could have been equal to the task, if only because no one else could attack marble the way Michelangelo did. 'I saw Michelangelo at work,' wrote Blaise de Vigenère in 1550: 'He had passed his sixtieth year and although he was not very strong, yet in a quarter of an hour he caused more splinters to fall from a very hard block of marble than three young masons in three or four times as long.' The result was that Michelangelo worked a piece of marble so finely that onlookers continually feared he would cut away too much or break it. 'He attacked the work with such energy that I thought it would fly into pieces,' Vigenère continued: 'With one blow he brought down fragments three or four fingers in breadth, and so exactly at the point marked, that if only a little more marble had fallen he would have risked spoiling the whole work.' All this is clear to see in Michelangelo's Florentine *Pietà*, where Calcagni's contribution is thin, elongated, meagre. Yet the face of Nicodemus, who supports both the dead Lord and the Virgin, is filled with emotion – a portrait, as Vasari tells us, of Michelangelo himself.

On my first visit to Florence cathedral, as on many subsequent visits, I relished a particular example of Vasari's own work: the fresco of the Last Judgement inside the dome of the cathedral, a fresco he was working on at his death in 1574 and Federico Zuccari completed. Climbing the dome offers much closer views of the promised torments of the damned (infinitely more fascinating, considered as works of art, than the rewards of the saved). You follow the same corridors and the 463 steps used by those who built the dome, between its two shells and then up a flight of iron steps to the beautiful marble lantern. Then the whole city lies at your feet.

This then is Florence cathedral, in Matthew Arnold's judgement the most beautiful church in the world. (He excluded the interior from this praise.) He added: 'it always looks to me like a hen gathering its chickens under its wings, it stands in such a soft, lovely way, with Florence round it.'

In front of the cathedral on Easter Sunday is re-enacted the medieval religious ceremony quaintly known as 'Exploding the Cart'. The cart

is a huge gilded pagoda on wheels, decorated with tassels and surmounted by a crown. It trundles into the cathedral square. Then a
representation of the Holy Spirit, in the form of a dove on a wire,
swoops from the high altar through the open doors of the cathedral
into the pagoda, which bursts into flames.

Next to the cathedral is its free-standing bell-tower, the famous
Campanile:

Giotto's tower,
The lily of Florence blossoming in stone,

as Longfellow described it. Giotto in fact designed at most the first
storey when he became cathedral architect in 1334. Intricate white,
green and red marble decoration on the bell-tower matches the cathedral facade. The statues on this elegant bell-tower are nearly all
noteworthy, though the lower ones have been replaced simply because
the originals by Donatello, Andrea Pisano and Nanni di Bartolo have
weathered so badly. (They are now in the Museo dell'Opera del
Duomo.) Look for the casts of prophets and sybils designed by
Donatello for the niches in the second storey, and for the reliefs done
by Luca della Robbia on the north face.

What makes this 85 m high tower so elegant is not, however, its
decoration or its sculptures but its beautifully modulated windows –
the first two storeys with a pair of double-arched openings, rising to
the third with its single, triple-arched opening beneath the cornice.

Across the cathedral square stands the gleaming Baptistery, which
Florentines habitually describe as the oldest building in the city, though
they rarely agree when it was built. The question first raised in the
minds of the British is generally a different one: why is it so huge? The
answer lies in the fact that when it was first built (and for long
afterwards) baptism was performed usually no more than once a year,
when the number of candidates and their supporters would readily fill
it. And it also served for other acts of worship.

The building, which today is exquisitely faced with geometric patterns of green and white Pisan marble outside (and black and white
patterns of marble inside), stands on the site of a Roman palace dating
from the century before Christ. A Christian baptistery was almost
certainly in existence here by the seventh century. The present eight-
sided building probably dates from the tenth century and initially had a

semicircular apse, replaced three hundred years later by the present rectangular one. The pyramid-shaped roof above the three-storeyed walls hides a dome. As for the porphyry columns on either side of the great doors facing the cathedral, they are cast-offs. The Pisans sent them in 1135 to be used in the new cathedral. The cathedral architects thought them insufficiently sturdy and relegated them to the Baptistery, where their function is purely decorative and not at all structural.

Once these columns flanked beautiful bronze doors created in 1336 by Andrea Pisano. In the early fifteenth century they were relegated to the south door. In spite of this slight, they remain marvellous examples of gothic art: twenty-eight quatrefoil frames containing scenes from the life of John the Baptist as well as the theological and cardinal virtues.

Pisano's doors were removed after Lorenzo Ghiberti was commissioned, after a public competition, to design more bronze doors for the Baptistery. In the Museo Nazionale of Florence you can see the trial panel he submitted, alongside one by Brunelleschi, who tied with Ghiberti but refused to collaborate with him. Both panels depict the attempted sacrifice of Isaac by his father Abraham. I think I like Brunelleschi's best, for its vigorous angel who is actually seizing Abraham's arm to stop him slitting his son's throat. On the other hand, Ghiberti's donkey, poking its nose out at the onlooker, is much more vigorous than Brunelleschi's. And I like Brunelleschi's weedy twisted Isaac far less than the splendid naked youth portrayed by Ghiberti.

At any rate Ghiberti began work, and the age of Tuscan renaissance sculpture dawned. The briefest comparison between the north doors, which Ghiberti created between 1403 and 1424, and his east doors, dating from 1425 and 1452, shows it developing. In the first of the two sets of doors gothic quatrefoils of the kind used by Pisano still frame the scenes. The east door by contrast contains only ten panels. The gothic quatrefoils have disappeared, allowing the sculptor space for masterly essays in the new art of perspective. In the story of Jacob and Esau, for example, Ghiberti has emphasized this by making the youth in the centre actually turn his back on us and walk into the scene towards his father. Behind them successive Roman arches, with smaller figures amongst them, redouble this effect of perspective, while in the distance to the right a youth climbs a mountainside. The illusion that Ghiberti has so brilliantly created is of a space far deeper than the actual depth of the sculpture itself.

The interior of the Baptistery is as impressive. Twenty-five metres in diameter, and surrounded by Corinthian columns – almost certainly taken from an earlier Roman building – topped by a gallery of divided windows, its decorated thirteenth-century pavement is fascinating, with signs of the zodiac, motifs from the orient, and so on. The whole spirit is Byzantine, as is the spirit of the thirteenth-century mosaic that completely covers the dome. As in the cathedral I find the scenes of the Last Judgement marvellously savage. Notice the devil on Christ's left, with a terrified human being in his mouth, while two animals protrude from his ears to attack other damned souls.

When I was young the *Mary Magdalen* by Donatello, now in the Cathedral Museum, was the greatest work of art inside the Baptistery. Still there, happily, is the tomb he and Michelozzo created for Baldassare Coscia, who called himself Pope John XXIII but has since been dubbed an anti-Pope.

Where should one go, then, after the cathedral square? Obviously to see Michelangelo's *Pietà* and Donatello's *Mary Magdalen* in the nearby Cathedral Museum. Once there do not miss the famous *Singing Gallery* by Luca della Robbia, which was once set over the doorway to the north sacristy of the cathedral. There are ten of these sculptures, illustrating Psalm 150 ('Let everything that hath breath praise the Lord'). Luca della Robbia must be one of the few artists to have been paid more for his work by delivering late. By 1434 we know that four of the reliefs for the *Singing Gallery* were finished. A year later it was agreed to offer the sculptor extra money, because the work was proving harder than he had expected and because the carvings were proving so beautiful. As a second stroke of fortune he was able to enlist the help and advice of Donatello. The completed work is a triumph. Fat little boys dance to drums and pipe. Serious boys, such as we have seen in any school or church choir, sing with all the tension of trebles. And most enchanting of all, underneath the long trumpets of the musicians four unrestrained little girls dance for joy. 'Praise him with the sound of the trumpet. Praise him with the timbrel and dance.' And so they do.

The question 'Where next in Florence for artistic and historical delight?' the answer must be, 'Almost anywhere', with the promise that Florence offers its visitors much more than its art and history. But art and history do appear in Florence in the most unlikely places. Even the railway station is a notable mid-thirties construction, and on a nearby wall a notice tells you that here Shelley composed his 'Prometheus Unbound' and the 'Ode to the West Wind'. Not far away along Via Nazionale, at the corner of Via d'Arriane, a grimmer plaque records the extraordinary height reached by the waters when the city was flooded in November 1966.

Although Florence has some half a million inhabitants and at the height of the tourist season most of them seem to be causing traffic jams in the city centre, in truth they nearly all live in the sprawling suburbs. The human scale of the city that until the First World War was surrounded by fields, hills and vineyards can still be savoured. In quiet squares and narrow streets you can often escape the traffic. Here craftsmen open their workshops to the street. However much visitors complain about fighting for accommodation in midsummer, at other times of the year I have never found it difficult to find a palatable *pensione* in one of these areas.

It is undoubtedly best to walk about Florence. You can cross the city on foot in just over half an hour, but if you do so you are walking too fast. If you must ride in the city centre, take a bus. (You buy your ticket in a tobacconist's or in a bar.) Florence needs leisurely strolls to appreciate its merchants as well as its medieval, renaissance or elegantly twentieth-century streets.

Thousands of shops and open-air stalls in Florence sell ceramics and leather goods, jewellery and figurines of Michelangelo's *David*, pottery and mosaics, glass and embroidery. Florence is a centre of fashion, the great houses concentrated in Via Tornabuoni. Close by are less expensive boutiques – cheaper, but still selling clothes and accessories that have written all over them the quality that is Florence. The Florentines revel in notebooks and stationery made of delightfully marbled paper.

They also love markets. The Mercato Nuovo in the Via Porta Rossa opens every day in summer (Tuesday to Saturday for the rest of the year). In Florence it is known as 'il Porcellino', from the ugly bronze boar which Pietro Tacca copied from an antique statue in the Uffizi. Cosimo I set up the Loggia in the middle of the sixteenth century as a market for gold and silk. Today the Mercato Nuovo has come down a little in the world and devotes itself to selling straw hats, ceramics, leather goods, lace and the other knick-knacks that appeal to the heart of every tourist.

Like every other city in the world, Florence boasts a flea market, the Mercato delle Pulci in the Piazza dei Compi. (It operates on Saturdays and Tuesdays from eight in the morning to seven in the evenings, with a long break for lunch at one.) Another open-air market, selling the souvenirs which always seem much better value in Florence than anywhere else, sets up its stalls every day (save Saturdays in summer and Mondays in winter) on the Piazza San Lorenzo, behind the Palazzo Medici-Riccardi and beside San Lorenzo – the church which Brunelleschi rebuilt as a fitting last resting-place for the Medici dynasty.

None of these is my favourite Florentine market. I can think of no greater pleasure in Florence than to wander north of San Lorenzo through the open-air stalls along the Via dell'Ariento, across the Via Panicale (where clothes are sold from more open-air stalls), to the huge Mercato Centrale. The Mercato Centrale is no tourist market, but the city's main food market, open every weekday morning and all day on Sundays. You can park underneath it. Its nineteenth-century cast-iron hall (built by Giuseppe Mengone in 1874 and beautifully restored in 1980) is stupendous. Upstairs you buy fruit and vegetables. Downstairs is a cornucopia of deer, quail, pigeons, grouse and – sold by the butchers – wild boar. I still find it bizarre to see the head and shoulders of a boar glaring at me, while his rear parts have already been neatly sliced away and sold to customers. One morning in the Mercato Centrale I saw a butcher call to two extremely pretty girls who were coquettishly walking by and then stroke the horns of such a boar. The Italian word *cornuto* means both a horned animal and a cuckold, an inspired connection lost in English since Shakespeare's Forester in *As You Like It* cried, 'The horn, the horn, the lusty horn/Is not a thing to laugh to scorn'.

Most tourists will no doubt buy fruit for picnics but also want to patronize the restaurants of Florence. There are of course many expensive ones; but the intimate, homely *trattorie*, filled with workmen and businessmen from the immediate neighbourhood, have their own entrancing savour. In my early days in Florence I used to eat very well and cheaply at the *mense* (students' canteens) at no. 2 Piazza Santissima Annunziata and no. 25a Via San Gallo, but I can no longer prove I am a student. (There are other *mense* at no. 66 Via dei Servi and no. 51 Viale Morgagni. They open from 11.45 to 14.15 and from 19.00 to 20.45.) Ice-cream and cake shops, delicatessens and bars fit themselves into every nook and cranny of the city. In the bars you pay considerably more to sit down and be served. The locals eat standing up, paying at the till for their sandwich and *cappuccino* before being served at the bar. The English phrase 'snack bar', with its unfortunate connotations 'cheap and nasty', is a singularly bad translation of Florence's delightfully named and usually excellent *rosticcerie*, *tavole calde* and *fiaschetterie*.

Students and young people will relish the cafés and bars around the Piazza San Marco, which are populated by their opposite numbers from the nearby university and Academy of Art. The Dominican church and convent that gave the square its name stand to the north of the piazza. San Marco is a church that assumed its present grandeur only gradually. Michelozzo restored it in 1452; Giambologna added two splendid side chapels in 1580; and three hundred years later Fra Gioacchino Pronti gave it a baroque facade. Michelozzo also gave the monks their fine Cloister of San Antonio, a lovely renaissance building, and the pilgrim's hospice which now houses a collection of works by Fra Angelico, many of them brought here from other churches in the city. There are splendid works of art among them, but no one in Florence should miss the celebrated frescos which Fra Angelico and his pupils painted in the corridors, cloisters and dormitory cells of their monastery.

You get in at no. 3, to the right of the church of San Marco. The most famous fresco in the whole convent is, I suppose, the *Annunciation* which Fra Angelico painted on the wall of the upper corridor opposite the staircase. To my eyes, equally fine is the *Noli Me Tangere* he painted in the first dormitory cell to the left of this *Annunciation*. Whereas the *Annunciation* is total stillness, his *Noli Me Tangere* almost moves as you look at it. A half-turning Jesus gently prevents the half-kneeling Mary Magdalen from clasping him. His haloed head is silhouetted against a fence behind him, the Magdalen's against the tomb. The colour of her long golden hair matches his. And this is a Tuscan garden.

Yet if I were to choose the one fresco that most moves me in the convent of San Marco I should choose neither of these but the uncanny *Mocking of Christ* in cell seven. Jesus sits blindfold on a podium, dressed in a white robe, wearing the crown of thorns and carrying a sceptre in his left hand and an orb in his right. In front of him are seated the Virgin Mary and St Dominic. They seem to play no part in what is happening. Mary contemplates, one hand on her cheek. St Dominic, hand to his chin, is reading. What adds a remarkable *frisson* to the whole composition is the way Fra Angelico has portrayed those mocking Jesus. They appear merely as disembodied hands, beating and pulling at him, as a face which spits at him, and a fifth hand which cruelly feigns to worship him by raising a cap from a non-existent head.

Walk from here past the university along Via Giovanni Battista and you reach another church which Michelozzo rebuilt in his masterly fashion. The church of Santissima Annunziata was founded in 1250. Michelozzo was required to extend it because of the enormous crowds who came to see a painting which had apparently been miraculously finished overnight by an angel while the artist slept. That painting is still there, in an enormous tabernacle designed by Michelozzo. But – artistically at any rate – of far greater interest are many other paintings in this church: the *Birth of the Virgin Mary* by Andrea del Sarto, in which the model for the Virgin was his wife; a *Coming of the Magi* by the same artist, in which this time he has portrayed himself (in the right-hand corner); a splendid mannerist *Visitation* by Jacopo Pontormo; and a still greater mannerist masterpiece, Rosso Fiorentino's *Assumption*.

Enjoying Florence is a mixture of shopping, eating, talking, walking and looking at some of the greatest works of art and architecture ever produced. At least one day, on however short a visit to the city, should be devoted to exploring that part of Florence lying south of the River Arno. From the cathedral square Via dei Calzaiuoli leads past the guildhall and chapel of Orsanmichele on its way to the Piazza della Signoria. Orsanmichele is, I think, an acquired taste. The problem is scale. Orcagna's famous tabernacle is really too huge for the place. (It conceals one of Orsanmichele's ten pretty little rose-windows, for instance.) The detailed, delicate work on the tabernacle itself was designed to be examined from all sides, but its situation by no means makes this immediately apparent and one can easily miss the fine death and assumption of the Virgin at the back.

Outside, the rich diversity of the early renaissance sculpture in its niches is hard to take in at one go. Even so anyone who persists in exploring it is richly rewarded. The very first niche where the Via de'Lamberti joins the Via dei Calzaiuoli contains the first full-size renaissance statue to be cast in bronze, Ghiberti's *St John the Baptist*. Beyond the door you find what is, in my view, Andrea Verrocchio's supreme achievement: the figures of Christ and doubting Thomas. Vasari's description of this masterpiece has never been bettered. For a long time, he tells us, the niche was left empty because so many sculptors, with their rival supporters, craved this commission. Finally the statues were allotted to Verrocchio. Vasari continues:

Andrea made the models and the moulds and cast them and they came out so sound and complete and well-made that the casting was exquisite. Then he chased and finished them and brought them to their present state of perfection, which could not be greater. In Thomas you see at the same time both doubt and a desire to find out the truth, combined with the love with which he places his hand on the side of Christ. Christ himself, in whose figure is all the grace and divinity that art can give, raises his arm with a gesture of great freedom and opens his robe to dispel the unbelief of his incredulous disciple.

Verrocchio was not the greatest sculptor of the fifteenth century. That palm must go to Donatello. Walk further around Orsanmichele to find his agile, beautifully modelled relief of St George killing the dragon, with the rescued maiden watching in an exceedingly winsome pose. (This, incidentally, is a copy of the original, which is now in the Bargello.) Further on, just before the statue of the Madonna and Child, is his magical *St Mark*, with his mobile drapery and pensive, bearded face. In 1411 when he began work on this masterpiece, Donatello was only twenty-five.

All this is delaying a visit south of the river, and the marvellous statues and buildings around the Piazza della Signoria threaten to do the same. Created in 1307 as the Piazza del Popolo, it stands on the site of Roman baths, a reminder that Florence was founded by Julius Caesar. Here is the elegant Loggia dei Lanzi, with its famous statues, designed by Orcagna and built in the second half of the fourteenth century.

It needs a strong will to walk on, ignoring the Palazzo Vecchio, with its celebrated asymmetrical tower, 95 m high. Arnolfo di Cambio designed this severely magnificent building at the very end of the thirteenth century, and its exterior has scarcely changed since then. Other artists and architects have enriched its interior. The huge 'Salone dei Cinquecento' was built in the 1490s by Simone Cronaca and decorated with frescos by Vasari. When Cosimo I defeated the Sienese,

Vasari had the excellent idea of commemorating the victory by erecting here a statue of *Victory* which Michelangelo had sculpted in the 1530s, intending it for the tomb of Pope Julius II. (Michelangelo eventually signed a new contract which cut down by half the number of statues for this tomb, leaving this one homeless. Eventually his nephew gave it to Cosimo.)

Vasari also created in the Palazzo Vecchio a charming private study (which, like much else in the palace, is today open to the public), and Vincenzo Borghini decorated it with brilliant mannerist allegories. But all this must be renounced for another day in order to reach the treasures that are south of the Arno.

Cross the river by the Ponte Vecchio.

> Taddeo Gaddi built me. I am old;
> Five centuries old,

Henry Wadsworth Longfellow apostrophized this remarkable bridge . . .

> And when I think that Michel Angelo
> Hath leaned on me, I glory in myself.

His fellow-countryman Mark Twain, on the other hand, made fun of it, and the river too:

It is popular to admire the Arno. It is a great historical creek with four feet in the channel and some scows floating around. It would be a very plausible river if they could pump some water into it. They call it a river, and they all think it *is* a river do these dark and bloody Florentines. They even help out the delusion by building bridges over it.

In my view the poets have it against Mark Twain. Add Byron to Longfellow:

> Along the banks where smiling Arno sweeps
> Was modern Luxury of Commerce born,
> And buried Learning rose, redeemed to a new Morn.

In the sixteenth century Grand Duke Ferdinand I banned from the Ponte Vecchio the butchers who had sold meats there for two hundred years, replacing them with aesthetically more acceptable workers in precious metals. Gradually these newcomers extended their shops, building outwards over the water and propping up three storeys with precarious brackets. (Happily they are likely to stand for many more years, as a result of the 1966 floods which forced the city to restore them.) In the 1560s the Medici built a covered passage above these shops, along which they could walk from their offices in the Uffizi to the Pitti Palace – one of our ultimate objectives on this ramble. As you thread your way through the goods and trinkets spread out on cloths by the merchants of the Ponte Vecchio, notice the bust of Benvenuto Cellini, himself a master medallist and goldsmith, erected here in 1900, four centuries after his birth.

So the Via Guicciardini leads up to the Pitti Palace. Of all Florence's fifty-seven palaces built as private homes, this is the biggest. Luca Pitti began building it in 1440; it seems to me a crude way of showing off. He went bankrupt. In 1549 the unfinished building was bought by the wealthy wife of Cosimo I, and Bartolommeo Ammannati set to work enlarging it and built the grand staircase. He put the superb renaissance windows in the ground floor of the facade. By 1616 this facade had reached its present proportions, 227 m long and incorporating twenty-three windows. To complete the building, over the next two centuries a couple of wings were added. Naturally King Vittorio Emanuele II used it as his palace between 1865 and 1871, when Florence was the capital of Italy. He gave it to the state in 1919.

Today the Pitti Palace is an art gallery, housing no fewer than eight Tintorettos, eleven works by Raphael, twelve by Rubens and fourteen Titians.

I find the palace imposing. I find its gardens magnificent. The Boboli Gardens, as they are called, began to be laid out by Niccolò Tribolo for Eleanor of Toledo. When he died Ammannati, Buontalenti and others continued the work. Restored Roman statues, new works by renaissance sculptors, fountains, grottoes, magnificent cedars of Lebanon, and a great amphitheatre designed by Ammannati laid the foundations which others enriched. Alfonso Parigi the Younger planted the magnificent avenue of cypresses in 1637. Giambologna created the famous fountain of Oceanus. He was also commissioned to sculpt a portrait of Giovanna of Austria, wife of Grand Duke Francesco II, but when Francesco fell in love with Bianca Cappello, the project came to an end. Later one of his successors, Ferdinand II, had the colossal statue completed, erecting it in the Boboli Gardens to symbolize 'Abundance', as a tribute to his own benevolent self.

William Beckford visited the Boboli Gardens in 1780 and was entranced.

> I ascended terrace after terrace robed by a thick underwood of bay and myrtle, above which rise several nodding towers and a long sweep of venerable wall almost entirely concealed by ivy. You would have been enraptured with the broad masses of shade and dusky alleys that opened as I advanced, with white statues of fauns and sylvans glimmering amongst them, some of which pour water into sarcophagi of the purest marble covered with antique *rilievos*.

He rested on capitals of columns and ancient friezes scattered about as seats. He then followed a winding path as far as Forte di Belvedere, the huge fortress designed by Buontalenti in the shape of a six-pointed star. He returned to his lodgings 'delighted', as he put it, 'with a ramble that had led my imagination so far into antiquity'.

Beckford could not in those days step from the Boboli Gardens into the fortress. We can, to be offered superb panoramas in all directions. The way out leads directly to the best stretch of the old thirteenth-century city walls. From the Porta San Giorgio the steeply descending Via di Belvedere leads alongside the wall past olive trees to the fourteenth-century arch known as Porta San Miniato. Above us is the church of San Miniato al Monte, and (slightly lower down) the Piazzale Michelangelo. This *piazzale* offers what is certainly most visitors' favourite view of the entire city and beyond to the Apennines, impressive, even though it cannot compare with the panoramas from Forte di Belvedere. Some of Michelangelo's statues are reproduced here including of course his *David*, looking very much 'the presiding genius of Florence', as D. H. Lawrence called him.

It is time to go to see his tomb in Santa Croce. The road leads down to the narrow medieval Via di San Niccolò. This street leads into the equally entrancing medieval Via dei Bardi (so named because of the palaces of the rich Bardi family who lived here), but to walk to Santa Croce we must turn right just as we reach it. Cross the Arno by the Ponte alle Grazie and walk along Via dei Benci, turning right to the church along Borgo Santa Croce.

Santa Croce is the Westminster Abbey of Florence. Machiavelli is buried here. So is Galileo. In 1564 Michelangelo's body was brought from Rome to lie in the tomb made for him by Vasari. Rossini is buried here, though he died in Paris. Here is a monument to Dante but not his body. Bernardo Rossellino created here a lovely mid-fifteenth-century tomb for the Florentine humanist Leonardo Bruni. Antonio Canova sculpted an impressive neo-classical monument to the poet Vittorio Alfieri.

The fine monuments of Santa Croce are not all funerary ones. The pulpit by Benedetto da Maiano, a contemporary of Rossellino, bears exquisite carvings of the four virtues and scenes from the life of St Francis. Giotto painted frescos for the Peruzzi Chapel and the Bardi Chapel (including one of St Francis receiving the stigmata). In the second Bardi Chapel is a crucifix by Donatello. And Donatello sculpted the Madonna in the *Annunciation* on the south side of the main church (next to the door). With her long slender neck and her elegance, she seems to me to hover very much on the borderline between the sacred and the profane.

Santa Croce is the finest Franciscan church in Florence, basically dating from the early fourteenth century. The monks were given a marvellous renaissance chapter house when Brunelleschi built for them the Bardi Chapel in the 1430s. He also designed their great cloister. Their former refectory is now a museum.

Santa Croce had no bell-tower until Gaetano Baccani built the present one in 1847. Worse, the facade was left unfinished until 1853, when a benevolent Englishman, Francis Joseph Sloane, paid the Florentine architect Niccolò Matas to create the three delightful gables and for the facade a coloured marble pastiche of the style of the thirteenth century.

To the north of Santa Croce, Via delle Pinzóchere leads to Casa Buonarroti, made out of three houses Michelangelo bought in 1508. Today it is an art gallery and museum devoted to his memory. Here you can see Michelangelo's earliest surviving sculpture: the *Madonna of the Stairs*. The Virgin is immensely solemn, as a fat little Jesus pushes his head inside her dress to her breast. Clearly we are to understand that she foresees her son's passion. And with the utmost subtlety the sculptor has suggested this in the carving of the infant's arm, which hangs limply as if dead, and by an unfinished child in the background who seems to be carrying a cross.

No doubt few will manage to complete such a long ramble in one day. If by now it is time for lunch, the Piazza Santa Croce, surrounded by seats, makes a fine spot for a summer picnic. If it is time for supper, the surrounding *trattorie* are excellent.

6

A Canter through the Uffizi

The Uffizi in Florence, housing one of the greatest collections of art in the world, certainly the finest in Italy, is itself a work of art. Giorgio Vasari designed it in 1560, to serve as offices (*Uffizi*) for Cosimo I, and after Vasari's death the work was completed by Bernardo Buontalenti.

Right away let it be said that the seemingly endless rooms of this fantastic art gallery can be daunting. When Mark Twain and his companions visited the city, he recalled that, 'We wandered through the endless collections of paintings and statues of the Pitti and Uffizi galleries, of course,' adding apologetically, 'I make that statement in self-defence; there let it stop. I could not rest under the imputation that I visited Florence and did not traverse its weary miles of picture galleries.'

The problem (if I dare use such a word about the Uffizi) is that of *embarras de richesse*. Personally I have a lot of stamina in pursuing Tuscan art; nonetheless I have learned to take each visit to the Uffizi at a canter, so to speak, sometimes not remotely trying to see even the whole of one room, but choosing one masterpiece and enjoying that and that alone. But this counsel of self-protection keeps breaking down. How do you choose just one painting from a room containing Botticelli's famous *Primavera*, his *Madonna of the Magnificat*, his *Birth of Venus*, his *Calumny of Apelles*, his *Man bearing a Medallion of Cosimo il Vecchio*, his exquisite *Annunciation*, and his *Adoration of the Magi*? To mention here only two of the incidental delights of these Botticellis: the artist himself appears in two of these pictures (he is probably the man bearing Cosimo's medallion, and he appears again, dressed in yellow, on the right of the *Adoration of the Magi*);

and Lorenzo il Magnifico is also painted on the left in the foreground of this lovely *Adoration*, arrogant and quite as prominent as all Biblical figures who have much more right to be there.

In addition to these rich Botticellis, this same room contains a superb painting, bought in Bruges by a banking agent of the Medici: Hugo van der Goes's *Adoration of the Shepherds*. Because Ghirlandaio and Filippino Lippi found particular inspiration in this *Adoration*, the authorities at the Uffizi have decided to hang here an *Adoration of the Magi* by Ghirlandaio and Filippino's picture of the Infant Jesus with St Jerome. The decision to place these paintings together was inspired, but it does make it difficult for the tourist to move on to explore the rest of the Uffizi. More: near by in the same room is Roger van der Weyden's extremely moving *Entombment of Jesus*. Indeed the only painting in this room that I do not reckon an absolute masterpiece is Lorenzo di Credi's crude *Venus*.

The richness of this particular room in the Uffizi is almost matched by one you pass through in reaching it. Room 7 in the gallery houses one third of Paolo Uccello's *Battle of San Romano*, which we British know from our own third in the National Gallery and the French know from their third in the Louvre. Lorenzo il Magnifico used to lie in bed and admire all three. Here too are the magical portraits which Piero della Francesca painted of Federico da Montefeltro and his wife Battista Sforza. Fra Angelico's delicate fragmentary *Virgin and Child* makes this room yet more special; and as a further delight here are hung a *Madonna and Child with St Anne* by Masaccio, and Domenico Veneziano's *Madonna with Four Saints* (they are St Francis, St John Baptist, St Lucy and St Zenobius).

As a gallery whose international collection vies with the best in the world, the Uffizi obviously offers far more than merely Tuscan paintings. In fact its role as a gallery began with sculpture, not paintings. The first main exhibition room of the gallery, along the east corridor, is filled with fine statues from classical antiquity whose rediscovery helped to create Italian renaissance sculpture. One impressive example of the way artists thus spoke to each other across the centuries can be seen in this room: the splendid *Hercules and the Centaur*, first created in late-Hellenistic times and then restored in 1589 by the Florentine sculptor Giovanni Caccini.

But I come to the Uffizi chiefly to see Tuscan paintings. Even the gentlest canter through its exhibition rooms, simply picking out a picture here and there without any pretence at comprehensiveness, affords an unforgettable insight into the works of the remarkably fecund artists who have flourished in this region.

The earliest Tuscan art in the Uffizi represents both Florence and Siena, in the persons of Cimabue and Duccio di Buoninsegna. Giovanni Cimabue was born in Florence around 1240 and trained in the Baptistery workshop, where he helped to create the *Scenes from the Life of Joseph*. He travelled to Rome and Assisi, continually seeking a fresher interpretation of the themes of religious art. You can see him – for example in the picture of St Francis with the Virgin Mary, painted for the lower church at Assisi – taking such a traditional motif as the devotion of the mother of Jesus – and then imbuing it with a new tenderness and pathos. Cimabue was gradually transforming the old Byzantine style. In the year 1275 he was back in Florence, creating the massive *Madonna in Majesty* for the church of Santa Trinità. Today it hangs in the second exhibition room of the Uffizi. It is Cimabue's masterpiece: at once the culmination of Byzantine art in Tuscany and a pointer to the developments that were to come.

Nearly everyone in Tuscany who aspired to be a great painter at that time seems to have come to Assisi to learn from Cimabue. Duccio was one. Duccio was a volatile man who clearly could channel his personal emotions into his art. The first work we know of by him is a commission of 1278, when he decorated twelve chests which held the official papers of the commune of Siena. Then in 1285 he was commissioned to paint a Madonna for the church of Santa Maria Novella in Florence. This picture, known as the *Rucellai Madonna*, today hangs in the Uffizi, alongside Cimabue's Santa Trinità altarpiece.

The influence of Duccio's teacher Cimabue is so evident in the pupil's Madonna that for centuries this painting was in fact thought to be by the older man, and only documentary evidence of Duccio's commission persuaded critics to change their minds. Can we today make out differences in the way the pupil adapted his master's teaching? I do think I can. The drawing of the Virgin herself seems to be freer in Duccio's picture, and the line of the hem of her cloak seems to display a controlled turbulence, akin to the turbulence which Duccio had to control in his public life, quite alien to Cimabue's work. The colours are still wonderful, especially, I think, the green in the clothes of the middle angel on Mary's right. True there is still a stern, hieratic Byzantine note in the composition of the *Rucellai Madonna*; but its spirit is nearly the gothic.

Twenty-five years after Duccio created this masterpiece Giotto painted the *Madonna* that hangs in the centre of the same room in the Uffizi. Giotto was born in 1266 at Colle i Vespignano in the Mugello. Tradition says he started life as a shepherd boy who seems always to have retained a pleasingly rustic sense of humour. Knocked down by some pigs in the street one Sunday, he simply picked himself up with the words: 'No wonder they knock me down. In my time I've made thousands of *lire* out of their bristles and never given them even a bowl of soup in return.'

Giotto joined the mosaic workshops of the Baptistery in Florence and then trained as an artist in Rome, where around 1300 he created a remarkable mosaic for St Peter's: *The Ship of the Church*. Contemporaries were immediately impressed by the unusually vivacious expressions Giotto had given to the people he depicted. The papal financier Enrico Scrovegni commissioned him to decorate the Arena Chapel in his palace at Padua. (His scene of devils tormenting the damned in this chapel is still terrifying, with wretches hanging from trees – one woman from her braided hair.) He also went to Assisi, to work in the upper chapel on the great series of frescos devoted to the life of St Francis. Here already the Byzantine habit of placing saints against a flat, usually golden background, has been abandoned. The backgrounds of Giotto's frescos now are far more realistic, and they have their own dramatic role to play in the pictures. In the *Deposition*, for instance, the mourners in the foreground are strikingly enfolded by the converging hillside behind them.

Twenty years later Giotto, now back in Florence, was to paint a yet greater, even more dramatic version of the legend of St Francis, for the Bardi Chapel of the church of Santa Croce. And for the church of Ognissanti he created the *Madonna* now in the Uffizi, equally dramatic, equally vivacious, even though the artist has deliberately chosen here to use more traditional elements – the throne, the golden background, the solemn angels. The Mother and Child are both gentle and at peace. On either side two men peer through the carved panels of the Virgin's throne, the one on the right especially yearning and deeply serious.

The whole scene is instantly appealing. Giotto, said John Ruskin, was the 'first Italian, the first Christian, to arrive at some kind of understanding of the virtues of domestic and monastic life and to portray them for the benefit of all and sundry – from the prince to the shepherd, from the wisest philosopher to an untaught child'. Ruskin added that by all means if you choose call Giotto's Holy Family the Madonna, St Joseph and the child; only remember that essentially he painted 'Mamma, Papa, and the Baby. And all Italy threw up its cap –"*Ora ha Giotto il grido.*" ' The truth of Ruskin's judgements is utterly confirmed by Giotto's Uffizi *Madonna*.

The artist died at Florence on 8 January 1337 and was honoured by burial in the cathedral at the expense of the commune. In 1490 Politian composed an epitaph for him:

> I am the man who brought painting to life when it was dead,
> whose hand combined sure accuracy with masterly ease.
> Whatever is to be found in nature may be found in my art.
> To no one was it given to paint more or to paint better.
> I am Giotto – what need was there to say it?
> This name itself will for many years suffice as an epitaph.

Sienese masters of the fourteenth century dominate the next room in the Uffizi. Its pride is an *Annunciation with St Ansano and St Margaret* by Simone Martini. As well as in his native Siena, Simone had worked in Assisi, in Naples and in France. He ended his days at Avignon. He also clearly loved the gothic style patronized by the French court at this time. The French equally took to him. In Naples King Robert of Anjou knighted him and gave him a stipend of fifty ounces of gold.

Simone could people his works with realistic children or old men, set in recognizable landscapes. (One of his paintings shows a horseman who has fallen into a crevasse in the hills south of Siena.) For his masterpiece in the Uffizi he went back to the golden background of the old Byzantine style. But, as Enzo Carli has written, 'The painting takes the Gothic taste for sheer line to the extreme limits of melodic expressiveness, and it is this line, with its impetus, its inflexions, its sinuous cadences, that expresses the very bodilessness of the Angel and the Madonna, whose gestures seem perfectly weightless, on the point of vanishing into the great gold light of the background.'

This triptych is signed both by Simone Martini and his brother-in-law Lippo Memmi, and dated 1333. Critics usually assign to Memmi the portraits of St Ansano and St Margaret, on no documentary evidence whatsoever. An interesting – and also virtually impossible – task is to try to figure out any differences of style between these two saints and the central panel. To my mind there aren't any.

Florentine disciples of Giotto take up most of the next exhibition room. In contrast to the treatment of Lorenzo il Magnifico in Botticelli's *Adoration of the Magi*, Orcagna and his brother Jacopo di Cione have left us here a painting of scenes from the life of St Matthew in which the donors are smaller than the saints – displaying a proper perspective in both the artistic and the spiritual sense.

The exuberant late Gothic artists crowd into the next two rooms of the Uffizi. Here I must admit to liking best a work that is not by a Tuscan but by the Umbrian painter, Gentile da Fabriano. Gentile did in fact work in Florence, as well as Venice and Rome. His *Adoration of the Magi* is brilliant, the figures in rich clothing (the influence, perhaps of the Venetians), the sensation of depth magical.

Gentile painted this *Adoration* in 1423 for the Palazzo Strozzi. Horses, birds, human beings, a couple of monkeys, a dog, a donkey and a cow crowd into this picture, painted in remarkable naturalistic detail. It is hard to guess whether the man in a hat to the right of the picture is trying to catch a dove or marvelling at the symbol of the Holy Spirit. In the background the lengthy caravan of the Magi winds its way to Bethlehem in a virtuoso display of perspective and composition. To the left one of the three kings, his crown discarded, kneels before the Infant Jesus who gently pats the old man's bald head.

As I warned at the beginning of this chapter, there is little chance of cantering through Room 7 of the Uffizi. My choice here is Masaccio's *Madonna and Child with St Anne*. Masaccio was a young man (he was born at Castello di Val d'Arno in 1401 and died in Rome only twenty-seven years later) profoundly dissatisfied with the flamboyance of late gothic art. He still utilized the innovations in perspective and composition that his predecessors had made, but he sought a sterner kind of realism.

To give a feeling of depth to his paintings, Masaccio used light and shadow in a completely revolutionary way. His finest work in Florence is not in the Uffizi but in the church of Santa Maria del Carmine: a series of frescos illustrating the life of St Peter, which the rich merchant Felice Brancacci commissioned from him in the mid-1420s. Here the artist has chosen significant moments from the stories about Peter and then dramatized them by vividly emphasizing the reactions of the onlookers. His use of light and shade here is brilliant, for the painted light and shade of the frescos corresponds uncannily with the natural light from outside as it illuminates the Brancacci chapel. As if to show us that he knows precisely how brilliant is his revolutionary deployment of light and shade, Masaccio has included in the series of frescos (which he did not live to complete) the incident where St Peter heals by means of his own shadow!

The church of Santa Maria Novella, filled as it is with many masterpieces of Florentine art, contains one by Masaccio well worth seeking out. Over the fourth altar of the north aisle is his fresco of the Holy Trinity, along with the Virgin Mary, St John the Evangelist and portraits of those who commissioned the work. Mary is drawing the onlookers into the picture by turning to us and pointing to the crucified Jesus. This is the very first work of art to make use of the one-point system of perspective, which serves still more to draw the observer into the whole scene.

Masaccio's *Madonna and Child with St Anne* in the Uffizi is sterner than anything else I know by him. His reaction against Burgundian gothic has led the artist here to return to the canonical forms of the thirteenth century. He has relaxed a little, perhaps, in depicting the angels (unless these have been softened by Masolino da Panicale, who also worked on this painting).

Lovers of perspective done *con brio* adore the third of Paolo Uccello's *Battle of San Romano* in the same room. The story goes that when his wife called him to bed, he would simply go on painting, murmuring what a sweet thing is perspective. In truth his skills in this respect were far inferior to Masaccio's. In the refectory of Santa Maria Novella he painted a very entertaining fresco of the Flood in which his use of perspective is self-conscious almost to the point of absurdity. Nearly everything recedes to one vanishing-point. Most of the people and objects are painted exactly at a right-angle to the plane of the picture. So bizarre is the effect that even Uccello's extremely strong sense of fun (seen here, for example, in the poor fellow in a circular tub desperately floating away) is for once almost overwhelmed.

The undoubted bizarreness in Uccello's work is reflected in a delightful story recounted of him by Vasari. When Paolo was commissioned to do some paintings in the cloisters of San Miniato al Monte (fragments of which have recently been rediscovered), he painted the fields blue, the cities red and the buildings in whatever colour that came to his mind. The abbot of San Miniato, for his part, fed the artist almost entirely on cheese. Paolo was such a mild-mannered man that instead of complaining he gave up the work. If he saw a pair of monks from San Miniato in the city, he would take to his heels. Finally two of the monks ran after him to find out what was wrong. 'It's entirely the fault of your idiot abbot,' replied Paolo. 'He has so stuffed me with his cheese pies and cheese soups, that soon I'm afraid people will be using me for glue.' The monks fell about laughing, went and told their abbot, and Uccello was enticed back to work with the promise of different fare.

In the room of the Uffizi that houses Paolo's *Battle of San Romano* is Domenico Veneziano's altarpiece of *The Madonna and Child with Four Saints*. By contrast with the Uccello, Veneziano has created an extremely gentle painting that uses perspective with the same delicacy as it deploys exquisite greens and pinks and blues. Originally painted for the church of Santa Lucia dei Magnoli in Florence, it portrays St Lucy herself as a meek and pretty young woman whose blond hair is severely tied back. Domenico has painted a triple arcade, hinting at what would once have been a triptych. He has subtly indicated that the Virgin Mary is a real woman and not some stone Madonna in a niche, by carefully bringing her forward, out of the niche at the back of his picture (another brilliant example of his skill with perspective).

A Venetian by origin, Domenico came to Florence in the 1430s to work on the choir of the church of Sant'Egidio. His assistant was the young Piero della Francesca, whose panels with the portraits of Federico da Montefeltro and his wife are the fourth outstanding masterpiece in this room. They face each other, the duke with his bizarrely broken nose, caused by an accident in a tournament which also cost him an eye. His olive skin contrasts with the duchess's ivory face, his short curly hair with her braids, his vivid red hat with her brocaded sleeve.

Go behind the panels to look at the duke and duchess painted on the other side driving towards each other in triumphal chariots, attended by the virtues, he drawn by white chargers, she by unicorns. Behind both their profiled busts and their triumphal drive, Piero has magically painted distant prospects of their domains. The red harnesses of the duke's horses are set against a white lake on which five ships are sailing. His chariot is set with red and yellow draperies, his faldstool crimson, yet this is no match for the crimson, white and grey dress of his twenty-year-old duchess, who sits meekly reading.

Piero della Francesca painted this superb double diptych in 1465, when his patron was in fact Count of Urbino. (He became duke later.) Kenneth Clark made an interesting observation about Federico's portrait bust. The line of his neck was originally drawn further in, Piero then altered it to the present outline, in order to accentuate the monumental character of the silhouette.

We do not know when Fra Angelico's *Virgin and Child* in the same room of the Uffizi was painted. Once it formed part of a much larger altarpiece, and the fragmentary inscription at the base of the painting probably refers to the donors.

Fra Angelico, Vasari tells us, 'was a simple man and most holy in his ways'. Gentle and temperate, 'he lived chastely, removed from the cares of the world. He would often say that whoever practised art needed a quiet life and freedom from anxieties, and that he who occupied himself with the things of Christ ought always to be with Christ.' It is said that he never took up his brush without praying first, and never made a crucifix without weeping as he did so.

His models were the paintings of Giotto – not because he failed to understand the newer developments of fifteenth-century Italian art, but because he consciously saw this style as the finest for his own devout purposes. So this exquisite *Virgin and Child* is something of an oddity in an exhibition room that also houses Uccello, Masaccio, Veneziano and Piero della Francesca. What is undeniable is the immense charm of his Madonna: her gentle eyes, her long slender fingers and the Child that ethereally balances on her arm are a perfect expression of what Henry James called Fra Angelico's 'passionate, pious tenderness'.

My favourite painting in Room 8 of the Uffizi is Filippo Lippi's *Madonna and Two Angels*, one of which is looking slyly over his shoulder. Filippo Lippi was Masaccio's only pupil, and he in his turn taught Botticelli, so Botticelli's *Madonna of the Rose Garden* is in this room. It would be good to see here one day a painting by Botticelli's own pupil, Filippo's son Filippino.

To be fair, in the very next room of the Uffizi is a painting said to be by Filippino Lippi, though a number of scholars contest the attribution. Here too is Botticelli in an unusually bloodthirsty mood, depicting Judith hurrying away from Holofernes's camp, leaving her enemy dead in his tent. But this room is really devoted to the brothers Piero and Antonio Pollaiuolo. Antonio was multi-talented: goldsmith, sculptor, engraver and architect as well as painter. What made him special was his fascination for anatomy, a passion he passed on to Leonardo da Vinci. Antonio is one of the first artists to have dissected a corpse. You can see his fascination with the play of muscles in the tiny panels depicting *The Labours of Hercules* in the case between the windows of Room 9. Even more spectacular (though still small) is his bronze statuette in the Bargello of Hercules squeezing the breath out of Antaeus. Hercules' shoulder muscles and shoulderblades are straining; he has hollowed out his back to lift Antaeus on to his chest; and Antaeus is bursting with pain.

So to the room (or rather four rooms combined into one) containing Botticelli's famous *Primavera* and his equally entrancing *Birth of Venus*.

Both come from the villa of a cousin of Lorenzo il Magnifico. For this young man Venus symbolized (as Marsilio Ficino told him in a fascinating letter) Humanitas: 'a nymph of excellent comeliness, born of heaven and more than all others beloved by God on high. Her soul and mind are Love and Charity, her eyes Dignity and Magnanimity, her hands Liberality and Magnificence, her feet Comeliness and Modesty. The whole, then, represents Temperance, Honesty, Charm and Splendour.' To create such a goddess visually is no light task. Botticelli succeeded, seemingly effortlessly. This effortlessness is that of genius. He takes us back into classical mythology, precisely as Ficino's symbolism does. For me *Primavera*, painted around 1480, achieves this supremely by means of Botticelli's three enchanting Graces. The beauty of these three young women, dancing in a wood, their nudity scarcely veiled by transparent drapery, is unparalleled. The figures are placed in an olive grove representing the Garden of the Hesperides. Venus stands in the centre, demure, even devout. Above her a chubby, blindfolded Cupid is about to loose an arrow towards the dancing Graces. Beyond the three Graces, a nonchalant Mercury, one hand on his hip, reaches for some fruit. Finally, on the right of the painting, Botticelli has depicted Ovid's tale of the metamorphosis, by the touch of Zephyr (and a rather truculent, blue Zephyr he is), of the shy earth-nymph Chloe into the peaceful, luxurious Flora, who is dressed in the spring flowers that grew in the garden of his patron's villa.

As another of the young man's tutors, Politian, wrote:

> *Ben venga primavera*
> *che vuol l'uom s'innamori.*
> *E voi, donnzelle, a schiera*
> *con li vostri amadori,*
> *che di rose e di fiori*
> *vi fate belle il maggio,*
>
> *venite alla frescura*
> *delli verdi arbuscelli.*
> *Ogni bella è sicura*
> *fra tanti damigelli;*
> *chè le fiere e gli uccelli*
> *ardon d'amore il maggio.*
>
> [Welcome spring,
> that desires men to fall in love.
> You young girls too, in a crowd
> with your lovers,
> you who with roses and flowers
> make yourselves beautiful in May,
>
> come to the shade
> of the green bushes.
> Every lovely one is safe
> among so many young men;
> for the beasts and the birds
> burn with love in May.]

Ten years after painting *Primavera*, Botticelli created his *Birth of*

Venus. In the meantime he had visited Rome to see for himself the fabulous statues of classical antiquity that were being excavated there. In the *Birth of Venus* Zephyr and Chloe are now lusciously entwined, as they blow towards the shore modest, naked Venus, floating in her scallop shell. The white foam of the waves represents the seed of Uranus who created her. This Venus symbolizes two sides of love, the pure and the impure. Exquisitely sensual, she partly conceals her nakedness with her flowing red hair and with her left hand over one breast. Ashore, the Hour of Spring, her dress covered in daisies and cornflowers, holds a wind-filled crimson cloak, fully to clothe this nakedness – for sacred mysteries should be hidden from the vulgar.

Before leaving this room take at least one look at the artist's self-portrait in his *Adoration of the Magi.* Here Botticelli has painted everyone in modern dress. But there is much symbolism too. The ruined walls among which the Holy Family sits represent for Botticelli the crumbling away of the old order with the coming of Christ. Already they are sprouting weeds and creepers. Behind to the left are the ruins also of classical building. Aged Joseph lays his head on his hand. One of the Magi, kneeling, clasps the Infant Jesus's feet. And from this painting one man looks directly at us: the artist himself.

When Leonardo da Vinci left Florence in 1481 he had left unfinished a huge, ambitious *Adoration of the Magi.* You can see this today, still unfinished, in Room 15 of the Uffizi (a room which also contains work by Leonardo's teacher Andrea Verrocchio). The monks of San Donato a Scopeto, outside the city walls, had commissioned the work at a time when Leonardo had decided precisely how he was to develop his art. Chiaroscuro, *sfumato* (a technique which dissolves contours to create a greater illusion of reality), and a way of filling his canvases with figures while keeping tight control of the main ones in a central triangle were some of his new ideas. All these techniques he clearly intended to deploy in the Uffizi *Adoration.* The canvas is crowded and exciting. At the sides are two still figures: youth and age. In the background are prancing horses and curious architectural forms, with trees growing on top of them and figures descending steps. So brilliant is its construction that in spite of its diversity and the vitality of its many individual figures, your eye is drawn back again and again to the Madonna and Child at the centre. But, alas, all that the artist has completed is the preliminary chiaroscuro drawing, done in a pigment made from red earth.

An altogether different picture, though one with many delights, is also hung in this room: *Perseus Freeing Andromeda*, which Piero di Cosimo painted in 1589. The style of this entertaining artist was obviously influenced by Leonardo (and also by the Umbrian painter Luca Signorelli). He loved ancient mythology, especially of a bizarre or recondite kind. The Perseus myth is not particularly bizarre, but Piero di Cosimo has made up for this by portraying an astonishingly evil beast, with the hero delicately balancing on his back.

Briefly go left into Room 16 for the pleasure of seeing the maps of Tuscany which Stefano Buonsignori painted on its walls in 1589, and to enjoy the rich ceiling painted by Jacopo Zucchi, before walking on to look at Andrea Mantegna's *Virgin of the Cave* in the next room. Mantegna is not a Tuscan artist (he was born in Padua in 1431 and died at Mantua in 1506), and although he was influenced both by Uccello and by Donatello, I find his work harsher, less warm than that produced by most artists of this region.

Before leaving this room (which, unfortunately, is not always open), I always take a fascinated look at the statue of a sleeping hermaph-rodite, sculpted in the second century BC, in preparation for admiring the Uffizi's most celebrated statue: the Medici Venus, a beautiful copy made in the first century BC of a Venus sculpted three centuries earlier.

The Medici Venus was discovered in Rome in the sixteenth century and brought to Florence in 1777. Nathaniel Hawthorne fancied he detected a slight degree of alarm in her face; 'not that she really thinks that anybody is looking at her, yet the idea has flitted through her mind and startled her a little'. He perceived in her a 'chaste and naked grace'. He added delightedly, 'The Venus de Medici has a dimple in her chin.' The impressive octagonal room in which she stands, its dome made of mother-of-pearl, was built by Bernardo Buontalenti in the late 1580s to house the finest statues then possessed by the Medici, and it remains today a home worthy of this Venus.

We are here, however, principally to look at paintings, and the Uffizi from now on, while not neglecting great Tuscan artists, begins to demonstrate its stature as a national and international gallery. Room 19 contains masterpieces by Luca Signorelli and Pietro Vannucci, Verrocchio's Umbrian pupil who is generally called Perugino. The following room houses a select group of lovely German paintings. Lucas Cranach's portrait of Luther and his wife shows them serious, sympathetic, almost wistful. In this room Cranach's *Adam and Eve* has been sensitively hung opposite Albrecht Dürer's study of the same subject, both beautifully painted, fine German renaissance nudes but quite different from the luscious women of renaissance Tuscany.

The next room displays the gorgeous Venetians, Bellini (whose father had worked in Florence as a pupil of Gentile da Fabriano) and Giorgione, and some excellent if lesser Venetians such as Bellini's pupil Vittore Carpaccio.

Another room leads through more German and some Flemish works on to Room 23 (with, amongst other paintings by Antonio Correggio, a splendid *Adoration*) and through to the welcome break of the south corridor. This corridor offers a marvellous view of the city – San Miniato al Monte on the left, the cathedral and the Palazzo Vecchio ahead, the Arno and its bridges, and south of the river the dome and bell-tower of Santo Spirito and the dome of San Frediano, almost (not quite) enough to make you neglect the fine antique sculptures alongside you.

This is a brief respite, for Room 25 at the end of the south corridor is where the Uffizi displays Michelangelo. Incredibly the famous tondo of the Holy Family failed to satisfy the Florentine merchant Agnolo Doni, who commissioned it from Michelangelo in 1503. They had an acrimonious dispute about payment.

This is Michelangelo's first known painting. He once asserted that 'painting and sculpture are one and the same thing', judging that 'painting should be considered excellent as it approaches the effect of a relief'. (He did not believe the reverse. 'A relief,' he added, 'should be considered bad precisely in so far as it approaches the effect of painting.') The Doni Tondo in the Uffizi reveals exactly this ideal of a painting that seems to be three-dimensional. The colours are polished like marble. No doubt this masterpiece owes something to the artist's study of the monumental figure painting of the by then unfashionable Masaccio; but in the extremely unusual positions of Mary, Joseph and the Infant Jesus, where the mother leans over backwards towards her son and Joseph bends anxiously forward, the painting charts out new ground in Italian high-renaissance art. And the five naked youths lolling in the background, who clearly have nothing to do with the subject, are unmistakably the work of Michelangelo and no one else.

Raphael is by far the major artist in Room 26 of the Uffizi, but if we are to stay with Florentines, look out Andrea del Sarto's painting of *St James with Two Children*. Vasari called the paintings of this tailor's son 'faultless'. Later critics have described them as dreamy, sometimes (in Browning's words) even silvery-grey and placid. I personally think I detect much tension beneath Andrea del Sarto's apparent easy harmony. And Browning also put a famous defence into Andrea's own mouth:

> I, painting for myself and to myself,
> Know what I do, am unmoved by men's blame
> Or their praise either . . .
> Ah, but a man's reach should exceed his grasp,
> Or what's a Heaven for?

As it can do when you least expect it, the Uffizi now springs a surprise. The next room contains four works by Jacopo Pontormo, of which the finest, I think, is the *Supper at Emmaus*, painted in 1525. Pontormo was a pupil of Andrea del Sarto, whose delicacy he retained but whose colours in Pontormo's works become increasingly pale and strange. Along with another of del Sarto's pupils, Rosso Fiorentino (whose work you can also see in this Uffizi exhibition room), Pontormo vehemently rejected the naturalism and balance of high-renaissance art, and the two men became virtual anarchists in their artistic style. In his *Madonna with Four Saints*, now in the Uffizi but painted in 1518 for the church of Santa Maria Nuova, Rosso displays a wild disregard of the aesthetic canons worked out by his immediate Italian predecessors.

Largely because of the pioneer study, *Über Greco und der Manierismus*, written by M. Dvořák in 1921, these artists are now generally known as Mannerists. They loved to set themselves intricate problems of composition. They relied much less on antique models while still referring obliquely and intellectually to them. Jacopo Pontormo also warmed to the angular art of Albrecht Dürer. All these influences came together in the *Deposition* he painted in 1525 or thereabouts for the church of Santa Felicità in Florence. His colours here are extraordinarily delicate mauves and pinks and greens, the figures elongated and unnaturally entwined, the different actors in the drama united by exaggerated gestures which also draw in the onlooker. Even the dead face of Jesus is looking out towards us!

Elsewhere in Tuscany Pontormo's special vision reappears: in the great cloister of the Certosa at Galuzzo (from where the Uffizi *Supper at Emmaus* comes) and in a beautiful pastoral lunette painted for the Medici villa of Poggio a Caiano.

Mannerism spread to Rome and elsewhere in Italy, as is instantly clear in Room 28 of the Uffizi from the impressive, bizarre *Madonna with the Long Neck* by the Emilian artist Francesco Parmigiano. But to reach this you pass through a room filled with Venetian masterpieces by Titian: his *Venus of Urbino*, who has a little dog on her bed; another *Venus*, this time with Cupid; the painting of *The Genius of Venice*, which the Florentines lent to the Royal Academy, London, in 1984; the portrait of a splendidly devout Knight of Malta. Standing in front of Titian's *Venus of Urbino* Mark Twain found her obscene. 'I saw young girls stealing furtive glances at her; I saw young men gaze long and absorbedly at her; I saw aged, infirm men hang upon her charms with a pathetic interest,' he wrote. His fellow-countryman Nathaniel Hawthorne described her as 'naked and lustful'. But in the less prudish eighteenth century the English traveller Tobias Smollett confessed himself charmed by the painting, 'which has a sweetness of expression and tenderness of colouring not to be described'.

Great Tuscan paintings are absent from the last few rooms of this astounding gallery, which now rests content with displaying some unmissable masterpieces from other parts of Italy and from the rest of Europe. In Room 34 is a superb *Holy Family* by Veronese. In Room 35, among many marvellous paintings by Tintoretto, I make first for the beautiful *Leda* he painted in 1570. And in the next room open to the visitor (no. 41) I always pause for the sensitive, loving study by Rubens of his wife Isabella Brandt. Still to come are eighteenth-century French paintings, more Flemish works, Dutch landscapes, a *Young Bacchus* by Caravaggio, and two portraits of Maria Theresa by Goya.

But if this canter round the Uffizi is not to slow down to a weary plod, make the last room no. 44. Here are three amazing portraits by Rembrandt van Rijn, one of an old man and two of himself, the greatest an unwavering depiction of his old age.

Then walk to the bar at the end of the corridor, taking a glass out on to the terrace over the Loggia dei Lanzi, to breathe the fresh air and gaze over the Piazza della Signoria as far as the distant hills of Fiesole.

7

The Wine and Food of Tuscany

'It is undoubtedly a golden age,' wrote the Florentine Marsilio Ficino in 1492, 'which has restored to the light the liberal arts that had almost been destroyed: grammar, poetry, eloquence, painting, sculpture, architecture, music.' What Ficino failed to mention was Tuscan food and wine – but maybe the traditions that have created both were never in any danger of being lost, even in the dark ages. When Catherine de' Medici married the king of France she took no chances with French cuisine but brought along her own Italian cooks (and also, incidentally, taught the French to use forks).

Fine cooking demands fine ingredients, and Tuscany provides these in abundance. The flat region to the south, the Maremma, is still roamed by wild boar. Sheep placidly graze on the rolling hills of the region. The best beef in the whole of Italy is raised in the Val di Chiana, south of Arezzo. The Tyrrhenian Sea supplies the ingredients for the stew known as *cacciuco* (which is included among the Tuscan recipes later in this book). Restaurants on the coast often offer breaded seafood that has been fried in oil and is served still hot, with a slice of lemon. They call it *fritto misto di mare*. *Fritto misto* is popular throughout Tuscany, but inland it will be made from sliced veal, chicken or sweetbreads, sometimes even cheese or vegetables.

Traditional Tuscan dishes vary from region to region, and have still not been muscled out of every restaurant by so-called international cuisine. In the Tuscan gazetteer of this book I have indicated from time to time specialities of various towns and cities, all of them worth tasting, many of them a delicious surprise.

All traditional Tuscan restaurants ultimately derive their cuisine from the skills of the Italian housewife. Even in cities today, most

Tuscan housewives still cook two daily meals, shopping for fresh ingredients each morning. I first came across their formidable skills some twenty years ago when an old friend, an Italian lawyer (a man of amazing hot temper outside court, so what he was like inside I dread to think) had done some favour for a client who was a farmer. In return the farmer invited him to his home for a meal. I was taken along. We drove out into the countryside to the farm, where in the open air a huge table was already laden with hams and meats and dry cakes (to provoke a thirst for wine). As the afternoon came and went, and the children ran after little chickens, more and more dishes were brought out, an astonishing variety, entirely created by the farmer's wife and daughters and all derived from the produce of their farm.

In my experience, dishes travel in Tuscany and subtly change as they do so. *Panforte*, for example, is a traditional Sienese cake, made from shelled almonds, hazelnuts, cinnamon, honey, sugar, candied fruit, cocoa, flour, the rind of oranges and lemons, and spices. It is exceedingly good for the constitution, and you need to drink a strong wine with it (or at least black coffee). Siena, it is said, was a resting-place for caravans from the Orient, which brought many recipes for spicy rich sweets. An alternative theory is that the recipes were brought back by Crusaders. Whatever the explanation, Siena is a haven for those with a sweet tooth. Try Sienese *ricciarelli* or Sienese *cavallucci*. But such dishes can be found elsewhere in Tuscany. I have eaten *panforte*, for instance, in San Gimignano and found it there to be darker and if anything more powerful than the Sienese variety.

Variety too is provided by the rivers that water the region. Trout and eels, sweet-water crabs, tench, pike and frogs are found in abundance in the locality of these rivers and not elsewhere. Similarly, expect to find prawns and shrimps, squid and crawfish, bream, bass, mullet and mackerel, mussels and clams near the Mediterranean and not inland.

Over the centuries Tuscan cuisine has incorporated new ingredients and ideas. The ubiquitous tomato, for instance, was virtually unique to Sicily until the soldiers of Garibaldi brought it north in the nineteenth century. Another late arrival was maize, which now is the basis of a staple Tuscan dish: the excellent (and filling) *polenta*, a kind of corn-meal that is usually served with a tomato or meat sauce. Beans too are intruders into Tuscan cooking, a late addition to the traditional courgettes, black cabbages, artichokes, fennel and peas of the region. Now bean and cabbage soup (*ribollita*) has become a classic Tuscan dish, and later I give the recipe.

The one permanent ingredient of Tuscan cooking over the centuries has been olive oil. The best is from Lucca, green, rich, thick, beautiful. John Evelyn described it as 'smooth, light, and pleasant on the tongue', and he was obviously referring to the least acid of the oils (now officially designated as having less than 1 per cent acidity). Tuscan olives are harvested and crushed in late November. One of D. H. Lawrence's memories of February mornings in Tuscany in the 1920s was of the sun shining on the horizontal green cloud-puffs of the pines, the sky clear and full of life, and water running hastily, 'still browned by the last juice of crushed olives'.

The most famous Tuscan dish, *bistecca alla fiorentina*, perfectly illustrates the long traditions of country cooking that have also permeated the cuisine of the great Tuscan cities. The steak ought to have come from the white cattle of the Val di Chiano, killed furthermore just after they have ceased to be calves. It is cooked over an open fire, on a charcoal made from vine shoots and soft wood, sometimes entrancingly varied by the addition of branches of herbs. The *bistecca* is turned over once, and then is ready to be served, sprinkled as always with black pepper and a little salt.

Tuscan restaurants generally divide their menus into six sections:

Antipasti or 'appetizers' could be cold cuts of ham or meats, vegetables in olive oil, or the splendid *crostini*, i.e. warm canapés of, say, chicken liver;

Minestre, which include soups, broths, consommés, and such pasta dishes as *tortellini*;

Pietanze, namely the main dishes;

Contorni, which are the vegetable side dishes;

Formaggi, cheeses (though there are no nationally renowned Tuscan ones);

Dessert, which is self-explanatory, and *Vini*, which could simply offer: *rosso locale, bianco locale, birra alla spina* (pressurized beer), *aqua minerale, caffè espresso* and *caffè corretto* (i.e. coffee laced with, say, brandy).

Dessert might well be styled *Dolci* (i.e. sweets), and near the sea you find a seventh section: *Pesce* (fish). In these regions you find the delicious Tuscan speciality *cacciucco*, a fish stew whose recipe is given later in this book.

Thus a typical menu in countless Tuscan restaurants might read:

ANTIPASTI

Salsicce di cinghiale	wild boar sausages
Prosciutto e salami toscana	Tuscan ham and salami
Antipasto di mare	an hors d'oeuvre of seafood
Cinghiale in olio	slices of wild boar dressed in olive oil
Insalata sott'olio	salad dressed in olive oil
Carciofini sott'olio	artichokes dressed in olive oil
Funghietti sott'olio	mushrooms in olive oil
Olive verdi	green olives

MINESTRE

Consommé	clear soup
Pastina in brodo	pasta broth
Spaghetti in burro	spaghetti in butter
Spaghetti al pomodoro	spaghetti with a tomato sauce
Spaghetti alla vongole	spaghetti with clams
Spaghetti ragù di carne	spaghetti with a meat sauce
Tortelloni in brodo	small coils of pasta in broth
Penne all'arrabbiata	short pasta in a rich and spicy sauce
Penne alla boscaglia	short pasta 'country style'
Minestra di fagioli	bean soup

PIETANZE

Vitelle al forno	roast veal
Faraona al forno	roast guinea fowl
Pollo arrosto	roast chicken
Pollo alla cacciatore	chicken with tomato and pimento sauce
Petto di pollo	chicken breasts
Arrosto di maiale al forno	roast pork
Scaloppine al marsala	veal escalope cooked in a wine sauce
Galetto alla griglia	grilled young cockerel
Braciole (senza osso) ai ferri	boned grilled chops
Bistecche di maiale ai ferri	grilled pork chops
Fiorentine ai ferri (l'otto Hg)	one eighth of a hectogramme of grilled T-bone steak
Coniglio alla cacciatore	rabbit in tomato and pimento sauce

Cinghiale in salami	wild boar and salami
Agnello in umido con spinacio	slowly cooked lamb stew with spinach

CONTORNI

Insalata verde	green salad
Insalata mista	mixed salad
Insalata di pomodori	tomato salad
Fagioli lessi	boiled haricot beans
Funghi	mushrooms
Spinaci saltati	spinach
Patate fritte	fried potatoes

DESSERT

Riccio alla fiamma	roasted chestnuts
Panforte	see above in this chapter
Zuppa reale	trifle (often called *Zuppa inglese*)
Tartufo	truffles
Coppa (or *Gelato*)	ice-cream
Torta brasiliana	Brazilian cake

As for Tuscan wine, the word *locale* on a menu can often point towards an unexpected treat. The whole Tuscan coast, for example, produces wines that have no national fame, no official *appellation*, and yet much character. Around Porto San Stefano and Porto Ercole, for instance, and nowhere else in Italy, you can drink excellent wine called Parrina, both red and white (the red based on the sangiovese grape, the white on trebbiano). Some of these local wines are now being granted the coveted DOC (*Denominazione di Origine Controllata*), which once was applied to no more than 12 per cent or so of all the wines of Italy – though the percentage has begun to rise. This accolade has been granted, for instance, to a red wine of the hills outside Lucca, Rosso delle Colline Lucchesi. Lucca also produces fine white wines that have next to no fame outside their own area. Fame counts for little. These wines, and the equally little known *rosé* (*rosata*) wines from the country around Livorno, I have found to be extremely drinkable, DOC classified or not.

The most famous wines of Italy are certainly Tuscany's Chiantis. They vary enormously. Over 150,000 acres of vineyards produce this one wine, with some 7,000 registered producers. Does quantity drive out quality? One of my preferences is for the Chianti grown around Radda in Chianti, but that preference does not arise from sampling every other Chianti in this enormous acreage! The best, most delightful way of deciding for yourself is to drive south from Florence to Siena by way of the N222, or to give it its more romantic name, Via Chiantigiana – the Chianti Road. The route takes you through enchanting villages: such as pretty Greve, and even more delightful Panzanio, with its twelfth-century oratory of Santissima Annunziata, beautifully restored inside. (The doors of the church, made in 1982, depict Pope Paul VI receiving the Ecumenical Patriarch; look out also for a portrait of Pope Paul's predecessor John XXIII on the same doors, as well as Jesus in the carpenter's shop and St Francis.)

All along the route you can stop at a *fattoria* to buy and taste Chianti. If you want to stay longer there are many small hotels, a good number with swimming-pools. The hillsides are covered in vineyards, dotted here and there with olive groves and tall evergreens. Stuck on posts are signs advertising the wines of the *gallo nero* (black rooster) consortium, a group of Chianti producers whose integrity guarantees the quality of their Chianti. Their chief rivals are the *putto* consortium, whose emblem is a baby Bacchus. For several years such groups have been letting their wines age, where appropriate, rather than looking for quick sales. A Chianti described as *vecchio* must have aged for two years and a *riserva* for three. Chianti *classico* must also have an alcohol content of at least 12 per cent (as opposed to the usual 11.5 per cent).

In addition, good Chiantis now often carry the accolade DOCG (*Denominazione di Origine Controllata e Garantita*) as a further reassurance of their quality. Happily, none of this has produced an over-regimented wine. Chianti grapes vary, though the basis of the wine must always be principally red sangiovese. Trebbiano toscano and malvasia del Chianti are used to lighten the wine, and canaiolo neri adds fragrance. In addition Chianti producers are allowed to mix up to 15 per cent of wine from other regions of Italy. In short, as always in the wine world, you must rely in the end on the skill and integrity of those who bottle it for you. Size is not always an indication of quality. (Of the seven distinct Chianti zones Rufina, the smallest, makes some of the finest. The other six zones are Colli Senesi, Colli Fiorentini, Colli Aretini, Montalbano and Colline Pisane.)

When Chianti is good it is marvellous, and often surprisingly un-expected in its savour. In 1983, for instance, I drank a 1975 *gallo nero* Chianti Classico, San Donato, DOC, costing 8,000 lire – much less than the price of the cheapest wine in a British restaurant. It was much smoother than I expected, smoother than the usual Chianti, delicate and musty, almost nutty.

If Chianti is the best-known Tuscan wine, it is not the best. Nearly every connoisseur will agree that this must be Brunello di Montalcino, a wine treasured by the Lombards in the eighth century. The brunello grape is a variant of the sangiovese that makes Chianti, but it produces a stronger wine, a lovely deep red in colour, that grows browner with age. Brunello is expensive, and it is nearly always at least five years old. Sangiovese also is the basis of the pleasing red wine called Morellino di Scansano from the vineyards around Pitigliano. Here, too, you can drink an excellent *bianco*, to my mind more a pale yellow than white, slightly bitter, very lovely.

Another fine Tuscan red is produced around Montepulciano, a wine that I would say is indistinguishable from excellent Chianti (if such a statement were not considered heresy by the producers of that region). Once the product of local nobility (and, some say, intended for use at Holy Communion), the best wines of Montepulciano in consequence carry on their labels the additional accolade *nobile*.

One distinct curiosity among Tuscan red wines is Sassicaia. In this region of Italy the splendid cabernet sauvignon grape helps to create a wine that is not allowed to compete for DOC status. Yet cabernet sauvignon is the basis of the finest wines from Bordeaux, and anyone who relishes good claret will adore Sassicaia. The cabernet grape also adds its own distinction to Carmignano, a superb red wine produced west of Florence and much favoured in the eighteenth century by the Grand Dukes of Tuscany.

My favourite white Tuscan wine is Vernaccia, which comes from San Gimignano. You can buy wine in San Gimignano from shops around the main square and also from the former Franciscan convent of the city (which also boasts a superb view over the Tuscan hills outside). Vernaccia is also the name of the grape from which this full-bodied white is made. Its producers dub the wine *riserva* after it has aged in oak for only one year. White Tuscan wine is also a speciality of the Island of Elba, where the basic grape is trebbiano (and thus the taste is quite different from that of Vernaccia). The Elbans call their white wine Procanico, and also produce a fizzy, sparkling version. Trebbiano is also essential to the production of Bianco della Lega, a white wine particularly valuable on hot afternoons in Tuscany by being low in alcohol content.

More and more white wine is being produced in Tuscany. The consortia of the Chianti region are making it from their surplus grapes (Bianco della Lega and Galestro are two recent innovations). But what the Tuscans themselves love (apart from what they have produced at home from their own rows of vines) is called Vino Santo, usually sweet (though very occasionally dry), made traditionally from grapes that have been hung in kitchens and become a little smoky; it is kept for five years or more and then served both as an aperitif and with delightful dry cakes.

It was Vino Santo that sent me to sleep that hot summer afternoon when the lawyer and I went to eat with his satisfied client in the Tuscan campagna.

8

A Tuscan Gazetteer

As Fanny Burney declared, back home after an Italian tour, 'There's no looking at a building here after seeing Italy.' This gazetteer concerns itself with buildings. But it also tries to set out other Tuscan delights: special events throughout the Tuscan year, markets and shops, regional delicacies, and such like.

It should be used in conjunction with the index to this book. For example, chapters 5 and 6 of the book have already been devoted to Florence, so that the entry on Florence in the gazetteer simply aims at supplementing what is written there (and elsewhere on that city throughout the text). Other cities are dealt with by means of guided tours (for instance, Lucca, Pisa, Siena, San Gimignano), though these, I hope, are more gentle saunters, so that visitors following the tours can find time to savour shops and bars, and find their own nooks and crannies in these enchanting places.

Believing that writers are best appreciated where they lived and were inspired, I have mentioned at appropriate points in the gazetteer such poets as the tormented lover Cino da Pistoia and the sunny, happy Folgòre da San Gimignano, as well as Henry James's temporary drunkenness in much underestimated Pescia.

Artistically Tuscany is the richest region in Italy, and I have tried to show this. When I had finished this long section of my book, I think I had come to understand Leigh Hunt's remark that 'a red cap in Italy goes by you, not like a mere cap, much less anything vulgar or butcher like, but like what it is, an intense specimen of the colour of red'.

ABBADIA ISOLA, see under MONTERIGGIONE.

ABBADIA SAN SALVATORE derives its present-day prosperity from its role as a centre for winter sports, capitalizing on its situation 812 m high on the eastern slopes of Mount Amiata. It once was famous as the site of the richest abbey in Tuscany. The Cistercians rebuilt the abbey church in 1036, but retained the huge eighth-century crypt with its splendid pillars and capitals. The crucifix dates from the twelfth century. The gothic and renaissance old town is a virtually perfect survival of the past.

Monte Amiata, once a volcano, is at 1,739 m the highest peak in southern Tuscany, capped by a great iron cross and festooned with ski lifts.

ABETONE, 49 km north-west of Pistoia, lies 1,388 m high in the Apennines and offers superb and sometimes difficult ski-runs. The town is situated on the border of Tuscany with Emilia, surrounded by a protected forest of some 3,700 ha. In summer the hoteliers of Abetone offer hospitality to climbers and to those who enjoy long walks, swimming and tennis.

Winter-sports resorts abound in this region. On the road that leads south-east from Abetone lie first **Cutigliano**, on the left bank of the River Lima, which lives off tourism, and then **San Marcello Pistoiese**, the most important town in this part of the Apennines. Cutigliano boasts a Palazzo Pretorio built in the fourteenth century.

ANGHIARI, see under AREZZO.

ANSEDONIA. The Romans built a port here in 273 BC and called it Portus Cosanus. They also dug a canal, the Tagliata Etrusca, to connect their port with Lake Burano. Ansedonia is today the southernmost town of the Tuscan province of Grosseto. Recently archaeologists have excavated an impressive Roman villa, dating from the first century BC. The excavations, with fine mosaic pavements and wall-paintings, can be visited. The walled citadel, capitol and forum are particularly delightful. So is the medieval aspect of a town built on Etruscan and Roman foundations. Puccini lived in the Torre della Tagliata while composing *Tosca*. If you eat in Ansedonia and have a strong stomach you will relish the powerful local fish soup. Lake Burano is now a bird sanctuary.

ARCIDOSSO. Beautifully situated on the western slopes of Monte Amiata, Arcidosso has preserved its medieval quarter while developing also as a modern holiday resort. Above the town are the ruins of a fourteenth-century castle. The road from here to Montelaterone passes by the thirteenth-century romanesque church of Santa Maria ad Lamulas and the renaissance church of Madonna Incoronata.

AREZZO. Prosperity has encircled this exquisite old city with unattractive modern buildings. Inside it retains its ancient charm, in spite of the ravages of the Second World War. Built on Etruscan foundations, Arezzo had become a free city by the tenth century, and managed to preserve its independence, in spite of the hostility of Florence, until 1384. Here lived Guido Monaco, generally known as Guido d'Arezzo, who died in 1050 having invented the modern musical scale. Each year in late August a musical festival dedicated to his memory is held in the city. Petrarch was another son of Arezzo, born here in 1304 because the Florentines had forced his father into exile. Other famous citizens of Arezzo were Pietro Aretino, the writer, and the artist, writer and architect, Giorgio Vasari. No. 55 Via XX Settembre, where Vasari was born, contains frescos he painted in 1542, some of them portraits of his fellow-artists. There is also a Petrarch Academy at no. 28 Via nell'Orto, where the poet was born, even though he had left the city for good and was living at the papal court in Avignon by 1312.

The city is rich in ecclesiastical buildings. In the Piazza della Libertà is the cathedral, facing the fourteenth-century Palazzo del Commune. Built at various times from the thirteenth to the twentieth century, Arezzo cathedral boasts a gothic facade finished in 1914 and a bell-tower constructed in the mid nineteenth century. Inside in the north aisle is a fresco of St Mary Magdalen by Piero della Francesca, and a splendid marble tomb behind the high altar, the Arco di San Donato, made in the mid fourteenth century to house the remains of the city's patron saint, St Donato, who was martyred in AD 361. A finer tomb still is that of Bishop Guido Tarlati, which Giotto designed in 1330. Here too is buried Pope Gregory X who was visiting Arezzo in 1276 when he died.

More bones of St Donato are to be found in a silver-gilt reliquary in a far greater church than the cathedral, the Pieve di Santa Maria, in the Piazza Grande. Built in the twelfth and thirteenth centuries, this remarkable romanesque building has a celebrated facade,

1. *The powerful Forte della Stella, built by Cosimo de' Medici in the sixteenth century to defend Portoferraio, the most important town on Elba*

2. *Napoleon's bedroom in the little palace he created out of two windmills during his exile on the island of Elba*

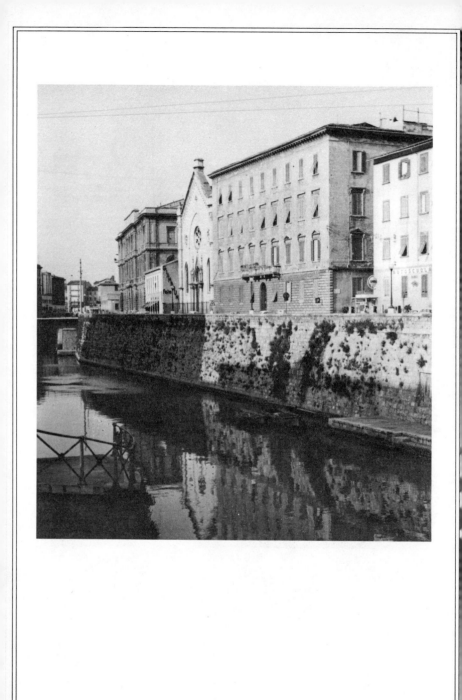

3. Livorno, a port whose prosperity was much enhanced by the brilliant maritime constructions of the Elizabethan Sir Robert Dudley

4. *The seaside resort and fishing village of Levanto, not far from La Spezia, where the drowned body of Shelley was washed ashore*

5. *The delightful fishing village of Marciana Marina, Elba*

6. The necropolis at Populonia, the grave of Etruscans over six centuries

7. The poet Giosuè Carducci rhapsodized over the famous avenue of cypresses
at Bolgheri, planted in 1801

8. *The tower of the early-fourteenth-century Palazzo Vecchio, Florence, rising 95 m above the city*

9. *The Pitti Palace, Florence, transformed in the sixteenth century by the architect Ammannati for Eleonora di Toledo*

10. *Michelangelo's disturbing statue of* Night, *sleeping ill at ease in the Medici chapel, Florence*

11. *In a cell of the convent of San Marco, Florence, Fra Angelico's fresco* Noli Me Tangere *depicts Jesus as the gardener gently dissuading Mary Magdalen from clasping him*

12. *The shady courtyard of the Palazzo del Bargello, Florence*

13. *Giambologna's superb* Rape of the Sabine *(1583), in the Piazza della Signoria, Florence*

14 (top). *The dome designed by Brunelleschi magnificently crowns the cathedral of Florence*

15 (left). *One of the bronze doors designed by Andrea Pisano for the Baptistery of Florence cathedral, depicting scenes from the Life of St John the Baptist, and four of the cardinal virtues*

16 (right). *The campanile of Florence cathedral, begun by Giotto in 1334, continued by Andrea Pisano and finished by Francesco Talenti in 1359*

17. *The fifteenth-century Palazzo Pretorio of Certaldo*

18. *At Fiesole the slender bell-tower of the cathedral, built in 1213, rises above the Roman amphitheatre, which has existed here since* I BC

19. At San Quirico d'Orcia romanesque lions and caryatids support the south door of its collegiate church

20. The brooding ruins of the fortress at Chiusi still speak of the savagery of twelfth-century Tuscany

21. *Santa Maria della Spina, Pisa, a tiny gothic masterpiece built on the bank of the Arno to house a sacred spine from Christ's crown of thorns*

22. *Francavilla's statue of Cosima I guards the entrance of the spectacular Palazzo dei Cavalieri, Pisa, sumptuously decorated by Vasari in 1562*

23. *In the Baptistery of Pisa is Nicola Pisano's exquisite thirteenth-century pulpit*

24. *The Rocca of Volterra, whose massive middle tower the citizens dub 'il Maschio',*
built by Lorenzo il Magnifico in 1472

25. *The excavated Roman amphitheatre and baths at Volterra*

26. *At Lucca the fourteenth-century tower of the Palazzo Guinigi is bizarrely topped by oak trees*

27. *The romanesque façade and bell-tower of the church of San Michele in Foro, Lucca*

28. The magical façade Siena's cathedral

29. Outside the Palazzo Pubblico, Siena, the she-wolf feeds the city's legendary founders, Romulus and Remus

30. The thirteenth-century Palazzo del Capitano in the shady Via di Città, Siena

31. *The twisting medieval Via Ricci at Montepulciano*

32. *In the Piazza Grande, Montepulciano, stands the fourteenth-century Palazzo Comunale*

33. The church of Madonna di San Biagio, which Antonio Sangallo the elder built
just outside Montepulciano in the first half of the sixteenth century

34. There is every historical possibility that on his way to Rome St Peter himself landed
at the spot where the lovely eleventh-century church of San Piero a Grado now stands

sculpted with the Virgin Mary, saints and depictions of the seasons of the year. The bell-tower, finished in 1330, has forty double openings and has become the symbol of the city.

The Piazza Grande itself is a masterpiece of harmonious Italian architecture. Vasari built a loggia here in 1573. The Palazzetto della Fraternità dei Laici, built between the fourteenth and the sixteenth centuries, is an amazing blend of gothic and renaissance. Here are ancient shops. And here on the first Sunday of each September takes place the annual Joust of the Saracen, when two knights from each of the four quarters of Arezzo tilt with lances at a shield on a post. As if this were not enough, the Piazza Grande is the site of an antiques fair on the first Sunday of every month.

Other important churches in Arezzo include San Francesco, San Domenico and Santissima Annunziata. The Franciscans never got round to finishing the facade of the church they built between the thirteenth and fifteenth centuries, but the interior is famed for Piero della Francesca's frescos on the subject of the discovery of the True Cross, as well as for a rose-window with stained glass depicting St Francis and Pope Honorius III (done by a Frenchman, Guillaume de Marcillat in 1524, who also made stained glass for the cathedral). The late-thirteenth-century church of San Domenico (with a gothic bell-tower) was designed by Nicola Pisano. Over the high altar is a crucifix by Cimabue. Santissima Annunziata is a renaissance church built in 1490.

Of the two major museums of Arezzo, the Galleria e Museo Medioevale e Moderno, no. 8 Via S. Lorentino, is the fifteenth-century Palazzo Bruni-Ciocchi, built by Donato Bruni. The Museo Archeologico Mecenate, with its Etruscan art, is housed in the renaissance convent of San Bernardo, which was itself built in the ruins of the Roman amphitheatre. If you prefer the open air to museums and art galleries, don't miss the Fortezza Medicea, with its splendid panoramic views, or the Prato Gardens, where stands a statue of Petrarch. (With the unconscious arrogance of the British upper-crust of yesteryear, Lady Morgan in 1820 observed of Arezzo that 'its subtle air has been particularly favourable to genius; and in fact, under many moral disadvantages, it has produced men of eminent talent, from Maecenas to Petrarch'.)

Not 2 km south of Arezzo, by way of the Via Michelangelo, is the exquisite fifteenth-century church of Santa Maria della Grazie, whose high altar in terracotta and marble is by Andrea della Robbia. And 28 km north-east of Arezzo lies the walled medieval town of **Anghiari**. Here the Florentines defeated the Visconti of Milan in 1440. Here, too, the French defeated the Austrians in 1796. Anghiari boasts a renaissance Palazzo Taglieschi, now a museum of local art. At nearby **Monterchi** (on the road to Citta di Castello) was born the mother of Piero della Francesca. In the local cemetery is one of his most remarkable paintings, the *Madonna del Parto*, depicting two angels pulling back a curtain to reveal the pregnant Virgin Mary, pointing proudly to her womb. As Kenneth Clark wrote, this is

one of the few great works of art which are still relatively inaccessible, and to visit it offers some of the pleasures of a pilgrimage. Only after much wandering and misdirection do we reach a rustic cemetery on a hill a few miles outside the village of Monterchi, where the custodian seems to understand the nature of our quest; and it is with scepticism and apprehension that we see her open the doors of a tiny graveyard chapel. In this heightened state of perception we are suddenly confronted with the splendid presence of the Madonna, rising up, 'full without boast', only a few feet away from us.

Kenneth Clark added that it is deeply characteristic of Piero della Francesca 'that this refined and sacred style should be united to an image as natural and shameless as the speech of a peasant'.

ARTIMINO is a walled village 22 km west of Florence, with a late-twelfth-century church. Bernardo Buontalenti built here a villa for Ferdinand de' Medici the first. Close by is the Etruscan cemetery from whose stones the church was built. Known as Pian di Rosello, it was constructed in the seventh century BC and rediscovered in 1970. Take the opportunity of sampling some of the local wine.

ASCIANO. Asciano retains much of its wall, built in 1351. Twenty-six kilometres south-east of Siena, it displays an important collection of Sienese art in the Museo di Arte Sacra, which is situated next to the romanesque, eleventh-century church of Sant'Agata. The former church of San Bernardino is now the Etruscan museum, containing treasures mostly from the necropolis of Poggiopinci (5 km to the east).

Eleven kilometres south of Asciano is the remarkable early-fourteenth-century convent of **Monte Oliveto Maggiore,** still inhabited by monks. A superb gateway (decorated by Della Robbia terracottas); a marvellous avenue of cypresses; a cloister with frescos by Luca Signorelli and Giovanni Sodoma illustrating the life of St Benedict; the pharmacy, its old recipes and jars still intact (dating from the seventeenth century); the baroque church of 1772; the marquetry stalls inside the church, created by Giovanni da Verona in 1505; all add up to an unforgettable visit.

BAGNI DI LUCCA, known as a health resort for six hundred years, lies on the N12 some 29 km from Lucca. Possibly the mild climate and the gentle walks beneath the plane trees contribute as much to health as the internationally renowned salt and sulphurous waters. Today the nineteenth-century bathhouse in the Palazzo del Bagno is a ruin, as is the neglected Protestant cemetery where Ouida is buried.

BARGA lies 42 km due north of Lucca in the wooded valley of the River Serchio known as the Garfagna. The town offers superb views of the valley, as well as a romanesque cathedral containing a twelfth-century sculpted pulpit and in the apse a huge statue of St Christopher from the same century. Those interested in the pre-history of the Garfagna can study it in the museum housed in the Palazzo del Podestà. Opera lovers come here for an annual festival each July and August.

BIBBIENA stands in the Casentino, the upper valley of the River Arno. The fifteenth-century church of San Lorenzo contains terracottas attributed to the school of Della Robbia. Opposite this church stands the early-sixteenth-century Palazzo Dovizi. The patron saint of Bibbiena is Saint Hippolitus, and the twelfth-century church of SS Ippolito e Donato contains the remains of late medieval frescos as well as a triptych painted by Bicci di Lorenzo in 1435. A clock-tower is a desultory reminder of what was once a fine castle.

Bibbiena is celebrated for its salami and for the 'Bello ballo', a fourteenth-century dance still performed on the last day of Carnival. From the central piazza you can see **Poppi** and **Camaldoli.** Poppi boasts a thirteenth-century Palazzo Pretorio and arcaded streets. Inside the castle are fifteenth-century frescos and a chapel with frescos done a century earlier. The sculptor Mino da Fiesole was born here.

Mino da Fiesole painted a Virgin Mary in the monastery church at Camaldoli which St Romuald founded in 1012. Lorenzo il Magnifico was a patron of this monastery, whose buildings today date mostly from the seventeenth and eighteenth centuries. (An exception is the pharmacy of 1543 which retains its old pots and carved cupboards.) The monks published works on the care of fir trees, and the region is still wooded. About 2.5 km above the monastery is a baroque church and eight cells, where the monks could live in complete isolation, following the example of their founder. In contrast to the baroque church of Il Salvatore is the charming chapel of San Antonio.

Twenty-three kilometres east of Bibbiena is the monastery of **La Verna**, founded by St Francis of Assisi. Here the saint is alleged to have received the stigmata, and there is a Cappella delle Stimmate with a crucifixion painted by Salvi d'Andrea in 1480. The Franciscan church was greatly enlarged on the orders of Pope Eugenius IV in 1433. Here too is a splendid basilica built in the late fifteenth century, as well as a charming church of Santa Maria degli Angeli, basically early thirteenth century though with lovely renaissance choir stalls.

BIVIGLIANO, north-east of Florence is today a holiday resort, with lovely panoramic views. In religious history it is famous for its convent of Monte Senario. Here in the early thirteenth century seven wealthy councillors of the city of Florence set up the order of the 'Servites' (or Servants of Mary), eating little, fasting and praying. To commemorate the appearance of the Angel Gabriel to Mary they later founded the church of Santissima Annunziata in Florence; but their mother house – now consisting mostly of eighteenth-century architecture – was here.

BÓLGHERI, see under CÉCINA.

BORGO SAN LORENZO, 29 km north-east of Florence, suffered almost complete destruction by an earthquake in 1919. The rebuilt town is devoted to agriculture and industry, though it retains its romanesque church of San Lorenzo (partly rebuilt in the sixteenth century) with its hexagonal bell-tower of 1263. Three kilometres to the north is the eleventh-century church of San Giovanni Maggiore.

Close by are Vespignano, the birthplace of Giotto (his house has allegedly been identified) and Vicchio, the birthplace of Fra Angelico (see under MONTE SENARIO).

BOSCO AI FRATI, see under SCARPERIA.

BUONCONVENTO, see under MONTALCINO.

BUTI, a village east of Pisa at the foot of Monte Pisano. The road to Buti skirts the Monte Serra and is picturesque. The villagers make notably fine wickerwork baskets.

CALCI lies 12.5 km from Pisa (by the Via Garibaldi) at the foot of Monte Pisano in the Val Graziosa. The pretty eleventh-century church was to have had a massive bell-tower; it remains unfinished. One kilometre to the east is the splendid Pisan charterhouse (Certosa di Pisa), which was founded in the fourteenth century but now includes a baroque church (with rich frescos of the seventeenth and eighteenth centuries and a high altar with stalls of the fifteenth century), a small fifteenth-century cloister and a greater one with a seventeenth-century fountain. The charterhouse lies amid chestnuts and pine trees, as does Calci.

CAMALDOLI, see under BIBBIENA.

CAMPALDINO is a plain where in 1289 a decisive battle was fought between the Florentines and the people of Arezzo. A column pinpoints the site of the battlefield, just north of Poppi (which lies 5 km north-west of Bibbiena), along the N70.

Dante, who was a young man, fought on the side of Florence, which won. The Florentine historian Giovanni Villani recreated the victory, in which, he recorded:

between horse and foot more than 1,700 were slain, and more than 2,000 taken, whereof many of the best were smuggled away, some for friendship, some in return for ransom; but there came of them bound to Florence more than 740. Among the dead left on the field were M. Guiglielmino de Pazzi of Valdarno and his nephews, the which was the best and the most experienced captain of war that there was in Italy in his time.

This region is known as the **Casentino**. Today it is a lovely wooded valley, watered by the upper reaches of the River Arno. Here the exiled Dante was given refuge by the friendly Guidi. Continue north (towards Pratovecchio) and you see to the left the eleventh-century Castello di Romena, now a ruin (which you can visit) and close by, the romanesque church, the Pieve di Romena.

CAPALBIO, 10 km north-east of Lake Burano, lies at the heart of the Maremma game park. The local restaurants of this walled village specialize in succulent wild boar and various kinds of deer.

CAPRAIA, an island whose surface area is no more than 19 km², lies in the Tyrrhenian Sea north of Elba, between Corsica and the mainland. In the early centuries of the Christian era it was an ideal home for monks withdrawing totally from the world. The road south-west from its only town, Capraia Isola, leads past San Stefano, built on the site of a fifth-century church erected by these monks. Later, part of Capraia was used (and still is) for criminals forcibly segregated from the world and forced to work on the land. For a very short time (1767–81) Capraia existed as an independent state.

Formerly volcanic, Capraia today is divided by a ridge between 300 and 400 m high, creating two slopes. The slope to the west of the island is wild and creased by ravines. That to the east of the island is much gentler, with valleys and navigable coves. Here is the inhabited part of the island and the village of Capraia, though paths lead nature-lovers into the wilder part. One such path leads to Il Laghetto, a lake in what was once the crater of a volcano. Another leads to the so-called 'Semaforo', giving an impressive view of the sea towards Corsica.

Capraia attracts lovers of underwater swimming and nature watchers. Its old watch-towers, in particular the Torre dello Zenobito at the southernmost tip of the island, speak eloquently of a less civilized time when the inhabitants were continually in danger of piracy. Another relic of that era is the sixteenth-century castle built by the Genoese at Capraia. Just below the Torre dello Zenobito is the remarkable Cala Rossa, a series of craters of red rock, close to which modern holiday-makers enjoy wind-surfing and fishing. The island can be reached in a couple of hours by boat from either Livorno or Portoferraio on Elba. There are some hotels – though not enough for all those who wish to stay during the high summer.

CAPRESE MICHELANGELO is the village where the artist and poet was born in 1475. It lies 45 km north-east of Arezzo, and you can visit the house where he was born – the Casa del Podestà, close by the fourteenth-century castle – and the thirteenth-century church of San Giovanni Battista where he was baptized.

CARRARA, wrote Charles Dickens, 'shut in by great hills, is very picturesque and bold'. In his day few tourists stayed there and nearly everyone he met was connected in one way or another with the working of marble.

Few tourists even visited Carrara in those days. (Dickens reached the quarries by pony.) The work was arduous, for marble was hewn by dangerous explosives from the fissures on Monte Altissimo, and then hauled down by sluggish, sad oxen. Even when Edward Hutton visited the place a hundred years later, he found the same methods and the same 'poor capering, patient brutes' dragging immense wagons over sharp boulders and dazzling rocks, 'grinding them in pieces, cutting themselves with sharp stones, pulling as though to break their hearts under the tyranny of the stones, no less helpless and insensate than they'. Hutton even found the people ugly, without sweetness, overburdened by toil, and he got away as soon as he could.

In comparatively recent years all this has changed. The construction industry of the Middle East (and the love of marble displayed by Arabs) means that something in the region of 10,000 m³ of marble a year are cut from Monte Altissimo. Compressed-air drills, electrical power-saws with carborundum teeth, cut out 100-tonne rectangular pieces of marble. Then mechanically driven steel wires cut these to the builders' and artists' specifications. Sculptors drive in from Pietrosanto near by, and along the main road from Querceta, to choose their marble. Today good metalled roads lead from the coast. (**Marina di Carrara** is the northernmost seaside resort of Tuscany, and in the nearby port you can see lovely white blocks of marble waiting for shipment abroad.)

Some 300 caves (as the quarries are known) around Carrara support a town of over 70,000 inhabitants. They continue, in modern ways, an industry known since the Romans, who quarried the marble of these Apuan mountains centuries before the Christian era. Marble is in fact ancient limestone that has been crystallized by enormous pressure and tremendous heat, over hundreds of millions of years. Carrara white marble is prized above all other kinds because of its purity of colour and because its grain is so fine. And

Monte Altissimo (*not* in truth the highest peak of the Apuan Apennines, since it rises to fewer than 2,000 m above sea-level) represents some six square miles of perfection. This mountain provided the marble for the great Italian sculptors and architects of the Renaissance. Commissioned by the Medici to design a facade for the church of San Lorenzo, Michelangelo lived here to supervise the cutting and shaping of his marble; and in the Piazza Duomo, Carrara, you can see a plaque over a bar proclaiming that this was his home.

Dickens had a higher opinion of the inhabitants of Carrara than did Edward Hutton, and so do I. (Dickens found they had built a beautiful little theatre, and heard there a chorus of labourers, self-taught, sing a comic opera by ear; 'and they acquitted themselves very well'.) They also eat well, specializing in *testaroli* (green vegetables in a mould); *tortelli* and savoury rice.

If you press your way through the modern town, you are rewarded with a splendid romanesque cathedral, with a facade bearing a gothic upper storey and an intricate fourteenth-century rose-window. You can find the Teatro degli Animosi (1840) where Dickens heard comic opera, in the Piazza C. Battisti. Only a keep remains of the old Fortezza; but a ducal palace, built by Alberico Malaspina in the sixteenth century, is now the Accademia di Belle Arte. The Piazza Alberica also contains the eighteenth-century Palazzo dei Conti del Medica. There is a seventeenth-century church of San Francesco. And of course there is the Professional Institute of Marble Workers (Istituto Professionale del Marmo) which is well worth a visit.

CASCIANA TERME is a spa, 38 km south-east of Pisa, situated amidst vineyards and olive groves 160 m above sea-level. Restaurants specialize in eels and fish from the Arno.

CASCINA, on the N67 east of Pisa, achieved fame in 1364, when Florence defeated Pisa at a battle here. The church of Santa Maria is an unspoilt twelfth-century building; and the fourteenth-century Oratorio di San Giovanni was decorated with frescos by Martino di Bartolomeo in 1398. Today the citizens mostly earn their living by making furniture.

CASTAGNETO CARDUCCI, see under CÉCINA.

CASTELLINA IN CHIANTI, as its romantic name implies, both boasts a fifteenth-century Rocca (citadel) and was the first base of the League of Chianti producers. There are Etruscan ruins dating from the fourth century BC.

CASTELLO, 3 km north-west of Florence, is the site of no fewer than three Medici villas (see the index, under Villas). The oldest, Villa di Careggi, had been a medieval house until Cosimo il Vecchio commissioned Michelozzo to alter it in the early fifteenth century. Today, however, most of the buildings date from the restorations of the sixteenth century. The second oldest was also based on a medieval building: Villa della Petraia was rebuilt for the Medici family by Buontalenti in 1575 – though he did not destroy the medieval tower. Giambologna created the statue of Venus on the upper terrace, close by a fountain by Tribolo. The third villa, Villa di Castello, retains the famous garden which Tribolo laid out in 1537. Visitors are welcome only at the Villa della Petraia and to the garden of the Villa di Castello.

Here are fine sandy beaches, rocks, and a pine forest. Close by are the remains of the Etruscan city of Vetulonia and the ruins of the Roman villa of the Gens Clodia (to which family Catullus' beloved Lesbia belonged).

CASTELNUOVO DELL'ABATE, see under MONTALCINO.

CASTELNUOVO VAL DI CÉCINA is a little-known medieval town due south of Volterra, retaining the thirteenth-century tower of its former castle, a town-hall dating from the fourteenth and fifteenth centuries, a parish church (San Biagio) that is partly romanesque, partly gothic, and – because of its site, 600 m above sea-level – marvellous views across chestnut forests.

CASTIGLIONCELLO, 2 km south of Livorno, was once inhabited by the Etruscans and then declined in importance, frequently the victim of pirates until Cosimo I de' Medici built its protective tower in 1560. In recent years its position on a promontory has made Castiglioncello a favoured seaside resort. Etruscan museum and tomb.

CASTIGLION FIORENTINO, on the N71 south of Arezzo, is a walled town noted for its art gallery, a castle, the sixteenth-century Loggia del Vasari and a thirteenth-century church of San Francesco. The Collegiata was restored and altered in 1853, but it retains fine paintings by Lorenzo di Credi, Bartolommeo della Gatta and Segna di Bonaventura; in what remains of the old parish church (to the right of the Collegiata) is a fresco by Luca Signorelli of the Deposition. Four kilometres south is the thirteenth-century Castello di Montecchio Vesponi, which the citizens of Florence gave to the English *condottiere* Sir John Hawkwood (see John Hawkwood in the index).

CASTIGLIONE DELLA PESCAIA, situated on the coast west of Grosseto and now the chief seaside resort in the Maremma, retains its medieval walls and its fifteenth-century Aragonese castle. Here in Roman and Etruscan times a lighthouse guided shipping into the landing-place known as the 'Salebro' (now called 'Serrata Martini').

South of Castiglione della Pescaia is the famous Tómbolo pine wood.

CASTIGLIONE D'ORCIA is an extremely attractive little town, situated 540 m above sea-level on the slopes of Monte Amiata, 46 km south-east of Siena and nestling under its ruined Rocca. Its frescoed medieval parish church boasts a fifteenth-century facade and a fourteenth-century *Madonna and Child* by the imposing Sienese artist Pietro Lorenzetti. The painter and sculptor Lorenzo di Pietro (who was called Vecchietta) was born here in 1392, and a *Virgin and Child with Angels* by him can be seen in the church of Santa Maria Maddalena (which also possesses a *Madonna* by a pupil of Lippo Memmi).

To the north-west is the medieval village of **Rocca d'Orcia**, still proud of its powerful, though ruined, fourteenth-century Salimbeni castle.

CAVO, see under ELBA.

CÉCINA, a town of around 25,000 inhabitants today, was created in the nineteenth century as a result of the draining of the Maremma. It lies 36 km south of Livorno, a few minutes (by car) inland from its excellent seaside resort, **Marina di Cécina**, where the River Cécina flows into the sea. The road leads down the coast to San Vicenzo, 25 km to the south and another favoured seaside town. Half-way to San Vicenzo you can drive left to the hillside villages of **Bólgheri** and (a little further south) **Castagneto Carducci**.

These two villages derive their fame in Italy as the childhood scenes of the poet Giosuè Carducci, who was born in 1835 and died in 1907. Carducci clearly did not love his memories of his childhood, save in some masochistic fashion. Bólgheri is famous today for an exceedingly impressive avenue of cypresses, almost 5 km long, which was planted in 1801 by Camillo della Gherardesca. Carducci wrote a gloomy, celebrated poem about them.

Indeed, his verse displays much pessimism about this ravishing part of Tuscany, with its nature reserves and delicious coastline. By contrast, Carducci tends to speak of *'quella foresta d'abeti e pini ove al confina nereggia'* ['that forest of firs and pines where the edge blackens'] and of silent, sad nostalgic farewells to chestnut trees. As for the sea, he watches the stars descend into its midst *'e si spengono i canti entro il mio core'* ['and the songs die inside my heart'].

None of this gloom should remotely dissuade the twentieth-century tourist from visiting this entrancing region. Higgledy-piggledy Bólgheri and the blue-brown walls and steeps of Castagneto are lovely.

CERTALDO. Half-way between Florence and Siena, at the confluence of the Elsa and the Agliena, is a town in two parts. The lower part is modern. The old upper town was for most of his life the home of Boccaccio, and here he died in 1375. His alleged home, restored in 1823, was destroyed during the Second World War and has been rebuilt. In the church of SS. Michele e Iacopo (thirteenth century, restored with the addition of a cloister two hundred years later) he lies buried. (A cenotaph to him, erected in 1503, was destroyed in 1783 by those who disapproved of his writings, though the portrait bust by G. F. Rustici remains.) The Palazzo Pretorio was built in the fifteenth century and has contemporary frescos by Fiorentino, though again much of the building is a nineteenth-century restoration. In the Via Rivellino is the former chapel of San Tommaso, displaying a graceful romanesque-gothic facade and flanked by a romanesque cloister of 1210.

CERTOSA DEL GALLUZZO is the site of a former Carthusian monastery founded 6 km to the south of his native Florence by Niccolò Acciaiuoli in 1342. Acciaiuoli had been high steward of the kingdom of Naples, and his foundation – though inspired by deep devotion – displays the hand of a man who had known earthly splendour. The site alone, on a hill above the Via Cassia, is impressive. And the monastery lives up to the site, for just as Acciaiuoli had prospered in affairs of state, now he and his followers became great in affairs of the church. Successive generations of Cistercians at Galluzzo continued to enrich the foundation.

After his call to the spiritual life Niccolò Acciaiuoli still firmly intended to make his mark on the world, and he commissioned the splendid gothic Palazzo degli Studenti at Galluzzo (the architect was Fra Jacopo Passavanti) where young Florentines might study the liberal arts. (Niccolò was a close friend of both Boccaccio and Petrarch.) Its gallery has five frescoed scenes from the passion of Christ, done by Jacopo Pontormo when he came here in 1522 to escape the plague that had attacked Florence. (Pontormo was a pupil of Andrea del Sarto, but these five lunettes also display the influence of his other master, Dürer.) The gallery does in fact possess some German masterpieces – by Dürer himself, for instance, and by Lucas Cranach.

Monks need space to walk, meditate, and (at stated times) converse, and the Carthusians at Galuzzo created for themselves not one but three splendid cloisters for these purposes. The Great Cloister boasts sixty-six terracotta tondi (representing saints and Old Testament prophets) by Andrea and Giovanni della Robbia. (Pontormo's frescos of Christ's passion were originally also in the cloister, but were later detached for display in the gallery.)

The chapter-house where the monks transacted their daily business was not left unornamented: the Florentine Mariotto Albertinelli (d. 1515) was commissioned to paint here a fresco of the crucifixion. The monks also embellished their 'Colloquio' with sixteenth-century stained glass.

They dedicated their church to San Lorenzo. Its glory is the marble tabernacle over the high altar, designed by Giambologna, the mannerist genius who settled at Florence in 1555. In the sixteenth century these Carthusians gave their church a gothic facade. At the same time they commissioned fine stalls for themselves when at worship. They built a choir for the lay brothers, above a crypt containing the tomb of the founder (who died in 1365) and the sixteenth-century tomb of Cardinal Agnolo il Acciaiuoli.

Today you can also visit the refectory and a monk's cell (which turns out to be more sumptuous than one expected, since each monk has three rooms as well as a little garden and a loggia).

Certosa del Galluzzo is still a monastery – though since 1958 occupied not by Carthusians but Cistercians (who till then had not established a community in Italy since the Grand Duke of Tuscany expelled them 176 years previously).

On your visit to the old pharmacy before leaving the monks will sell you a fragrant, if slightly cloying, liqueur of their own making.

CETONA, see under SARTEANO.

CHIANCIANO TERME. The Romans called Chianciano Terme 'Fontes Clusinae' and relished its thermal springs. Eighty-five kilometres south-east of Siena and 9 km south-east of Montepulciano, it is now one of the world's noted spas, its unique *acqua santa* water reputed to cure liver and bilious problems. Those suffering nervous strains are offered help by carbonic mud baths, especially from the potent Silene spring. The Fucoli spring is said to be excellent for stomach and duodenal complaints. The healthy can indulge in tennis and other sports in the Parco di Fucoli. Those interested in the medieval parts of old Chianciano (18 m lower down than Chianciano Terme) will find the Palazzo del Podestà of the thirteenth century, decorated with fifteenth- and sixteenth-century escutcheons; the Collegiata, with its thirteenth-century porch and its wooden crucifix of the fourteenth century; and the eighteenth-century Palazzo dell'Arcipretura, which is now a museum of religious art. There are nightclubs in the modern spa, and food specialities include roast young pig and cheese made from the milk of sheep.

CHIUSI lies just off the Autostrada del Sole just south of the Lago di Chiusi. It was one of the twelve cities which formed the Tuscan confederation in the seventh century BC, and in 508 BC its king Lars Porsena even attacked Rome, according to the celebrated legend, which may have some history behind it. In the early third century BC Chiusi, then known as Camars, became subject to Rome, which renamed the town Clusium.

Much of this Etruscan–Roman history is still visible in the architecture and surroundings of Chiusi. The romanesque cathedral was built on Roman columns of varying styles and the builders utilized countless Etruscan and Roman materials. The Museo Nationale Etrusco, to the left of the cathedral, is filled with Etruscan cinerary urns, sarcophagi, statues. The town is surrounded by

Etruscan tombs which can be visited: the tombs of the Pilgrim and the Grand Duke date from the third and second centuries B C; the tombs of the Ape and the Casuccini from the fifth century B C; the tomb of Tassinaie from the first century B C. The fifth-century *hypogeum* of Gaiella is said to house the tomb of Lars Porsena. Etruscan galleries run underneath the town itself.

The other buildings well worth seeing in Chiusi are the medieval ruined Fortezza (thirteenth century or even older) and the church of San Francesco (fourteenth century). See Etruscans and Chiusi in the index.

COLLE DI VAL D'ELSA, 25 km north-west of Siena, is divided into Colle Basso and Colle Alto. The architect Arnolfo di Cambio was born in a tower-house that still survives in the upper town. Here too remain part of the medieval ramparts, with a grim, impressively castellated Porta Nuova; the Palazzo Campana of 1539; the Palazzo Pretorio, built in 1335; the late medieval Palazzo dei Priori, now the civic museum; the Palazzo Vescovile, now the museum of religious art; the church of Santa Maria in Canonica, begun in the seventh century, but basically today twelfth-century romanesque (with lovely warm brick embellishing the walls and an early, simple and satisfying rose-window at the west end); and the baroque cathedral, built in 1619, with a bronze crucifix attributed to Giambologna and a graceful pulpit, on four classical pillars, dating from 1465 and attributed to Giuliano da Mariano. The upper town is on the ridge of the hill, offering some splendid views (especially from the bridge and the Palazzo Campana).

In the lower town, in Via dei Fossi is the church of San'tAgostino. This began as a humble oratory dedicated to John the Baptist, but was greatly amplified in the thirteenth century. It remains un-finished, its west end proffering roughly hewn stones to have been covered with marble that was never bought. The interior is a delightful surprise: sixteenth-century renaissance, designed by Antonio da Sangallo the Elder, with paintings by T. di Bartolo and by Ghirlandaio. Also in the lower town is the fine church of Santa Maria a Spugna, built first in the tenth century and rebuilt in the eighteenth.

Craftsmen of Colle di Val d'Elsa produce excellent traditional glass and crystal ware.

COLLODI, 17 km north-east of Lucca, was the home of Carlo Lorenzini (1826–90) who took the pen-name Carlo Collodi and created the character Pinocchio. The Parco di Pinocchio contains a bronze monument of 1956, by Emilio Greco, commemorating the puppet and other characters from Collodi's fertile mind. Other sculptures in the park illustrate episodes from the book. In the Paese dei Balocchi, just south of the park, a fearsome fish, with menacing teeth and a great pink slab of a tongue was sculpted rising from an ornamental lake by Marco Zanuso and A. Piccoli. (It is called *il grande Pescecane*.)

Other attractions at Collodi are the Villa Garzoni, built between 1633 and 1662, with its elegant flight of steps and its seventeenth-century terraced gardens (partly altered in 1786), filled with fountains. The church of San Bartolomeo has fifteenth-century frescos and terracotta statues of the same date.

At Collodi they bake a cake known as a *torta coi becchi*.

CORTONA is one of the oldest towns in Tuscany. Thirty-two kilometres south-east of Arezzo, perched 650 m high on a spur of the Alta S. Egidio, it is very close to Umbria, and indeed was almost certainly founded by the Umbrians (though Virgil says it was founded by the mythical Dardanus). The Etruscans took it over as one of their twelve confederated towns. Cortona was allied with Rome in the fourth century BC and was made a colony by Sulla. The Goths captured the town in AD 490. It re-emerged as a free, democratic commune in the tenth century, was sacked by troops from Arezzo in 1258; regained its former prosperity, was taken by Ladislas, king of Naples, in 1409 and sold by him to the Florentines in 1411.

The Etruscan wall around Cortona once stretched almost two miles in all; much of it remains, including the sturdy Porta Montanina. The environs of Cortona are littered with Etruscan tombs, and the Palazzo Pretorio (built in the thirteenth century, extended in the seventeenth) now houses much Etruscan art, including funeral barques, vases, statues of warriors, and the famous sixteen-branched bronze candelabra of the fifth century BC (with its fearsome staring head). The Palazzo Pretorio also houses a priceless library of 133 incunabula, 1,172 parchments, 633 manuscripts and 2,200 printed volumes.

A reminder of Florentine domination of Cortona is the forbidding Fortezza Medicea, built by Laparelli in 1549 on the ruined Etruscan wall. The views from here are superb (including that to the east, to the old acropolis). Close by here St Margherita died in 1297. The sanctuary basilica of Santa Margherita da Cortona was built in her memory and to house her tomb (by the local artists Angiolo and Francesco di Pietro). This tomb, as well as a fourteenth-century crucifix, survives in the rebuilt church dating from 1856. Far more in keeping with the spirit of Cortona is the church of San Francesco, with its simple facade preserving a porch dated 1245. The steep flight of steps to the church is well worth climbing to see inside, behind the high altar, the tomb of St Francis's disciple, Brother Elia Coppi of Cortona. Here too is a reliquary containing what is believed to be a piece of the true cross. And in the crypt lies the body of Cortona's most famous son, the painter Luca Signorelli.

Signorelli's work can be seen inside the fourteenth-century church of San Niccolò (a fine banner) and in the church of San Domenico, just outside the town (a *Madonna and Child*, angels and saints; a *Deposition*). In the diocesan museum – housed in the former church of the Gesù, with Michelangelo Leggi's lovely wooden ceiling dated 1536 – is another, quite different *Deposition* by Signorelli; his *Last Supper*; a remarkable *Flagellation of Jesus*, where those who are whipping him are stripped for their work, while red-clad soldiers stand nonchalantly by; a beautiful *Nativity*, with the shepherds already worshipping the infant Jesus and the Magi in the distance, on their way; as well as the famous predella by Fra Angelico (who lived in Cortona) of the life of St Dominic and one of his splendid *Annunciations*. Here too are important works by Pietro Lorenzetti and his brother.

Other notable churches in Cortona include the late-thirteenth-century Sant'Agostino, the church of Santa Maria Nuova (1550), and the cathedral of Santa Maria, with a sixteenth-century portal by Cristofanello and a mid-sixteenth-century bell-tower by Francesco Laparelli. (The renaissance interior was redone in the early eighteenth century.) The church of Santa Maria delle Grazie was designed by Francesco di Giorgio Martini in 1485, and stands just outside the walls.

All this is set amid a most charming medieval city. The Piazza della Repubblica is quaint and impressive at the same time. The overhanging houses of the medieval Via del Gesù are entrancing. Cortona seems to relish fine flights of steps – up to the Palazzo Civico (thirteenth century with a sixteenth-century tower); up to the church of San Francesco. Brunelleschi built the Palazzo Lovari and the Palazzo Mancini. G. B. Caporali created the Palazzo Sernini and the Villa Passerini (also known as the 'Palazzone') in the early sixteenth century. The Palazzo Fierii Petrella dates from the fifteenth century; the Palazzo Ferretti from the eighteenth.

And the surrounding countryside is equally delightful. Terraced olive groves, dry-stone walls, villas, ilexes, pines, cypresses, surround churches and such stunning sights as the fourteenth-century Rocca di Pierle.

CUTIGLIANO, see under ABETONE.

ELBA, the largest island of the Tuscan archipelago, lies about 8 km from the mainland. The ferry (with accommodation for cars) takes about an hour from Piombino to Portoferraio.

The Etruscans named the island Ilva, which means iron, and for centuries it has provided Tuscany with iron ore. After the Etruscans came the Carthaginians, the Romans, the Pisans, the Genoese and the Spanish. Then Cosimo I de' Medici fortified the capital city, **Portoferraio**, as a precaution when he united Elba with his other lands in 1548. He arranged for the building of the powerful five-sided Forte della Stella and the Forte del Falcone. Cosimo's plans were not totally successful, for the Spanish contested his rule, endowing the town of **Porto Azzurro** with a fort in 1603. (It now serves as a jail.) The Spanish also built the sanctuary of Monserrato 6 km north of Porto Azzurro in 1650.

Elba continued to be contested by the Spanish, the Italians, the Turks and the French, to whom it was ceded by the Treaty of Amiens in 1802. Here, after his abdication in 1814, Napoleon was exiled by the allies, who granted to the former ruler of eighty million subjects sovereignty over this island 224 km square. Aided by his mother and his sister Pauline, he restlessly reformed the administration of the place, setting up a miniature court, before quitting Elba on 26 February 1815. After Napoleon's defeat at Waterloo, Elba became part of the Grand Duchy of Tuscany.

But Napoleon's two homes remain. Near the Forte della Stella,

Portoferraio, is the *palazzina* which he created out of two windmills, now called the Palazzina Napoleonica dei Mulini. He brought silver and books from Fontainebleau, as well as furniture from his sister's home at Piombino.

Six kilometres away is the Villa Napoleonica di San Martino, which the exiled emperor set up as his country seat. He transformed an old country house into a villa decorated in the neo-classical style. He filled it with mementoes of his former glory. He himself left an inscription: 'Napoleon is happy everywhere.' Close by this villa is a neo-classical art gallery – the Pinacoteca Foresiana – built in 1851. Five kilometres south-east is the spa Terme San Giovanni, with the remains of an imperial Roman villa.

Portoferraio (which means 'iron port') remains the largest town on Elba. Its blast furnaces survive. Its church of the Misericordia, built in 1566, displays one of Napoleon's deathmasks and is the site of a requiem for the emperor each year on 5 May. West along the coast from Portoferraio is the pretty fishing village of **Marciana Marina**. Further west, and inland, the village of **Marciana Alta**, from which you can take a cable car to the 1,018 m peak of Monte Capanne. Marciana Marina boasts a quaint twelfth-century tower on its mole, built by the Pisans, and at Marciana Alta is the ruined medieval castle of the Appiano dynasty who once ruled the island.

On the southern part of the island is the fine seaside resort of Marina di Campo (where there is a small airport). Here is the largest harbour on Elba. A radio beacon occupies the Medici Tower on the quay. Five kilometres higher up is the tiny village of San Piero, and another 5 km farther on the village of Sant'Ilario where the operatic composer Giuseppe Pietri was born. Two other seaside villages on the south shore of Elba are Lacona and Capoliveri (a town known in Roman times, which now produces wines as well as iron ore and offers a superb view of the island of Montecristo).

On the east coast of the island of Elba is Rio Marina, whose name comes from a pure water rising here from five springs. Not far from Rio Marina is a new village, **Cavo**, the nearest place on Elba to the mainland, which takes its name from the telegraph cable (*cavo*) linking it with Piombino. And just off Cavo is the Isola dei Topi (which means 'rat island'), rising no more than 3.7 m above sea-level.

But Elba's charm does not lie chiefly in its towns and villages. Its granite and porphyry landscape, its equable temperature – allowing a variety of vegetation and trees – make this island a rambler's paradise. The abundant fish of the Mediterranean, as well as the fine Moscato and Aleatico wines of the island, add to its paradisical qualities.

The other islands of the Tuscan archipelago are Capraia, Gorgona, Pianosa, Giglio, Giannutri and Montecristo. For CAPRAIA see the separate entry in this gazetteer. Pianosa is another jail. Montecristo houses a ruined Benedictine monastery, San Salvatore, and another monastery, San Mamiliano, which pirates pillaged in 1553. Legend had it that the monks hid their treasures before they fled, and this inspired Alexander Dumas's famous *Count of Montecristo*. Today the island is an uninhabited nature park, and can be visited from Elba. See also under GIGLIO.

EMPOLI, 33 km east of Florence, was the scene of a famous debate in 1260 when Farinata degli Uberti persuaded the Ghibellines not to destroy Florence. Here in 1554 was born Jacopo Chimenti, who called himself Jacopo di Empoli.

Empoli is a busy industrial town, well known for its glass-blowing. It is also graced by the collegiate church of Sant'Andrea which dates back as far as the fifth century but was rebuilt in the romanesque style in 1039. On top of this romanesque skeleton was applied a facade in green and white marble, in a gothic style that showed various modifications until the facade was finished in the eighteenth century.

Close by the Porta Pusano, which was built in 1487, stands the fourteenth-century Augustinian church of Santo Stefano, alas much damaged in the Second World War but still worth seeking out, especially for its frescos. The Museo della Collegiata, close by the church of Sant'Andrea, is also a treasure-house of religious art and today gives shelter to some of the frescos rescued from Santo Stefano after 1944.

Eleven kilometres north of Empoli is the village of Vinci, birthplace of Leonardo: see VINCI in this gazetteer.

FIESOLE, an Etruscan town 8 km north-east of Florence, is older than Florence herself. Rivalry between the two towns led to the destruction of most of Fiesole by the Florentines in 1125. But this act of cultural and political savagery could not efface the Etruscan and Roman remains of this city, which have revealed their extraordinary splendour and complexity in the age of excavation. Fiesole offers superb views of Etruscan walls, part of an Etruscan temple, the Roman arena which could hold up to 3,000 spectators, Roman baths and a Roman temple. Treasures from these sites can also be seen in the archaeological museum which looks like a Roman temple, but was in fact built just before the First World War.

When the Florentines destroyed old Fiesole, they left standing the cathedral and the bishop's palace. The cathedral is basically a building of the thirteenth and fourteenth centuries, restored in the late nineteenth century. It is certainly worth entering and visitors are well rewarded visually if they put a coin into the boxes that work the lights, both for the main basilica and the crypt. The ancient columns have splendid capitals. Explore the Capella Salutati to the right of the chancel, with its fifteenth-century frescos by Cosimo Roselli and its mid-fourteenth-century tomb of Bishop Salutati by Mino da Fiesole. Mino da Fiesole also carved the altar front, with the Madonna surrounded by saints. In the crypt are a granite font carved by del Tadda in 1569, fifteenth-century frescos, and the tomb of St Romulus. (Romulus, though no doubt a great saint, is not my favourite in connection with Fiesole. That palm goes to the humble ninth-century Irishman St Donatus, who slipped unobtrusively into an earlier cathedral here just as the citizens were about to elect a new bishop. In acclamation of Donatus, the bells are said to have rung spontaneously and the puzzled Irishman was unanimously elected. He ruled as bishop for forty-seven years.)

Climb back to the high altar to see its mid-fifteenth-century altarpiece by Bicci di Lorenzo. The vault of the apse is frescoed by the sixteenth-century painter Nicodemus Ferrucci. In the chapel to the left of the choir you can see statues of St Matthew and St Romulus by another Ferrucci, the Florentine sculptor Andrea (1465–1526).

The sculptor Mino da Fiesole (c. 1430–84) is commemorated now in the name of the Piazza Mino da Fiesole on which the cathedral stands and which was once the old Roman forum. To the east is the fourteenth- and fifteenth-century Palazzo Pretorio, next to which is the renaissance church of Santa Maria Primarana, which contains a couple of fine crucifixes: one, of wood, done in the fourteenth century, the other (in terracotta, with the Virgin and saints) by the school of Della Robbia. Della Robbia terracottas are also to be seen in the Museo Bandini, which is pleasingly intimate and also contains, for example, works by Nino Pisano and Bicci di Lorenzo.

But what helps to make Fiesole so rewarding to visit is the view of its former rival Florence, especially as seen from the vicinity of the convent church of San Francesco. In this convent (built in the mid fourteenth century, though the gothic interior of the church dates from the early twentieth century) are some fine paintings (including a fifteenth-century fresco of St Francis himself). St Bernardino of Siena once lived here – in one of the sparse cells in the cloisters. Since the Franciscans were enthusiastic missionaries, it is fitting to find here a missionary museum, with treasures brought from as far as Egypt and China.

The facade of San Francesco is fifteenth-century work. And just outside this church is another curiosity: the basilica of Sant'Alessandro – built on the site of a Roman temple and utilizing the old Roman columns.

Close by Fiesole is the Villa Medici, which Michelozzo built for Cosimo il Vecchio between 1458 and 1461. Unfortunately tourists at present are not allowed to visit this villa, which Georgina Masson has rightly dubbed 'the first true Renaissance villa of Italy'. (See in the index Villa Medici, Fiesole.) The route past this villa nevertheless compensates the disappointed visitor with stunning views of Florence. This steep old road (the Via Vecchia Fiesolana) leads to the hamlet of San Domenico di Fiesole, scarcely 2 km outside Florence. Here Fra Angelico was professed, in the monastery of San Domenico built in the early fifteenth century, and here he later became prior of his fellow Dominican monks. For the first altar on the north side of the monastery church he painted the lovely *Virgin with Angels and Saints*. The chapter-house of the monks also contains another *Madonna and Child* by Fra Angelico, as well as one of his apparently simple yet passionate frescos of the crucifixion.

FLORENCE occupies a whole chapter of this book and is referred to in the text more often than any other Tuscan city. This section of the gazetteer aims at supplementing what can be found by consulting the entry under Florence in the index.

The city lies almost at the mid-point of the Italian peninsula between the Adriatic and the Tyrrhenian Seas. The chief motorway of Italy, the Autostrada del Sole, connects Florence with Rome and Naples in the south and Milan and Bologna in the north. The motorway to the sea (Autostrada del Mare) connects the city to Prato, Pistoia, Montecatini, Lucca, Pisa and the western seaside resorts. A dual carriageway carries traffic from Florence to Siena. The city is served by the main national railway lines, and its nearest international airport is San Giusto, Pisa. (British Airways' address in Florence is nos. 36–38 Via della Vigna Nuova; Alitalia is at nos. 10–12 Lungarno Acciaioli.)

Much of the history of Florence is charted in the text of this book, at least as far as the eighteenth century when the Medici Grand Dukes were succeeded by the House of Lorraine. In 1860 Florence, along with the rest of Tuscany, became part of the Kingdom of Italy, and was its capital city from 1865 to 1871.

Florence is extremely well-equipped for tourism. Four hundred hotels and *pensioni* offer over eighteen thousand beds. Lists of hotels and much other tourist information can be obtained from Ente Provinciale per il Tourismo (no. 16 Via Manzoni) and Azienda Autonoma di Turismo (no. 15 Via Tornabuoni).

If you need the help of the British Consul, his consulate is at no. 2 Lungarno Corsini. (The American consulate is at no. 38 Lungarno Amerigo Vespucci, a fitting address.)

Sports facilities abound: swimming-pools, tennis clubs, golf courses, shooting ranges, etc. Florence boasts numerous nightclubs. The British Institute is in the Palazzo Antinori at no. 2 Piazza Antinori (for this palace, see this section of the gazetteer, under San Gaetano). Its library and reading room are at no. 9 Lungarno Guicciardini. The American Library is in Via dei Parione. And the Biblioteca Nazionale (a copyright library in which I have often worked with the minimum of difficulty or red tape) is in the Piazza dei Cavalleggeri.

Throughout the year Florence hosts numerous cultural and artistic activities. The annual music festival takes place in May. The Teatro Communale runs both summer and winter seasons of drama. The 'Exploding of the Cart' (see p. 89–90) takes place in the cathedral square on Easter Sunday. An entertaining historical pageant in the Boboli Gardens is held on 24 June, and another on St John's Day (with fireworks in the Piazzale Michelangelo). From the middle of September to the middle of October in odd-numbered years the city runs an antiques fair. An international festival of documentary films takes place each December. Cultural, tourist and artistic events are listed in *Firenze Oggi* (free, with English editions, from the tourist offices) and in the lively monthly journal *Firenze Spettacolo*.

Theatre, concert and opera tickets can be bought at Universal-turismo, no. 7 Via Speziali. Tours in the surrounding country-side – for wine-tasting and the like – are arranged by Agriturist, no. 10 Via del Proconsolo.

Florentine food specialities include huge T-bone steaks, grilled chicken, and beans dressed with olive oil. See also the index to this book under Cuisine.

As well as the many buildings and institutions listed in the index to this book, the following must be mentioned (re-membering always the judgement of J. P. Cobbett in his 1830 *Journal of a Tour in Italy* that there is no way of justly de-scribing such fine things, for 'Art has here brought fiction so near upon the verge of reality, that the line between them is too nice to be drawn by words'):

Accademia, in the Via Ricasoli, houses the original *David* by Michelangelo as well as four unfinished but beautiful *Slaves* by him. Although many of the finest Tuscan paintings from this gallery have been transferred to the Uffizi, a goodly number remain.

Archaeological Museum in the Via della Colonna – filled with Etruscan, Egyptian and Roman treasures, many from other parts of Tuscany.

Badia Fiorentina in Via del Proconsolo, is the Benedictine abbey founded in 978 and much altered over the centuries (so that, for instance, the ceiling inside is baroque, and the hexagonal bell-tower has a romanesque lower part and gothic upper storeys). Among the treasures inside is a tomb of Margrave Ugo of Tuscany, son of the foundress, by Mino da Fiesole. See also Badia Fiorentina in the index.

Cascine, once a dairy farm ('Cascina') is now a shady park, entered from Viale Fratelli Rosselli. Visitors can join its private tennis club and swimming-pool.

Castagno Museum, see below, under Sant'Apollonia.

English Cemetery (known to the Italians as the Protestant Cemetery), Piazzale Donatello, is where are buried (amongst many others) W. S. Landor, Arthur Hugh Clough and Elizabeth Barrett Browning.

Fortezza da Basso, a massive fortress built for the first Duke of Florence by Antonio da Sangallo the Younger in 1534, now stands on a traffic island in the Viale Filippo Strozzi. Here the duke was murdered by his cousin. Craft exhibitions are held in the Fortezza da Basso throughout the year.

Loggia di San Paolo, see below, under Piazza Santa Maria Novella.

Museo di Storia della Scienza. The Science Museum in Florence, in the medieval Palazzo Castellani east of the Ponte Vecchio in the Piazza dei Giudici,, houses an impressive collection of scientific instruments, including a pendulum clock designed by Galileo, and his telescopes.

Museum of Musical Instruments. This remarkable collection, at no. 80 Via degli Alfani, contains amongst many other treasures instruments made by Antonio Stradivari, including his famous Viola Medicea of 1690.

Ognissanti, the church of the Umiliati (a Benedictine order specializing in weaving wool), was erected in 1250. It stands on its piazza north of the River Arno, close by the Ponte Amerigo Vespucci. Its riverside situation was an ideal one for the monks' work, and soon the whole area was essential for the economy of medieval Florence. The facade is a very early example of Florentine baroque, designed by Matteo Nigetti in 1637. Giovanni da San Giovanni frescoed the dome in 1617.

The bell-tower dates from the original foundation, as does the tympanum *Coronation of the Blessed Virgin Mary*, a fifteenth-century enamelled terracotta by Benedetto Buglione. Inside is the family tomb of the Vespucci family, one of whose members, Amerigo, gave his name to America after two visits in 1499 and 1502. He is said to appear in one of the two frescos painted by Domenico Ghirlandaio over the second altar on the south side of the church.

(The alleged Amerigo Vespucci is between the Madonna and a man wearing a red cloak.) Simonetta Vespucci, who posed as a nymph for Botticelli's *Primavera*, also appears in this fresco.

Because of its position by the river, Ognissanti suffered a great deal during the 1966 floods, but it has been very carefully and well restored.

Palazzo Antinori, see below, under San Gaetano.

Palazzo Davanzati in Via Porta Rossa was built by the Davanzati family in the middle of the fourteenth century and now – with furniture from the fifteenth to the seventeenth century – offers the best preserved example of a medieval Florentine house. You can visit the palace each morning from nine o'clock (save Mondays). It closes in the early afternoon.

Palazzo Guadagni, see below, under Piazza Santo Spirito.

Palazzo Guicciardini, see below, under Santa Felicità.

Palazzo Larderei, no. 9 Via Tornabuoni, is a splendid, late-sixteenth-century, high-renaissance building by Giovanni Antonio Dosio.

Piazza Santa Maria Novella, opposite the railway station, is the site of two obelisks set on tortoises designed by Giambologna. These were erected in 1608 as the turning-point of an annual chariot race started by Cosimo I in 1563. On the south-west side of the piazza the Loggia di San Paolo was built between 1489 and 1496, based on Brunelleschi's Loggia degli Innocenti (see the index). The lunette under the arcade, depicting St Dominic meeting St Francis, is by Andrea della Robbia.

For the church of Santa Maria Novella see below, under Santa Maria Novella.

Piazza Santo Spirito, south of the Arno, not far from Ponte a Santa Trinità, has a daily market and is surrounded by medieval workshops. Its elongated, irregular form adds to its charm. No. 10 Piazza Santo Spirito is Palazzo Guadagni, built by Simone del Pollaiuolo (who was known as Cronaca) at the beginning of the sixteenth century.

For the church of Santo Spirito see below, under Santo Spirito.

Piazza Santa Trinità, see below, under Santa Trinità.

Ponte a Santa Trinità, the most beautiful of all the Arno bridges, spans the river east of Ponte Vecchio. First built in 1252, it was many times rebuilt. In 1567 Cosimo I commissioned the present superb design from Bartolommeo Ammannati (who enlisted the help of Michelangelo). At the end of the century, to celebrate the marriage of Cosimo II, marble statues representing the seasons were placed on the parapet (the work of Taddeo Landini and Pietro Francavilla). In 1944 the allies destroyed the bridge, and the present structure is a perfect reconstruction (save for the four statues by Francavilla, representing the seasons, which were recovered from the river) by the architect Riccardo Gizdulich.

Porcelain Museum. This fine collection of porcelain that once belonged to the Medici Grand Dukes and the House of Lorraine is displayed in the Boboli Gardens in the eighteenth-century Casino del Cavaliere.

Porta Romana, close by the Boboli Gardens and the most southern of the old gates of Florence, was built in 1326 and retains its original doors and a fourteenth-century fresco of the Virgin Mary.

Porta San Frediano, south of the river and west of Ponte Amerigo Vespucci, is part of the best preserved section of the city walls which the commune of Florence built between 1284 and 1333. There is some evidence that this gate and its high tower, along with its massive doors (still with their original locks) and ironwork, was designed by Andrea Pisano. Borgo San Frediano leads west to the church of San Frediano in Castello, rebuilt in the 1680s by Antonio Maria Ferri, who gave it an exceedingly fine dome.

San Felice, lies just north of the Pitti Palace. In 1457 Michelozzo gave this gothic church a renaissance facade, which makes the medieval interior something of a (pleasant) surprise. Its treasures include a crucifix by a pupil of Giotto and a *Virgin and Saints* by Ghirlandaio.

San Firenze is formed from three churches joined together in the eighteenth century to make one great baroque whole. In consequence its baroque facade, by Fra Zanobi del Rosso in the 1770s, has on either side two other facades designed by Ferdinando Ruggieri in 1715. A plaque on a wall of its square (Piazza San Firenze) marks the house where Elizabeth Barrett Browning died in 1861. Robert Browning described her death to her sister. She put her arms round him, whispering 'God bless you,' and kissing him repeatedly with such vehemence, 'that when I laid her down she continued to kiss the air with her lips and several times raised her own hands and kissed them'. He asked, 'Are you comfortable?' and she replied 'Beautiful.' Then the maid sponged her hands, and Elizabeth went to sleep. Browning raised her up, and she died peacefully in his arms, her head resting against his shoulder.

San Frediano in Castello, see above, under Porta San Frediano.

San Gaetano in Piazza Antinori, Via Tornabuoni, a splendid baroque church built by Matteo Nigetti and the brothers Silvani in the first half of the seventeenth century, is unfortunately open only for services. Opposite is the fifteenth-century Palazzo Antinori built by Giuliano da Mariano, the home today of the British Institute.

San Pancrazio, is reached by walking along Via de' Federighi from where Ponte alla Carraia spans the River Arno. An ancient ninth-century church (with a fifteenth-century renaissance portico by Leon Battista Alberti), it was deconsecrated in 1809 and used for many years as a warehouse. When restored, it is destined to become a museum of sculpture.

San Salvi, no. 16 Via San Salvi, once a Vallombrosan convent and now a mental hospital, boasts a church dating from the fourteenth century (restored and altered over the next two centuries) and (in the former monks' refectory) a superbly restored *Last Supper* by Andrea del Sarto. This famous masterpiece, other frescos by Andrea, and works by Ridolfo, Ghirlandaio, etc., are open to the general public.

Close by is the world-famous Sports Stadium (holding up to 66,000 spectators) built by Pier Luigi Nervi in 1932.

Sant'Ambrogio, a late-thirteenth-century church with a nineteenth-century facade in Via Pietrapiana, contains a superb tabernacle in the Cappella del Miracolo, made in 1481 by Mino da Fiesole, who died three years later and is buried at the entrance to this chapel.

Sant'Apollonia in Via Ventisette Aprile, a convent founded in 1339 and extended in the next century, boasts in its refectory the spectacular *Last Supper* by Andrea del Castagno (1423–57). This is but one of the monumental paintings by Castagno housed here, and the convent is now the Castagno museum.

Santa Felicità, the second oldest church in Florence (the oldest is San Lorenzo – see the index), has been much rebuilt over the centuries and now stands as it was left by Ferdinando Ruggieri in 1736. Ruggieri was a sensitive restorer and Santa Felicità still has the air of a fifteenth-century church. The architect did not disturb the portico built by Vasari.

The sacristy, clearly by a pupil of Brunelleschi, contains Neri di Bicci's *Saint Felicity and her Seven Children* and Taddeo Gaddi's *Madonna and Child with Saints*. But the two masterpieces of this church are to be found in the first chapel on the south side (the Capponi chapel): Jacopo Pontormo's *Deposition* and his *Annunciation*. Of the four Evangelists painted in the tondi of the dome, Angelo Bronzino (d. 1572) did one and Pontormo the other three.

Santa Felicità stands in its square in the Via Guicciardini, on the way to the Pitti Palace. No. 15 Via Guicciardini is Palazzo Guicciardini, built at the beginning of the fifteenth century and reconstructed in the seventeenth. The politician and historian Francesco Guicciardini was born here in 1483. His contemporary Machiavelli lived at no. 18.

Santa Maria Maggiore, on the corner of Via dei Percori and Via Vecchietti, was founded in the eighth century but the present gothic building dates from the thirteenth.

Santa Maria Novella, the great Dominican church to the west of the city opposite the railway station, has a superb polychrome facade created by Leon Battista Alberti in 1470. (Note the emblem of his patron Giovanni di Paolo Rucellai – a ship's sail – and of the Medici – a ring with ostrich feathers.)

The building is made to seem even longer inside by the way the width of the bays decreases as they approach the altar. Santa Maria Novella was begun in 1246 and was a long time building. Jacopo Talenti took charge of the work in 1330, and by 1360 the bell-tower was finished.

The interior is filled with treasures. The altar crucifix is by Giambologna. For the sanctuary Domenico Ghirlandaio, between 1485 and 1490, painted scenes from the lives of the Virgin Mary and John the Baptist. Buontalenti designed the glass of the rose-window. Paolo Rucellai lies in his sarcophagus near the Cappella Rucellai, which contains Nino Pisano's statue of the *Madonna and Child*. And Filippo Strozzi lies in his tomb (designed by Benedetto da

Maiano) in the Cappella di Filippo Strozzi. Here are the superb frescos he commissioned from Filippino Lippi, as well as the stained glass designed by the same artist. The Cappella di Filippo Strozzi is in the south transept, opposite the fourteenth-century Cappella Strozzi in the north transept, for which Orcagna painted an altarpiece, depicting Christ giving St Peter the keys of heaven and St Thomas Aquinas the book of knowledge. Dante had recently died and Orcagna (assisted by his brother) also painted for this chapel scenes from the *Divine Comedy*, depicting Dante already in Paradise.

Other masterpieces in Santa Maria Novella include Masaccio's fresco of *The Trinity with Mary and St John above a Skeleton on a Sarcophagus* and, near by, Brunelleschi's fine pulpit. Brunelleschi also made the wooden crucifix in the Gondi chapel (first left from the high altar). He is said to have carved it with the intention of showing Donatello how to represent the crucified Jesus. Giuliano da Sangallo decorated this chapel in coloured marble in 1503.

The peaceful cloisters contain Uccello's frescos of Old Testament stories from the Creation to the Flood and Noah's drunkenness (see Uccello in the index). These cloisters lead into the fourteenth-century Spanish Chapel, the monastery's former chapter-house, designed by Jacopo Talenti. Its frescos were painted by Andrea da Firenze in the 1360s.

Santa Trinità, on the left side of Via Tornabuoni going north from Ponte a Santa Trinità, is a church of the Vallombrosan order dating from the mid thirteenth century and gothicized (beautifully) in the fourteenth. The facade is by Buontalenti. The bell-tower was constructed in the late 1390s.

The Sassetti Chapel in the choir is frescoed with scenes from the life of St Francis by Domenico Ghirlandaio. (You can have them lit up.) Francesco Sassetti, who commissioned the series in 1483, appears in the scene where the saint receives the Franciscan rule from the pope. (So do Lorenzo il Magnifico, his sons and his tutor Politian.) This scene is set in the Piazza della Signoria, and elsewhere in the sequence you can recognize Ponte a Santa Trinità and Piazza Santa Trinità. Francesco Sassetti and his wife also appear kneeling in Ghirlandaio's altarpiece depicting the *Adoration of the Shepherds*. (Note the classical touch whereby Ghirlandaio has painted the manger as a sarcophagus) Francesco and his wife lie here in black marble sarcophagi made (probably) by Giuliano da Sangallo.

In the north transept three chapels are particularly worth searching out: the second chapel contains Luca della Robbia's superb tomb of Bishop Benozzo Federighi, done in 1455; the third contains a fifteenth-century *Annunciation* by Neri di Bicci; the fifth has a wooden statue of St Mary Magdalen, begun by Desiderio da Settignano and finished by Benedetto da Maiano.

The piazza outside contains a porphyry statue of justice carved by Ferrucci Tadda in 1581, and a granite monolith from the Baths of Caracalla, Rome, which Pope Pius IV gave to Cosimo I. There are no fewer than three fine palazzi here: no. 1 Piazza Santa Trinità, the Palazzo Bartolini-Salimbeni, was built by Baccio d'Agnolo in 1520 and is now the French consulate; no. 2 is the Palazzo Spini-Ferroni, a crenellated, three-storeyed fortress of 1289; and opposite is the Palazzo Gianfigliazzi of 1459, where (a plaque says) Alessandro Manzoni stayed in 1827.

Santo Spirito, south of the river over Ponte a Santa Trinità and along Via del Presto di San Martino, was commissioned of Brunelleschi in 1428 for the Augustinian convent that had stood here since 1250. He died before he completed the building, and succeeding architects may not entirely have kept to his designs, but it remains a superbly proportioned renaissance building. (See also under Santo Spirito in the index.)

In the south transept, in the third chapel towards the east, Fillippino Lippi painted a *Madonna and Child* – including in the painting the donors, Tanai and Nanna dei Neri – which is justly considered one of the finest of his works.

The sacristy was designed by Giuliano da Sangallo in 1489 as an architectural tribute to Brunelleschi. There are two fine cloisters, the first designed by the brothers Parigi in the early seventeenth century, the second (now a barracks) by Ammannati. The only surviving part of the former gothic monastery is the refectory. The rest was burned down in 1471.

Santo Stefano, to the right of Via Por Santa Maria going north from Ponte Vecchio, has a romanesque facade of 1223 and a seventeenth-century interior by Ferdinando Tacca (reasonably well-restored in 1947). Tacca also did the bronze altar frontal which depicts St Stephen being stoned to death. The flamboyant flight of steps leading to the altar came here from the church of Santa Trinità, for which they were made by Buontalenti in 1574. The church today is open only for exhibitions.

Sports Stadium, see above, under San Salvi.

Zoological Museum, known as 'La Specola' because the Grand Duke founded an observatory here in 1775, is housed in the Palazzo Torrigiani (no. 17 Via Romana), built specially for this purpose by Gaspare Paoletti in 1775. It opens rarely: Sunday and Tuesday mornings from nine o'clock and Saturday afternoons from two o'clock.

FOLLÓNICA, see under MASSA MARITTIMA.

FORTE DEI MARMI, see under PIETRASANTA.

GAIOLE is a little town among the vineyards 30 km north-east of Siena. Close by are monastic buildings dating from romanesque times which now devote themselves to sheltering wine-producers rather than men of God. (The village is called Badia a Coltibuono.)

GALLUZZO, see under CERTOSA DEL GALLUZZO.

GARGONZA, see under MONTE SAN SAVINO.

GIANNUTRI (ISOLA DI), see under MONTE ARGENTARIO.

GIGLIO (ISOLA DEL), though the second largest island in the Tuscan archipelago, is much smaller than Elba, lying 14 km from Monte Argentario, lapped by the waters of the Tyrrhenian Sea. This island, only 5 km wide and not quite 9 km long, is a paradise for underwater fishers, who crowd there in summer. Its mountainous interior is wine growing (the wine is mostly from the ansonico grape); the old city of Giglio Castello (which seems today little more than a village of narrow streets and medieval houses) is protected by its medieval walls. Campanese is where tourists find sand and sea, though many also sunbathe at Cala dell'Arenella and Cala delle Cannelle. Poggio della Pagana, 498 m above sea-level, offers the finest views. Boats (with car-ferrying facilities) sail here daily from Porto Santo Stefano.

GREVE, 27 km south of Florence on the wine route to Siena, has scarcely more than ten thousand inhabitants yet contrives to dominate the Chianti trade. Its September wine fair is a treat. The Piazza Matteotti has seventeenth-century buildings with delightful porticoes. Here lived the explorer of North America, Verrazzano.

GROSSETO, though capital of one of the nine Tuscan provinces, is as yet far too little appreciated by the visitor. The reason lies in the frightful conditions that existed in this province, the Maremma, until this century. The Grand Dukes of Tuscany had begun to drain the area, attempting to check the outbreaks of malaria that had reduced the region to penury and isolation. But only from the 1930s did any systematic reclamation of the land prove commercially attractive. To read nineteenth-century travel books is to receive repeated warnings *not* to visit this region. Today it is prosperous and in parts extremely beautiful. And in spite of savage air-raids during the Second World War, the capital city itself is remarkable, especially its ancient heart, protected by a six-sided brick rampart built by the Medici in the late sixteenth century (itself protected by six bastions, five of which are now lovely public gardens).

Grosseto also is imbued with history. The Etruscans founded this city. It was the seat of a bishop from the year 1138. The cathedral was built by the mid thirteenth century. Although many times restored, its character and beauty remain unimpaired. The facade boasts three sets of doors, each surmounted by a dignified romanesque arch, over which slender arcades seem to climb above the side doors to the arcade above the main portal. Little towers, like delightful pepperpots (or maybe a salt- and pepperpot) flank the pretty, delicate, central rose-window. All is white marble with thin strips of red. On the south side of the cathedral are gothic windows; and the bell-tower of 1402 is built of brick. Architectural 'purists' (or bigots) have been critical of this cathedral because the original work of the Sienese architect Sozzo di Rustichino was restored in the mid nineteenth century. In truth, the restoration was both sensitive and necessary (in view of the decayed state of the city in the 1840s); and the restorer, Caldana, took care to preserve what he could of the original, in particular Rustichino's carved symbols of Matthew, Mark, Luke and John on the capitals of the pilasters.

The interior is not so imposing though not, for that reason, to be missed. The baroque dome is not unimpressive. Antonio di Ghino made the font in 1470. He also designed a sumptuous retable in the left transept, containing an *Assumption* by Matteo di Giovanni, done in the fifteenth century.

Next to the cathedral is the stately Palazzo del Licio – stone

for the lower storeys, brick above – now housing the Museo Archeologico. The name should not mislead the tourist: this museum
contains many Etruscan archaeological finds; but it also houses
excellent Sienese paintings.

The citizens of Grosseto have made strenuous efforts to restore
their much ravaged city. The Palazzo della Provincia is a twentieth-
century reconstruction of Sienese gothic. The Piazza Indipendenza
boasts a modern statue of St Francis by T. Faccendi (1965) by the
thirteenth-century church of San Francesco, with its well-restored
cloisters (containing a lovely three-hundred-year-old well).

Grosseto deserves a visit simply for its unique cuisine: octopus
and mussels pickled in oil; risotto of crayfish; roast birds with
croûtons; marinated mountain goat; Maremman snails; and the
like. Its environs are also a delight. Ten kilometres north-east is the
Etruscan town of **Roselle**. Its Etruscan walls survive almost complete; its Roman forum and streets are visible, as is the amphitheatre, in spite of the fact that the Saracens pillaged it in 935 and
the town was two hundred years later completely abandoned.

Thirteen kilometres north-west of Grosseto, along the Via
Aurelia, lies (on a fine hilltop site to the right) **Monte Pescali**.
Matteo di Giovanni created the altarpiece in its parish church; and
in the church of San Niccolò are recently discovered frescos by
Bartolo di Fredi. Twenty-nine kilometres from Grosseto, in the
same direction, is an even greater village, **Vetulonia**, where the
Romans beat the Gauls in 224 BC. It is hard to believe that this
peaceful place, in spite of its still powerful citadel walls, was once
so important: a maritime city of great significance to the Etruscans
until the Maremma silted up; the city from which the Romans took
their symbol of the *fasces* and their *toga praetexta*. The necropolis
to the north-east of Vetulonia is still being excavated, revealing
remarkable tombs created eight centuries before the Christian era.
Soon, I think, the small Museo Archeologico will burst its walls in
Vetulonia.

The medieval villages around Grosseto are enormously seductive,
and often gastronomically rewarding too. And no more than 13 km
away is the beautiful **Marina di Grosseto**, with its lovely sands, its
pine forest, its warm (though sometimes dangerous) sea. See also
Maremma in the index.

IMPRUNETA. When Brunelleschi designed the dome of the cathedral in Florence he insisted that its tiles came from Impruneta, 14 km to the south. Terracotta remains part of the historical redolence of this town today, situated 275 m above sea-level in the Chianti country. The same clay as provided tiles for Brunelleschi enabled Luca della Robbia to create a terracotta tabernacle for the Chapel of the Cross which Michelozzo built in the church of Santa Maria dell'Impruneta. Luca della Robbia also created terracotta statues of saints Paul and Luke for the Chapel of the Madonna (also designed by Michelozzo) in the same church. Although the church itself was viciously bombed in 1944, it has been well restored and still presents a fifteenth-century aspect, with a bell-tower built two centuries earlier and a mid-seventeenth-century porch. The fourteenth-century cloisters are still happily intact.

Impruneta is famed not only for its wines but also for a horse and mule fair, held from 15 to 18 October (i.e. around the feast of St Luke) in the fine arcaded main square. As well as making tiles and wine, the citizens excel at creating straw hats.

INCISA IN VALDARNO derives its picturesque name from the deep gorge cut by the River Arno 36 km downstream from Florence.

LARI, south of Pisa, retains a fine military castle at the top of a steep flight of steps, as well as Della Robbia work in the old church. The village holds a cherry festival in May and a peach festival in August.

LA VERNA, see under BIBBIENA.

LIVORNO, whose great mole (and subsequent development as a port) was created by the Elizabethan knight Sir Robert Dudley, was for many years quaintly called Leghorn by the British. Situated at the northernmost part of its province, Livorno is the main port of the region, serving the archipelago and beyond. The Medici inherited a fortress that had been prized or coveted for centuries by the Genoese, Pisans and Florentines. They set about creating (with Dudley's help) a perfect renaissance port and town. The ravages of time were compounded by deliberate destruction in 1943, with the result that present-day Livorno has lost many of its ancient buildings. Instead, elegant bars and shops cater for tourist and businessman alike.

What remains from the past is by no means to be despised. The

British will warm to the Doric portico of the cathedral, since the original was designed by Inigo Jones. Alas, however, this fine building was rebuilt in the late 1950s. In the Piazza della Repubblica is the moated Fortezza Nuova, no longer new since it was built in 1590 by Buontalenti and Bonnano on behalf of the Medici. It was connected with the Fortezza Vecchia in the harbour, designed by Sangallo the younger in 1534. A reminder that once Livorno was a port of arrival for slaves is the monument to Ferdinand I facing the old harbour. Known as the Quattro Mori ('four Moors'), it comprises Ferdinand himself, sculpted by G. Bandini in 1595, and four bronze Moors added by Pietro Tacca twenty years later. Tacca also designed two bronze fountains to flank this group, but these instead were placed in the Piazza dell'Annunziata, Florence. (In 1964 the commune of Florence sent Livorno two copies of these fountains, which now stand at the entrance of the Via Grande.)

The Piazza della Repubblica also boasts at either end of its vast quadrilateral statues of the Grand Dukes Ferdinand III and Leopold II, erected respectively in 1847 and 1883.

Grand Duke Ferdinand I was a man of liberal principles quite unusual for the seventeenth century. He made Livorno a haven for the persecuted: Italians from other parts of Italy; English Roman Catholics; Jews and Turks. The city was the first in Italy to allow Protestants their own burial ground, and the now neglected cemetery (no. 63 Via Verdi) contains, among others, the remains of Tobias Smollett. See in the index Robert Dudley and Tobias Smollett.

Pietro Mascagni, who composed the opera *Cavalleria Rusticana*, was born at Livorno. So was the artist Amedeo Modigliani, who died in 1920 in Paris, whither he had fled in 1906, believing himself unhonoured in his own country.

Any visitor to Livorno will find a cornucopia of fish food: mullet (*triglie*); baby eels; cuttlefish; raw as well as cooked shellfish. All of these are complemented not only with wines from the mainland but also with Aleatico from Portoferraio and Muscatel and Passito from the Island of Elba. Livorno, as Charles Dickens observed after his visit in 1844, 'is a thriving, business-like, matter-of-fact place, where idleness is shouldered out of the way by commerce'. Even so, its citizens still relish the other pleasures of life.

LUCCA is where John Ruskin, by his own testimony, 'literally *began* the study of architecture'. Here he found himself 'suddenly in the presence of twelfth-century buildings, originally set in such balance of masonry that they could all stand without mortar; and in material so incorruptible, that after six hundred years of sunshine and rain, a lancet could not now be put between their joints'. It was a revelation to him. 'Absolutely for the first time I now saw what medieval builders were and what they meant.' Over a century later the buildings of Lucca remain as solid and beautiful as he described.

Archaeologists have revealed that this spot was inhabited at least fifty thousand years ago. Our knowledge of Lucca's history becomes detailed only when she became a Roman colony, in the second century BC (see Lucca in the index). Her situation, close by the sea, 22 km north-east of Pisa and 75 km west of Florence, made the city an important crossroads, and the peak of her influence and wealth came in the early fourteenth century under the warlord Castruccio Castracani (about whom Machiavelli wrote a largely imaginary biography). The city was one of the few that successfully resisted the hegemony of Florence, becoming part of the Grand Duchy of Tuscany only in 1847.

The city today has her sports facilities (particularly clay-pigeon shooting, football, basketball and tennis). There are antique dealers and hoteliers, restaurants that now aim higher (if that is the right word) than traditional local dishes, and modern shops in the narrow streets. But the city today lives chiefly off agriculture, olive oil, fruit, wine and small industry that has not spoiled its unique environment.

Lucca is built on the left bank of the River Serchio, which waters a fertile plain from which she derives her own distinctive cuisine (risotto with truffles; delicious grilled chicken and steak; lamb stewed with olives; grain soup; thrushes cooked on a spit). Once the Serchio overflowed its banks and began to flood the city. Happily a local saint took a rake and raked out a new route for the river, which ever since has behaved itself, apart from overflowing in 1812 (see below).

Thus blessed and protected, the city preserved for the most part its Roman street plan (and the plan of the amphitheatre as well, though the citizens built houses around it and so the seats have all

disappeared). As a further protection the Roman walls were sup-
plemented by the present 4 km (2½ miles) of wall, built over a
century and a half (beginning in 1594) out of masonry faced with
brick, surrounded by a moat 35 m wide. Some of the massive
bastions of these walls remain, adding to its fearsome aspect.
Altogether the walls of Lucca comprise ten bastions and one pro-
jecting platform (bizarrely dedicated to a saint, the sixth-century
Irishman Frediano, who founded a church here – now dedicated to
him – and is buried in it). The bastions had space underneath them
for ammunition and food. Only three gateways pierced these walls.
San Pietro, on the south side, has preserved its portcullis. The date
of its construction (1566) is carved on the arch inside. The gate
bears a portrait of the saint and the coat of arms of the republic of
Lucca, with its motto 'Libertas'. Porta San Donato lies to the north-
west of the city and was begun in 1629. Its two statues represent St
Paolino and St Donato, and were carved by Giovanni Lazaroni.

The oldest of the three gates, Santa Maria, guards the northern
wall and was built with a single arch (the two side-arches are
modern). Built in 1539, it was decorated with the marble *Madonna
and Child* in the 1590s and further embellished with a couple of
panthers, representing the city's coat of arms.

When the River Serchio overflowed again in 1812, saintly assis-
tance was no longer required, for the waters were kept out of the
city by these great walls. By this time Lucca had been presented by
Napoleon to his sister Elisa Bacciochi. She rushed back to the city
and was hoisted over the walls by a crane, since to open the gates
would have been disastrous. After Napoleon's fall, Lucca was given
as a duchy to Marie-Louise de Bourbon. She had much of the walls
transformed into public gardens. Trees and plants now make them
charming for picnics and walks, without destroying their historical
fascination. Outside is the outer ring-road, which helps to keep
Lucca virtually traffic-free. The neo-classical Porta Elisa, constructed in 1804, preserves the memory of Bonaparte's sister. Porta
Vittorio Emanuele, built in 1910 on the east side, reminds the visitor
of the first king of modern Italy. At the end of the nineteenth century
a gate was opened near the botanical gardens to let the tram through
on its way to Ponte a Moriano. Then an old secret entrance was
opened up to make a road from the cathedral to the railway station,

and yet another from Via Vittorio Veneto south-west to San Concordio.

A single tour of Lucca is impossible. You need to make four. Begin the first at Porta Elisa at the east flank of the city walls. Climb the ramparts and walk along them north as far as the great bastion known as San Salvatore. You descend into the city and reach, near Via dei Bacchettoni, the ruins of a great tower (known in Lucca as 'Il Bastardo') on which was built the Casa del Boia, the house of the city's public executioner.

Turn immediately left along Via della Quarquonia to reach on your left Villa Guinigi. Built in 1418, Villa Guinigi belonged to a rich nobleman named Paolo Guinigi and on his downfall was presented to the city. This brick building, with its pretty windows and jolly loggia, now houses the Museo Nazionale Guinigi. Etruscan vases and sculpture, Roman remains (including a first-century-AD pavement mosaic) and Hellenistic reliefs speak of Lucca's ancient past. Among the treasures from Lucca's medieval greatness displayed here are a thirteenth-century crucifix by Berlinghiero Berlinghieri and two lovely panels by Ugolino Lorenzetti depicting *St John the Evangelist* and the *Madonna and Child*. Here too are a couple of masterpieces by Fra Bartolommeo (both once in the church of San Romano): the *Madonna of Mercy* and a painting representing God the Father with Saints Mary Magdalen and Catherine.

Via della Quarquonia continues into Piazza San Francesco. At one end is a column, set up in 1687 by Giovanni Lazzoni and bearing a statue of the Virgin Mary with a great starry halo (the *Madonna dello Stellario*). Via del Fosso crosses the square, flanked by its little canal. And opposite is the thirteenth-century church of San Francesco. Its gothic portico leads into a vast single nave, covered with a wooden beamed roof. Here is buried the mighty adventurer Castruccio Castracani and also the musician Boccherini, who died in 1805. Don't miss the sixteenth-century tomb of Bishop Giovanni Giudiccioni, or the fifteenth-century frescos (in the chapel to the south of the high altar) depicting the life of the Virgin Mary. There are fourteenth-century frescos in the courtyard of the monastery formerly attached to this church, as well as the tomb of Bonagiunta Tignosini.

Cross the square and walk along Via della Fratta to Piazza San Pietro, whose church was founded by the Lombards, rebuilt in the twelfth century and finished two centuries later. The mid-thirteenth-century Lombard sculptor Guido Bigarelli created the carving on the architrave of the main entrance, depicting Christ giving the keys of the kingdom of heaven to St Peter.

Our aim on this first walk is to reach Porta Santa Maria, so we turn right along Via Busdraghi and then right again along Via Fillungo until we reach Piazza Santa Maria with a view of the old thirteenth-century gate, its twin arches and its circular defensive towers. And here is where our second tour starts.

Climb the ramparts of the city wall again and this time walk west to the bastion dedicated to San Frediano. The bastion looks southeast on to the massive bell-tower of the church of San Frediano, and you walk down into Piazza del Collegio for a closer look. The Irish saint after whom the church is named built here an earlier basilica which he dedicated to St Vincent. Prior Rotone began the present building in 1112. It took the rest of the century to complete, yet its proportions – three portals, pilaster strips and a colonnaded gallery making up the facade – are harmonious and simple. Berlinghiero Berlinghieri created the mosaic of the Ascension that tops the facade. The interior is a superb basilica with rows of columns that reach the far apse. The mid-twelfth-century font, whose reliefs tell the story of Moses, is sculpted like a fountain. One of its creators named Roberto inscribed his name on the front. Behind it Andrea della Robbia created the lunette of the *Annunciation*.

The old twelfth-century font is no longer in use, supplanted by another fine one made in the fourteenth century by Matteo Civitali. And here are two foretastes of treasures to come on this visit to Lucca. One is the fresco by Amico Aspertino of the arrival of the Holy Face in Lucca. He painted it in the second chapel to the north side of the church in 1509, along with other frescos, one of which depicts San Frediano leading the River Serchio away from the city.

The Holy Face will be seen in the cathedral of San Martino. Here too is the acknowledged masterpiece of the Sienese sculptor Jacopo della Quercia (1374–1438). Here in San Frediano in the Trenta Chapel (the fourth on the north side) is the much damaged tomb he made for Lorenzo Trenta and his wife. With the help of Giovanni da Imola he also made the impressive gothic altarpiece for this chapel, with a lovely marble group of the Madonna and Child with four saints.

Piazza San Frediano, on to which the church faces, leads south towards the site of the old Roman amphitheatre, whose elliptical arena was made into the enchanting Piazza Anfiteatro in 1830, long after its medieval houses had concealed the ancient seats. Wander all the way round the amphitheatre and back into Via Fillungo, which leads left, through ancient houses and medieval towers as far as Via Fontana, where you turn right along Via Fontana to find (at Via degli Asili) the delightful seventeenth-century Palazzo Pfanner, with its lovely external staircase and its eighteenth-century gardens. On the first floor is displayed a collection of eighteenth- and nineteenth-century costume. (It does not open on Mondays.) Then the road leads to the Piazza Agostino with its fourteenth-century church, whose bell-tower rests on the arches of a Roman theatre.

Walk now due south to the church of Santa Maria Certeorlandini, which was built in 1188. (The interior and facade, however, date from 1719.) This street is called Via Loreto because next to Santa Maria Certeorlandini is a chapel built in 1662 as a direct copy of the famous Holy House of Loreto. On the corner of Via Loreto and Via Santa Giustina is one of Lucca's finest sixteenth-century town houses, Palazzo Orsetti, with two lovely portals sculpted by Nicolao Civitali.

Via Santa Giustina leads west as far as Via Galli Tassi, where just to the left across the street is the superb Palazzo Mansi. Built in the seventeenth century, Palazzo Mansi was sumptuously furnished in the eighteenth. The former bedroom of Lucida (widow of Gasparre Mansi), who made a pact with the devil so as never to grow ugly, remains the most sumptuous of all. The palace is now a civic art gallery and museum (closed on Mondays). Its beautiful doors open on to works by Tintoretto and Veronese as well as Luccan masters. There are Medici portraits by Bronzino and Pontormo, and a *Madonna and Child with Saints Anne and John* by Andrea del Sarto. Some of the rooms of this palace are themselves of an extraordinary richness.

This tour now leads south to the crossroad with Via San Paolino and turns left along this street to the one renaissance church in Lucca, San Paolino itself, which Baccio da Montelupo and Bastiano Bertolani built in the first half of the sixteenth century in the form of a Greek cross. Inside, the apse is decorated with seventeenth-century frescos of the life of St Paul. This church also boasts an exquisite stone statue of the Madonna and Child brought from Paris in the thirteenth century when Luccan merchants traded throughout the known world.

Retrace your steps along Via San Paolino to the tree-lined Piazzale Verdi. To the right Via del Crocifisso leads to two eighteenth-century churches – a rare phenomenon in this city – the church of the Crocifisso dei Bianchi and the church of Santa Caterina, both built by the Luccan architect Francesco Pini. Piazzale Verdi leads to the old San Donato gate, shouldered to one side these days by the Porta Vittore Emanuele, which gives access to the motorway.

The third tour of this entrancing city takes in the cathedral. Start again at Porta Elisa but this time follow Via Elisa. At the very start of this street the church of San Ponziano, a romanesque church rebuilt in the seventeenth century, still preserves its beautiful four-teenth- and fifteenth-century cloisters. This is a street of churches: San Michelotto on the left (you can still see its romanesque origins in the architecture of the walls) and the sixteenth-century Santissima Trinità (which houses a splendid sculpture of the Madonna by Matteo Civitali). The sixteenth-century house opposite is the Villa Buonvisi. You cross the canal to be confronted unexpectedly with another defensive construction, the mighty thirteenth-century Porta dei Santi Gervasio e Protasio. A single round arch (with a dwelling above it) is flanked by a couple of menacing round towers, the left one without a single window. Beyond the gateway is Via Santa Croce, leading to the church of Santa Maria Forisportam.

The name means 'outside the gate', where once Santa Maria stood – when the city was still defended only by its old Roman ramparts. Most of this deceptively simple-looking church was erected in the thirteenth century. Its facade, though unfinished, is to me one of the most charming in Lucca: three doors, each topped by a romanesque arch. Above the central door are six blind romanes-que arches, while on either side four similar arches climb up to them above the outer doors. And a third storey of four blind rom-

anesque arches finishes the work. Everything is simple, everything perfectly at peace.

The interior seems suddenly more elaborate. Three aisles lead to
an apse and transepts that were rebuilt in the sixteenth century. A
remarkable curiosity is an early Christian sarcophagus that has
been transformed into a font – life in the midst of death, so to
speak. The north transept is the home of a beautiful picture of the
falling asleep and assumption of the Virgin Mary, done on gold by
Angelino Puccinelli in 1386.

As Via Santa Croce crosses Via Guinigi you can see to the right
the tower of Palazzo Guinigi, bizarrely growing holm oaks on top.
Via Santa Croce continues across Piazza Bernardini. The whole of
the north side of this square is taken by the renaissance palace built
by Nicolao Civitali in 1512. It stands so stern and regular, its
windows smaller closer to the cornice to give an illusion of height,
that one might think the Luccans had lost that playfulness which
created the delightful facades of their churches were not Palazzo
Bernardini also built out of an amazingly friendly yellow-hued
stone and brick.

My own relish for the marble facades of Luccan churches makes
me want to pick up speed here, leaving Piazza Bernardini by the
south corner along Via del Gallo and continuing across Via del
Battistero as far as the lovely Piazza Michelotti and the church of
San Giovanni. Ammannati is said to have helped to combine here
two romanesque churches into one. If so, he most tactfully kept the
romanesque columns inside. (Actually, one of them is Roman.) And
although the gleaming white facade was also redone in the seventeenth century, its lovely late-twelfth-century porch, with capitals
on which are jolly lions, remains intact, as does the fine brick bell-
tower.

Next to it is the cathedral square, Piazza San Martino. Though
not the most fantastic facade in Lucca (that has yet to come), that of
the cathedral is still remarkable – so much so that at first you
hardly notice the carving of its patron, St Martin, leaning from his
horse to slice his cloak in two for the beggar.

San Martino was built in the sixth century by St Frediano and
became the cathedral two centuries later. In the second half of the
eleventh century the Bishop of Lucca who later became Pope Alex-

ander II decided that his city needed a more imposing cathedral and began rebuilding. In 1204 Guidetto of Como added the facade, with its balconies and slender decorated columns. The porch was embellished with superb reliefs of the life of St Martin later in the first half of the thirteenth century. Nicola Pisano finally added the *Nativity* and the *Deposition*.

Inside Lucca's cathedral of San Martino are the two masterpieces hinted at in the second of these four tours: the Holy Face and the greatest work of Jacopo della Quercia.

Matteo Civitali created in the middle of the north aisle a splendid so-called *tempietto* in 1484 to enshrine the Holy Face – a hauntingly beautiful crucifix brought here in the eighth century from the east. Legends soon abounded in connection with its deeply moving Byzantine face. The stupidest suggested that it was the face of a girl named Uncumber, who grew a beard to avoid marriage and thus preserve her virginity. The most charming is that the crucifix was carved by Nicodemus, who fell asleep before he had finished the face, to awake and find that an angel had done the work for him.

I have seen this Holy Crucifix both bedecked for display and simply hanging as it was carved. For display the Christ is decked in a black velvet skirt heavy with golden ornamentation, and he wears on his head an enormous crown with yet another cross surmounting it. Around the Saviour's neck is hung an oversize gold necklace. He wears black velvet cuffs, again encrusted with gold. And a great golden medallion hangs on his chest.

In its original state the lovely Byzantine image is far more appealing. The crucified Saviour's feet hang pointing down. His robe is simply, marvellously modelled. His head hangs in sorrow, somehow far more appealing than when grandiloquently crowned.

In the north transept of the cathedral is the tomb which Jacopo della Quercia made for Ilaria del Carretto. She was the young wife of Lucca's ruler Paolo Guinigi. She lies here asleep on a cushion, narrow-waisted, beautiful, her hands crossed.

These are not the only masterpieces inside the cathedral at Lucca. The sacristy houses a *Madonna and Child with Saints* by Domenico Ghirlandaio. Giambologna contributes a *Risen Christ* on the so-called altar of liberty in the north aisle. Above all the cathedral is a treasure-house of works by Matteo Civitali (the pulpit, the tombs

of Domenico Bertini and Pietro da Noceto in the south transept,
two fine fonts), one of Lucca's unsung geniuses.

As you leave San Martino, look at the astounding romanesque
carvings of the tasks of the twelve months of the year embellishing
its porch. The work seems idyllic. The hardest task to my way of
thinking is killing the Christmas hog; the easiest certainly is that of
May, when a young man on a horse busies himself in bringing a
rose to his girl-friend.

Walk around the cathedral, across the Via dell'Arcivescovato,
and right along Via della Rosa to reach the church of Santa Maria
della Rosa, a pretty oratory built in 1309, with a fine fifteenth-
century porch from Matteo Civitali's workshop. This is the church
that preserves a section of the old Roman wall – great stone blocks
that you can see on the left inside, contrasting powerfully with the
slender columns that divide the church into three aisles.

Carry on down Via della Rosa and you reach the bastion of San
Colombano. A gentle walk towards the west along the ramparts
brings you to the sixteenth-century gateway of San Pietro, where
the third tour ends.

Here the last tour begins. Cross Corso Garibaldi and walk north
along Via Giglio to Piazza del Giglio, where Lucca's neo-classical
theatre stands. To the north of this square is the vast Piazza
Napoleone, sheltered by plane trees and boasting a statue of Marie-
Louise de Bourbon done by L. Bertoli in 1843. To the west of this
square is the huge Palazzo Pubblico, reconstructed in 1578 by the
Florentine Bartolommeo Ammannati, continued by Francesco Pini
in 1728 and finished by Elisa Bacciochi in the early nineteenth
century when she opened up the megalomaniac piazza. The
Bourbons lived here and employed Lorenzo Nottolini to build them
a monumental staircase in the palace.

You walk across Piazza XX Settembre to find on your left Piazza
San Giusto, with its little church, romanesque outside, renaissance
inside. The Palazzo Giglio is here, by Nicolao Civitali. Nicolao also
built the imposing Palazzo Cenami, just along Via Cenami (north
of the square) where it joins Via Santa Croce.

Cross over Via Santa Croce and immediately on your right is the
twelfth-century church of San Cristoforo. (The upper part of its
facade was not completed until the fourteenth century.) Via Fil-

lungo leads on to the old 'Torre della Lite' – the 'tower of rows', since rival families went to law over it in the middle ages. Its clock still keeps good time, and today it is known by the happier name of Torre delle Ore.

Just north of the Torre delle Ore you turn left along Via Buia to reach Piazza della Misericordia. Here is a lovely neo-classical fountain and the church of San Salvatore. Don't miss the twelfth-century carving of the miracle of St Nicholas in the architrave of the side door, signed by its sculptor Biduino. Then turn south down Via Calderia to Piazza San Michele.

The church of San Michele is a restoration/reconstruction in white limestone of an earlier eighth-century church. Here is my favourite Luccan facade, if only because it far outstrips the church that it is supposed to ornament. When the facade was built in the early thirteenth century, it was intended to raise the church higher. Money ran out and so the facade today in its upper reaches fronts nothing. There are four rows of arcades, with columns worked in many and variously intricate ways. Topping the whole is an enormous statue of a winged St Michael slaying a dragon. The bell-tower stands far back on the right-hand side, its openings successively rising from one to three on each side. Inside, Luca della Robbia created a *Madonna and Child* for the south aisle and Filippino Lippi painted a panel in the north transept with Saints Jerome, Sebastian, Roch and Helena.

Opposite the church is the Palazzo Pretoria which Matteo Civitali built in 1492 (his statue is in the portico) and others enlarged in 1588. And to the west along Via di Poggio is (at no. 30) the house where Puccini was born.

At the end of the Via di Poggio you reach the renaissance Palazzo Cittadella and turn left along Via Burlamacchi in order to walk as far as the church of San Romano. It was consecrated in 1281, and one wall, preserved because the tombs of old Luccan families abut against it, remains from the old building. In 1373 the apse was extended – in brick. The interior is mid-seventeenth-century baroque, and houses the tomb of San Romano created two centuries earlier by Lucca's marvellous Matteo Civitali.

Behind San Romano, Via Caserma runs south as far as Via F. Carrara, where you turn left in order to reach Piazzale Vittorio

Emanuele. Here is the bastion Santa Maria. Climb the walls and walk west for superb views of the Pisan hills, continuing under the shady trees until you reach the sixteenth-century Porta San Donato.

These four tours, I know, sound resolutely cultural and architectural. Lucca is such an intricate medieval town, with antique shops, workshops that pour metal bowls and copper kettles and all manner of trinkets into the streets, that the tours turn out to be nothing so arduous but rather a continual enchantment. Indeed, so many are the diversions that any tourist encounters, that I believe few will manage to complete them in one day or even two.

The city tourist office (Via Fillungo, just north of the Torre delle Ore) and the information office (Via Vittorio Veneto, just south of the Palazzo Pubblico) offer not only maps but also information on the many entertainments arranged for the visitor by this city.

Since both Boccherini and Puccini were born here, these include a music festival that lasts from July through August into September. And since churches – especially romanesque ones – make wonderful concert halls, Lucca offers endless treats to those who enjoy listening to sacred music in entrancing surroundings.

One music festival each summer is held just outside the city at **Villa Reale**, Marlia, 8 km towards Pistoia. This villa is well worth visiting at any other time in the year too. Villa Reale was the summer residence of Elisa Bacciochi. In the fourteenth century the local landowners were the Orsetti family, who converted their home into a renaissance villa in the sixteenth. In the second half of the next century the stupendous gardens were laid out: clipped yews creating garden rooms; potted lemon trees; a tremendous pool set amidst flowers; a fountain; statues of Harlequin and Columbine.

Elisa enlarged the villa and redecorated it in the style of the First Empire. The riding-school in front of the house was done away with to create a great sweep of lawn leading down to the lake, and a tremendous 'English' park. Finally Marie-Louise de Bourbon added a 'Temple of Urania' (really an observatory), a greenhouse, a coffee-house big enough to use as a ballroom, a library and a study. Villa Reale is open from 10.00 to 12.30 and from 15.00 to 18.00.

The outskirts of Lucca are particularly rich in fine villas. One and a half kilometres to the south is **Villa Torrigiani** (closed to the general public on Thursdays). This villa was inherited by the Torrigiani in the eighteenth century, and is reached along a superb avenue of cypresses. They too converted their garden into an 'English' park. The pools retain their baroque shapes, as does the marvellous facade of the villa itself. Fortunately Anglomania did not extend to converting the superb, complex seventeenth-century garden behind the villa. The nearest village is Camigliano.

Scarcely 7 km from Villa Torrigiani is **Villa Mansi** at Segromigno. A seventeenth-century villa in origin, today it is stamped by the eighteenth-century vision of the architect Filippo Juvara. The furniture, porcelain and plate of this villa enhance a visit. The garden has once again been redone in the 'English' fashion.

See also BAGNI DI LUCCA.

MAGLIANO IN TOSCANA is a former Etruscan town, situated 11 km north-east of Orbetello on the Via Aurelia. The citizens in the middle ages protected their town by still-surviving ramparts. Its Palazzo dei Priori was built in 1430. Two fine churches grace Magliano in Toscana: San Martino, first built in the eleventh century, redone in the fourteenth and fifteenth; and San Giovanni Battista, a romanesque church that embodies later gothic and renaissance features.

Two and a half kilometres south-east of Magliano in Toscana lies the ruined romanesque church of San Bruzio, near a large Etruscan necropolis. West of Magliano in Toscana, 450 m above sea-level, is the Sienese fortress of **Manciano**, from which the road leads north-west to nearby Montemerano.

Montemerano is yet another walled town – testimony to the fierceness of medieval Tuscany. Its church houses a lovely polyptych done in 1458 by Sano di Pietro.

Finally, just north of Montemerano lies **Saturnia**, again a walled town (though parts of the wall are said to be pre-Etruscan). Saturnia has a spring of therapeutic sulphurous waters, exploited by the Terme di Saturnia. According to legend, it was founded by Saturn, the Roman god of sowing.

MANCIANO, see under MAGLIANO IN TOSCANA.
MARCIANA ALTA and MARCIANA MARINA, see under ELBA.
MARESCA, see under PISTOIA.
MARINA DI CARRARA, see under CARRARA.
MARINA DI CÉCINA, see under CÉCINA.

MARINA DI GROSSETO, see under GROSSETO.

MARINA DI MASSA, see under MASSA.

MARINA DI PIETRASANTA, see under PIETRASANTA.

MARLIANA, lying 460 m high in the Pistoian hills north of Montecatini Terme, once possessed a castle first noted in history in 1137, but destroyed many times since then and now scarcely surviving at all. The present parish church of San Nicolao was once the castle church. The drive from Montecatini Terme to Marliana is breathtakingly beautiful and slightly hair-raising too, around dangerous bends, rising steadily through the chestnuts to this altogether charming spot.

MASSA, 45 km north-west of Pisa, is beautifully situated in the Apuan Alps, which – rising to 2,000 m – protect the town from the north. Protected too is its Marina. **Marina di Massa** is the gentlest coastal resort, with a wide, attractive beach and entrancing Mediterranean vegetation. In the mild climate lemons, limes, olives, palms and oranges flourish.

For 350 years (till 1790) Massa was the capital of the Dukes of Malaspina, who built the Rocca between the fifteenth and the sixteenth centuries, and in the seventeenth century created the lovely three-storey Palazzo Malaspina (as beautiful inside as out). They lie buried in the cathedral, which was begun in the thirteenth century, but now boasts a baroque interior and a modern marble facade. As well as the Malaspina tombs, the cathedral houses a fine marble high altar.

In the restaurants of Massa try *testaroli*, made from green vegetables.

MASSA MARITTIMA is divided into two parts, both fascinating. The lower walled city – the Città Vecchia – contains the superb cathedral, in itself a sufficient reason for visiting the place. Built between 1228 and 1304 in the Pisan romanesque style, it is dedicated to the Virgin in her Assumption and to St Cerbone (patron saint of the city), scenes from whose life you can make out in reliefs over the portal. The white, red and green marble of the facade presents seven blind arches, bearing a loggia of ten arches, the whole embellished with carved lions, horses, griffons and humans.

The interior of the cathedral is equally beautiful. The west end is frescoed, and incorporates a rose-window depicting in its stained glass St Cerbone visiting Pope Vigilius. In the first chapel to the right is a font made by Giroldo da Como in 1267. On it he sculpted scenes from the life (and death by beheading) of St John the Baptist, as well as numerous other finely realized figures from the Bible. (Giroldo did not make the tabernacle to the font, which is a marble gem of the mid fifteenth century and carries representatives of twelve patriarchs and prophets, above whom towers John the Baptist himself as the last great prophet.) A chapel close to the left of the high altar contains a painting of the Madonna, dated 1316, perhaps by Duccio di Buoninsegna. There is a charming fresco of the Madonna in the left aisle, and it is fascinating to compare the two treatments of the subject by different artists working in different media. The cathedral contains a fourth-century sarcophagus; and in the crypt is buried St Cerbone himself. He died around the year 380, but his present tomb is a magnificent marble creation of 1324, on which Goro di Gregorio sculpted eight scenes from his saintly life. (Note: you have to ask the sacristan to let you into the crypt.) The bell-tower, with its delicately balanced openings (increasing in number as you reach the top) was rebuilt in the present century. The cathedral stands opposite the Palazzo Communale, a palace made all the more entrancing by combining three buildings: a thirteenth-century tower, a fourteenth-century exterior and a sixteenth-century interior. Don't miss the she-wolf of Siena which Urbano da Cortona carved on the tower in 1468.

Massa Marittima was the main town in the Maremma until the seventeenth century. As its name indicates, it was once by the sea, till the land silted up. In Etruscan times it was already important for its copper and silver mines. There is an archaeological museum in the early-thirteenth-century Palazzo Pretorio (on which the magistrates of the city from 1426 to 1633 had their coats of arms carved), containing Etruscan remains as well as paintings of the Sienese school. (There are more Etruscan remains in the Museo Archeologico in the renaissance Palazzo delle Armi situated in the upper part of Massa Marittima.) Siena conquered the city in 1335 and built the Fortezza dei Senesi (now an impressive ruin) in the upper city – known as the Città Nuova. The finest church in this part of the city is gothic – Sant' Agostino, begun in 1299 but finished only in the fifteenth century. Close by this church is a mineralogical museum (Museo della Miniera) which those fascinated by copper mining through the ages will enjoy. The square Candeliere tower in the upper city contains the sole bell to survive from those that once hung in the thirteenth-century fortress of Massa Marittima.

In Massa Marittima try the unusual rosé wine from Monte Regio. And here, on 20 May and on the second Sunday in August, citizens dress in medieval costumes and shoot at mechanical falcons with crossbows.

This delightful city lies in the Grosseto, 64 km south-west of Siena. Not far away on the road to Siena lies the ruined Cistercian monastery of **San Galgano**, with its thirteenth-century church and sixteenth-century cloisters, marking the spot where St Galgano built a tiny hermitage in 1180. This is a super picnic spot; and it is well worth climbing up to the round romanesque church of Monte Siepi, with its frescos by the fourteenth-century Sienese artist Ambrogio Lorenzetti.

The road leads 19 km south-west of Massa Marittima to the popular seaside resort of **Follónica** with its lovely pine woods, its beaches (with views of Elba and Piombino) and also – it must be added – its industry.

MONSUMMANO TERME just south of the road out of Pistoia on the way to Montecatini Terme, is a spa whose waters are reputed to cure both gout and rheumatism. Once you have been healed, why not give thanks in the seventeenth-century church (with a loggia on three sides)? The frescos are by Giovanni da San Giovanni (1630). The church has a rich ceiling, and contains a monument (1879) to the local poet, Giuseppi Giusti.

The excellent local wine here is Chianti Putto from Monte Albano.

MONTALCINO lies on an Etruscan–Roman site 41 km south of Siena, surrounded by olives and vineyards. When Siena was under siege in 1555 its leaders took refuge here and since then have allowed the people of Montalcino place of honour in the great Palio procession. More pertinent to the thirsty tourist is the splendid wine produced here, Brunello di Montalcino. You can buy it everywhere in the town, and in particular in the mighty Rocca which the Sienese built here in 1361.

The walls of Montalcino date from the thirteenth century, as does the Palazzo Comunale in the Piazza del Popolo (the lovely arcades date from a century later). Higher in the town in the Via Ricasoli is the church of Sant'Agostino, a sturdy romanesque building containing a good rose-window in its facade, later gothic elements in its architecture, and pleasing fourteenth-century frescos. It abuts on the diocesan museum, which is chiefly devoted to Sienese works of the later middle ages.

Due north of Montalcino is **Buonconvento**, still retaining its thirteenth- and fourteenth-century walls and a fine medieval parish church, and boasting a museum of sacred art (which is rarely open – a couple of hours on Sunday, Tuesday and Thursday mornings, two hours on Saturday afternoons, and that is all).

Equally difficult to find open is a rare treat: the abbey of **Sant' Antimo**, 10 km south of Montalcino. (Usually you can get in on Sundays, though not at lunchtime; but at other times you can find the sacristan in the little village of **Castelnuovo dell'Abate**, higher up.) The Benedictines founded the abbey in the ninth century, and a couple of porches and the crypt of that foundation remain. The sacristy is frescoed. But the most amazing phenomenon of this church is its wonderfully luminous interior – derived from the fact that it is built partly out of alabaster.

MONTE AMIATA, see under ABBADIA SAN SALVATORE.

MONTE ARGENTARIO, due south of Grosseto, is a remarkable circular peninsula, close by Orbetello. (Three strips of land join Monte Argentario to the mainland; two bear pine woods; the middle one carries Orbetello. Once Monte Argentario was in fact an island, and its present connection with the mainland is entirely due to silting.)

You can drive around Monte Argentario, whose peak is 635 m above sea-level, visiting **Port'Ercole** (with its Spanish fortifications) to the south of the island, and **Porto Santo Stefano** to the north. Both are highly popular seaside resorts. The Romans appreciated the plentiful fish (now, as then) around the island – there are the ruins of a Roman villa on the island of **Giannutri**, just over 17 km away. There is also an extremely pleasant car-ferry from Porto Santo Stefano to the Isola del Giglio (see under GIGLIO).

MONTECARLO, see under MONTEVARCHI.

MONTECATINI TERME, situated by the road from Florence to the sea (and a half-hour's drive from both), has been a famous health resort since 1300 when the properties of its healing waters were popularized by an astute doctor named Ugolino Simoni. You both drink the water and bathe in it to alleviate ailments of the liver, intestines and stomach. The various establishments set up for this treatment – Stabilimento Torretta, Stabilimento Tamerici, etc. – are built in an astonishing, not-quite-ponderous classical style, set among gardens and parks laid out in the present century, with the lovely Tuscan countryside rising behind. (A twenty-minute drive takes you nearly 900 m above sea-level, among the firs and chestnuts of the Apennines.) These establishments are also cafés and are enlivened by musicians. Montecatini Terme has set itself up as an international resort, with many first-class hotels (and some *pensioni* too). The place is rich in swimming-pools, mini-golf courses, tennis courts and even a small race-course (for trotting), as well as mud baths. The Accademia d'Arte in the Viale A. Diaz houses modern art. Montecatini Alto (as **Montecatini Val di Nievole** is popularly known) is reached by a funicular railway – and also by car, if you wish. The funicular starts in the Viale A. Diaz. In the struggle between Guelphs and Ghibellines the Pisan Ghibellines defeated the Guelphs of Lucca here in 1316. There is a ruined medieval fortress. The romanesque church of Montecatini Alto has fourteenth-century frescos. There's a museum with late medieval and renaissance paintings. And of course magnificent panoramic views of the surrounding countryside.

MONTECATINI VAL DI NIEVOLE (or MONTECATINI ALTO), see under MONTECATINI TERME.

MONTEOLIVETO, a wooded hillside south of the River Arno close by Ponte della Vittoria, is noted not only for its many fine villas (which, as private dwellings, are not open to the public) but also for the church of San Bartolomeo, with many frescos and an altarpiece by Santo di Tito.

MONTE OLIVETO MAGGIORE, see under ASCIANO.

MONTEPULCIANO. 'I wouldn't for the world not have been there,' wrote Henry James of this town, situated 65 km south-east of Siena and 605 m above sea-level, on a hill which dominates the Chianti and Orcia valleys. Unfortunately, as he confessed, Henry James got a trifle drunk on Montepulciano wine, and so never managed adequately to explore the fascinating place.

I think my reason must have been largely just the beauty of the name (for could any beauty be greater?), reinforced no doubt by the fame of the local vintage and the sense of how we should quaff it on the spot. Perhaps we quaffed it too constantly, since the romantic picture reduces itself for me but to two definite appearances; that of the more priggish discrimination so far reasserting itself as to advise me that Montepulciano was dirty, even remarkably dirty; and that of its being not much else besides but parched and brown and queer and crooked, and noble withal (which is what almost any Tuscan city more easily than not acquits herself of).

James's tipsy drowsiness cost him several remarkable architectural pleasures in this city and made him denigrate Montepulciano unjustly, even though the vine he quaffed (to judge by what I have drunk in recent years here) would have been an undoubted treat. He never walked round the walls and fortifications which Sangallo the elder built at the behest of Cosimo I de' Medici. He did not find time to visit the cathedral, built between 1592 and 1630, still unfinished, though recently restored when Henry James was there. (The bell-tower, likewise unfinished, derives from the earlier parish church which the cathedral replaced.) Had he gone inside he would undoubtedly have marvelled at Taddeo di Bartolo's gilded, gleaming, multicoloured triptych of the Madonna in her assumption, surrounded by angels and saints. He scarcely saw the splendid Sant'Agostino, for which Michelozzo created a superb facade – a facade that is at once classical, even severe, and yet gracefully flowing. Inside he would have missed paintings by Lorenzo di Credi and Giovanni d'Agostino, and a fifteenth-century wooden crucifix. He never admired the fourteenth-century church of Santa Maria dei Servi, with its frescos. He would not have been quite able to walk through the Porta al Prato to see the fourteenth-century church of Sant'Agnese just outside. It would have been far too difficult in his merry condition for James to discover the urn containing the bones of St Agnese, patron saint of Montepulciano, or to trace his life in the frescos decorating the cloister attached to the church. James ought also to have taken a short walk outside the city to look at the altogether magnificent church of Madonna di San Biagio, built in the first half of the sixteenth century in a beautiful honey-coloured stone, displaying on its towers Doric, Ionic, Corinthian and Composite orders of architecture, and boasting a magnificent dome. Inside this church – which is in the style of a Greek cross – is a marble reredos created by Gianozzo and Lisandro Albertini in 1584. Next to the church is a superb well and also the beautiful rectory with a double loggia, built to the designs of Antonio da Sangallo the elder. Returning to the city centre by way of the Via di Voltaia nel Corso, Henry should have looked inside the church of the Gesù to admire the baroque splendour created by Andrea del Pozzo.

As for secular architectural treats in this far from dirty city Henry James would surely have admired the battlemented Palazzo Comunale, in the Piazza Grande next to the cathedral, built in the late fourteenth century with a facade said to be by Michelozzo. Climb the tower of this *palazzo* and you can see as far as Siena, 65 km to the north-east. The Piazza Grande itself is a marvel, with a delightful well, surmounted with two griffons and two lions (and known as the 'Pozzo dei Griffi e dei Leoni'). The delights of the Piazza Grande are not yet exhausted – for the square contains two other fine palaces, both by Sangallo the elder.

Montepulciano is in truth crammed with *palazzi*: the Palazzo Tarugi and the Palazzo Avignonese (nos. 82 and 91 Via Sangallo), both by the famous sixteenth-century architect Giacomo Barozzi (who was known as 'il Vignola'). He also built the Palazzo Grugni (no. 55 Via di Voltaia nel Corso) which contrasts with the massive Palazzo Cervini in the same street, built by Sangallo the elder for Marcello Cervini, who became Pope Marcellus II.

Amongst the famous sons of Montepulciano was Lorenzo de' Medici's tutor, the humanist Angelo Ambrogini (who took the name 'Politian' from the Latin name for the city, 'Mons Politianus'). A plaque on no. 5 Via dell'Opio indicates the fourteenth-century house in which Politian was born. Another son of Montepulciano was the famous counter-reformer Cardinal Roberto Bellarmine.

Although the city is itself 605 m above sea-level, you can climb still higher up the wooded Monte di Totona – 3 km along the road to Chianciano. The name of this mountain is Etruscan in origin, reminding one that Montepulciano is said to have been founded by the Etruscan king Lors Porsena himself. A further kilometre towards Chianciano is **Sant'Albino**, a village nestling under the Monti della Maddalena and known since antiquity for its sulphurous spring.

The waters are said not only to cure diseases of the skin and bones but also to improve the reproductive powers of women and alleviate most gynaecological ailments. Today a modern thermal bath, the Terme di Montepulciano, has been built at Sant'Albino.

Throughout the year some event or other seems to be taking place at Montepulciano. On the Sunday and Tuesday before Lent allegorical carriages are paraded through the streets. At Easter horse-racing takes place at the local track. A great country fair on 1 May marks the feast of the city's patron saint, Agnes. On the last day of July the city hosts an international conference of liberal studies. For the first two weeks of August the restored Fortezza of Montepulciano houses an international handicrafts fair. (Montepulciano is proud of its metalwork and woodwork, creating traditional renaissance-style furniture and wrought-iron gates.) During this same period the municipality sponsors a festival of culture in which up to three hundred participants from many nations perform. And during the last week of September and the first week in October an impressive festival of contemporary art takes place here.

But undoubtedly the two most picturesque annual events at Montepulciano are the Bruscello and the Bravio delle Botti. The Bruscello takes place on 14, 15, 16 August (i.e. around the feast of the Assumption). In the Piazza Grande some 150 costumed actors spectacularly re-enact scenes of Montepulciano's history, to much applause.

The Bravio delle Botti is yet more spectacular. On the last Sunday in August men from the eight ancient districts of the city engage in a barrel race, pushing unwieldy barrels through the streets to the Piazza Grande. The race is preceded by a flamboyant parade, with fourteenth-century costumes (the eight districts were set up in 1374), drummers, flags, pages, soldiers, priors, artists and the like all in procession. Finally a great victory banquet, in which everybody joins, is held in the open air in the streets around the Piazza Grande.

Probably, however, Henry James would have appreciated best the annual Baccanale, held here during the last week in August in honour of the Vino Nobile for which Montepulciano is famed. Open-air dances, popular games and a meal of local food specially designed to complement the Vino Nobile (including inevitably the excellent *panzatella*, which is made from stale bread that has been softened in water and seasoned with oil, vinegar, basil, onions, tomatoes and heaven-knows-what other spices).

Perhaps after such a meal few will want to visit the local Museo Civico (in the gothic Palazzo Neri-Orselli, no. 15 Via Ricci), but it does contain a fine, if small collection of Sienese and Florentine art, as well as lovely terracottas by Andrea and Luca della Robbia.

See also Montepulciano in the index.

MONTERCHI, see under AREZZO.

MONTERIGGIONE, 15 km north-west of Siena, is a marvellous little town, walled and with fourteen defensive towers. Dante, picturing the ninth circle of hell as encompassed with fearsome giants, compared them to these same towers:

> però che, come su la cerchia tonda
>   Monteriggion di torri si corona
>   cosi la proda che il pozzo circonda
> torreggiavan di mezza la persona
>   gli orribili giganti, cui minaccia
>   Giove del cielo ancora, quando tuona.

> [As with circling round
> Of turrets Monteriggione crowns her walls,
> Even thus the shore, encompassing the abyss,
> Was turreted with giants, half their length
> Uprearing, horrible, whom Jove from heaven
> Yet threatens when his murmuring thunder rolls.]

Monteriggione belies its former role as a Sienese fortress, ever-alert against the threat from Florence, by presenting today the aspect of a sleepy medieval town, with a lovely church, half-romanesque, half-gothic.

Three kilometres to the west lies **Abbadia Isola**, which has an eleventh- and twelfth-century church containing a fresco by Taddeo di Bartolo (of the Madonna and Child) and a late-fifteenth-century altarpiece by Sano di Pietro. The rectory near by houses another *Madonna and Child*, by Duccio, and some lovely Etruscan works of art.

MONTE SAN SAVINO, situated on a hill due east of Siena and south-west of Arezzo, offers a magical view of the valley of the Chiana. Here in 1460 was born the sculptor Andrea Sansovino, who re-ordered the fourteenth-century church of Sant'Agostino and also probably built the Loggia dei Mercanti in the Corso Sangallo. Antonio da Sangallo the elder designed the early-sixteenth-century Palazzo Comunale. In the Piazza Gamurrini is the church of Santa Chiara which houses terracottas by Sansovino and by the Della Robbias.

Close by, on the road west towards Siena, is **Gargonza**, a perfect walled medieval village which sheltered Dante when he was exiled from Florence.

MONTE SENARIO, 20 km outside Florence, above Pratolino, is where in the thirteenth century seven wealthy Florentine councillors, having renounced this world, founded a monastery where they lived an exceedingly rigorous life, fasting and praying. They became known as the Servites (or 'Servants of Mary') and in 1259, to commemorate the Annunciation, built the superb church of San-tissima Annunziata in Florence. The monastery they built remains at Monte Senario, exquisitely situated in the woods, 580 m above sea-level and with tremendous views (and modern hotels too). Their church, rebuilt in the eighteenth century, houses a crucifix by the Florentine sculptor Pietro Tacca (1577–1640). To the north of this monastery is the richly cultivated region known as the **Mugello**, that is, the upper basin of the River Sieve, an area long renowned for its wines. It also has nurtured great artists; if you drive or cycle 7 km south-east of Borgo San Lorenzo you reach **Vespignano**, where you can visit the house in which in 1266 Giotto was born. Further east you reach **Vicchio**, sometime home of the sculptor Benvenuto Cellini (he lived in the house adjoining the oratory in the Corso del Popolo), and birthplace in 1387 of the painter Giovanni da Fiesole, who became famous as Fra Angelico. Here is a pleasant little museum of religious art. Take the road west from Borgo San Lorenzo and you reach **San Pietro a Sieve**, with its sixteenth-century church that houses terracotta fonts of the previous century, made by the Della Robbias.

See also BORGO SAN LORENZO.

MONTEVARCHI lies thirty or so kilometres north of Arezzo and boasts an eighteenth-century collegiate church next to its Museo d'Arte Sacra. The town also keeps a collection of fossils in its Accademia Valdarnese (in the former convent of San Ludovico). Two kilometres north of Montevarchi is **Montecarlo**, where the convent possesses a lovely *Annunciation* once attributed to Fra Angelico and now thought to be by his pupil Zanobi Strozzi.

MONTICCHIELLO, see under PIENZA.

MONTI DELL'UCCELINA, due south of Grosseto, is the region of the Maremma Natural Park.

MUGELLO, see under MONTE SENARIO.

ORBETELLO, lying on a narrow neck of land that runs through the Orbetello lagoon to Monte Argentario, was founded by the Etruscans and achieved great importance in the mid sixteenth century, when the Spanish fortified the town and established here the celebrated 'Polveriera' (powder factory). Orbetello was capital of the Spanish garrison states (the 'Presidi') until the following century. The ramparts – started by Philip II in 1557 and finished by his successor in 1620 – retain their formidable gateways. And the Civic Museum (no. 26 Via Ricasoli) has some splendid Etruscan remains, including parts of the tremendous temple excavated at Talamone.

Orbetello cathedral, dedicated to Maria Assunta, was rebuilt in 1660, without however losing its extremely beautiful gothic facade and rose-window of 1376. And inside, in the first chapel on the south side, is a pre-romanesque marble altar.

The town was not linked to Monte Argentario until 1842. Its restaurants naturally specialize in seafood, particularly marinated and smoked eel, which I have found delicious.

See also in this gazetteer MONTE ARGENTARIO and TALAMONE.

PERETOLA, see under POGGIO A CAIANO.

PESCIA, a farming town lying 19 km north of Lucca on the powerful stream that bears its name, is famous for its asparagus and its flowers – especially lilies, carnations and gladioli. (There's a huge market hall specializing entirely in flowers.)

The River Pescia divides the city into two. On its left bank is the baroque cathedral, put into its present form in 1693 but retaining the old bell-tower of 1306. The facade is modern, by an architect named Castellucci. Inside is a fine renaissance chapel, the Turini

Chapel, built by Giuliano di Baccio d'Agnolo in the fifteenth century. A yet more rewarding visit is to the fourteenth-century gothic church of San Francesco, in the Via Battisti. Here in 1451 Brunelleschi's adopted son Andrea Cavalcanti Buggiano added the Orlandi-Cardini chapel. And here, only nine years after the death of St Francis in 1226, Buonaventura Berlinghiero painted six scenes from his life, almost certainly the most faithful likenesses of the saint. In the same street the fourteenth-century church of Sant' Antonio houses frescos by Bicci di Lorenzo and a thirteenth-century wooden *Deposition*.

On the right bank of the river, for the Piazza Mazzini, Buggiano in 1447 designed the Oratory of the Madonna di Pié di Piazza. Here too stands the Palazzo dei Vicari, built in the thirteenth and fourteenth centuries.

Pescia is a thriving town, making paper as well as selling more flowers than any other in Italy. It has a good civic museum and, at no. 9 Piazza Obici, a geo-palaeontological and geological museum. You can also eat succulently here, with (inevitably) asparagus garnishing the dishes, as well as Sorana beans. One speciality found nowhere else is a stew named *cioncia*, made from the edible parts of an ox's muzzle!

PIENZA, 52 km south of Siena, has been rightly called the pearl of the renaissance. Here once was a small village named Corsignano, where in 1405 was born the remarkable Aeneas Silvius Piccolomini, who became Pope Pius II in 1458. He ordered the architect Bernardo Gamberelli, known as Rossellino, to recreate the town. By papal bull Pius II changed the name of the town to Pienza. Rossellino's work was superb, and the Italians rightly dub Pienza a *città d'autore* – 'an authors' city', i.e. the creation of one guiding intellect. By ordering his architect to build a cathedral, Pius II also changed Pienza from a town to a city.

In Rossellino's plans everything ranges around the cathedral square, the Piazza Pio II, for which he designed a lovely well. His cathedral – long, tall and airy – was one of the first renaissance churches to be built in Tuscany. He carved Pius II's coat of arms on the pediment. He engaged Giovanni di Paolo, Vecchietta and Sano di Pietro and Matteo di Giovanni to paint altarpieces. He designed a font (in the crypt, which also houses fragments of romanesque sculpture from the former church of Santa Maria delle Nevi). He designed the splendid gothic canons' stalls.

An even finer building perhaps is Rossellino's Palazzo Piccolomini in the same square. He based it on the Palazzo Rucellai in his native Florence. Not only is the interior well worth visiting – for its great hall of arms, the pope's bedroom (with a portrait of Pius II) and the library; it also opens out into a loggia three tiers high (a feature not found at the Palazzo Rucellai), overlooking a delightful hanging garden and offering views of the Orcia valley as far as Monte Amiata.

Other lovely palaces enhance the Piazza Pio II. On the north side is the Palazzo Comunale of 1463, with its three arches and its crenellated tower surmounted by bells. On the east side is the gothic Palazzo Vescovile, once the Palazzo Pretorio and a present from Piccolomini to the future Borgia Pope Alexander VI. Cardinal Ammannati of Pavia built the Palazzo Ammannati here. One more palace, the Palazzo Canonici – now the civic museum, with a lovely cope that Pius II used to wear – brings this outstanding piece of architectural planning to a brilliant harmonious conclusion.

Two churches from old Corsignano survive in new Pienza. The church of San Francesco (behind the Palazzo Piccolomini), built in early gothic at the end of the thirteenth century, preserves four-teenth- and fifteenth-century frescos, a wooden cross painted in the style of Duccio and a *Madonna* by Luca Signorelli. And just outside the city, to the south, is the Pieve di San Vito dell'Antica Corsignano, with its oddly charming and simple cylindrical tower, a romanesque church of the eleventh and twelfth centuries, where Piccolomini himself was baptized as an infant.

The poet Giovanni Pascoli described Pienza as 'born of a tender feeling of love and a dream of beauty'. But the architect suffered some abuse in his time – partly because the Sienese resented a Florentine working in their town. Rumours reached Pius II that his architect had far outspent what he had been allowed. The pope inspected his work and then summoned Rossellino. 'You did well, Bernardo, in lying to us about the expense involved in the work,' was Pius's surprising comment. 'If you had told the truth you could never have induced us to spend so much money and neither this palace nor this church, the finest in all Italy, would now be standing.

Your deceit has built these glorious structures which are praised by all except the few who are consumed with envy. We thank you and think you deserve especial honour among all the architects of our time.' So Rossellino was given a scarlet robe and 100 ducats.

Two annual events add to the attractions of Pienza. On the first Sunday in September is the Cheese Fair. The aromatic herbs of the Orcia and Chiano valleys have for a millennium and more been used in making *il pecorino*, a lovely sheep's cheese; and this is what is chiefly prized in Pienza restaurants and sold at the annual cheese fair (which they call the 'Fiera del Cacio').

The second annual event is quaintly called 'A Meeting with a Master Artist', when Pienza's city council attracts to the town for the months of August and September an artist of the quality of, for example, Giorgio de Chirico or Carlo Carrà. The artist displays his masterpieces and meets the people.

Not far to the east (and south-west of Montepulciano) is the medieval village of **Monticchiello**, perched 546 m high on a hill in the Orcia valley. Etruscan in origin, this village was based on an old villa called Villa Clelia (hence the derivation of its name: 'Monte Cleli'). The Sienese built its lovely golden-brown defensive walls in the mid thirteenth century, and the citizens of Monticchiello thenceforth loyally fought on the side of Siena, defending it for instance against the forces of Charles V. When the Spaniards attacked the village, they bombarded its fortress's watchtower, which instead of falling down, simply inclined to one side. The thirteenth-century parish church is approached by a worn, charming flight of steps and boasts both a gothic west door and rose-window. Inside are frescos, a *Madonna* of Pietro Lorenzetti (1320) and a wooden crucifix of the early fifteenth century. During the last two weeks of each July a theatre group called Il Teatro Povero ('The Poor Theatre') mounts an entertaining festival here.

PIETRASANTA means 'Holy Stone', a name indicating the reverence in which the town's chief product, marble, is held. Thirty-five kilometres north of Pisa and no more than 3.5 km from the coast, the city (of some 26,000 inhabitants) is the main Tuscan centre for visiting sculptors – both professional and amateur, some of them staying all the year round and using the commercial and private studios that flourish here, or else drinking with the locals in the

Piazza Carducci (named after the poet Giosuè Carducci, who was born in 1835 at **Valdicastello** 3 km to the east, where you can also see the oldest church in the region, San Giovanni, dating from the sixth century).

Although a busy industrial city, and one that was much battered in the Second World War, Pietrasanta retains much charm. The Rocca dates from the twelfth century. The city's cathedral was built in 1330, its bell-tower fifty years later. Lorenzo Stagi created its marble choir stalls and pulpit in the early sixteenth century. Donato Benti created the lovely font in 1509. (Its cover was added a hundred years later.) Stagio Stagi designed its two magnificent candelabra in the sixteenth century. And next to the cathedral is the fourteenth-century church of Sant'Agostino, with its fine facade.

Each year from July to September local craftsmen organize an exhibition of their sculptures in the Consorzio Artigiani. And the coastline to the west includes amongst its fine resorts and beaches **Marina di Pietrasanta.**

The road north-west from Marina di Pietrasanta leads shortly to **Forte dei Marmi.** Its name derives from the fortress built here in 1788 and still dominating the centre of this seaside resort, with its cool pine-forests and clean, warm sands and a (fairly) safe beach. The town of Forte dei Marmi, when last I was there, was still suffering from the effects of a tornado in 1977, though the Italians were working hard to restore the old elegance of this attractive resort.

PIOMBINO, the principal port for Elba, at the south end of the Massoncello promontory, is now much industrialized but once must have been extremely pretty. In 1805 Napoleon gave it to his sister, Elisa Bacciochi, Princess of Lucca and Piombino.

The Piazza Verdi retains a few vestiges of the old city walls, as well as the early-thirteenth-century tower of the Porta Sant'Antonio. The fifteenth-century parish church is packed with renaissance funeral monuments and also boasts a font created by Antonio Guardi in 1470. The Palazzo Comunale in its present form dates from the fifteenth century and its belfry was added in 1598.

You reach the ferries for Elba at Porto Vecchio.

PISA, lying on the River Arno some 10 km from the Ligurian Sea, is famed above all for its leaning tower, 'like pine poised just ere snapping', as Herman Melville observed. 'You wait to hear it crash.'

I think that such breathless waiting for an inevitable disaster (the tower sinks another millimetre each year) unfortunately makes many visitors forget to look at this campanile in all its remarkable beauty. (There are, after all, other leaning towers in northern Italy – two very boring ones in Bologna, for instance.) Historically the one at Pisa is fascinating because its builders decided to go on with the work when the tower had already begun to lean. The cathedral bell-tower was begun in 1173 and had risen scarcely more than 10 m when it began to keel over. The first architects tried their best to remedy this; but when they failed Tommaso di Andrea da Pontedera took over in the mid fifteenth century and resolutely finished it.

Yet it *is* bizarre, and statistics help to expound its bizarreness. The Leaning Tower of Pisa is nearly 56 m high. It weighs about 14,500 tons. Its eight storeys support seven bells (why not eight?), each one sounding a note of the scale. The outer diameter of the base is 15·48 m, the inner diameter 7·36 m. Two hundred and ninety-four steps spiral to the top, from which you can see Monte Pisano, the Apuan and Garfagnana mountains, the forests of Migliarino and San Rossore and the fertile plain leading to the sea. 'I take it to be one of the most singular pieces of workmanship in the World,' wrote John Evelyn, who visited Pisa in 1644; 'how it is supported from immediately falling would puzzle a good Geometrician.'

From the top of the Leaning Tower Galileo dropped objects to disprove long-held views about the speed of falling bodies. Pisa's greatest son, Galileo was (as everyone knows) condemned by the Vatican for attempting to prove that the earth went round the sun and not – as church teaching then held – that the sun went round the earth. He had, incidentally, unwisely mocked Pope Urban VIII in a humorous dialogue. He has since been rehabilitated.

But the Leaning Tower is not the only or most important aspect of this great Tuscan city. Its design is but one example of a sudden spurt of creativity that was to inject an enormously powerful charge into architecture throughout the rest of this artistically fecund region.

Pisa in the eleventh century was rich enough to lead the rest of the region in repulsing the Saracens who were attacking from the sea. The Pisans allied with the Genoese to expel the Saracens from Sardinia, and in 1163 the city's powerful navy was able to sack the Saracen stronghold of Palermo. Only after 1284, when the Genoese defeated the Pisan fleet at the Battle of Meloria, did Pisa begin to decline. Even then the city's trade continued to bring wealth to the merchants, who were also her patrons of religious and secular art. The consequence today is that Pisa is one of Tuscany's most entrancing cities.

To my way of thinking what creates the truly magical complex of architecture in the Piazza del Duomo is the combination of Leaning Tower, Baptistery and cathedral, all set on a green sward scarcely believable in Tuscany. When I first came here thirty years ago, cameras were not designed for incompetents of my sort. Nonetheless I attempted to photograph all three buildings, and wondrously the picture was a success. Back in Britain I gazed and gazed on it, with the bell-tower peeping slyly round the south side of the cathedral to see what I was trying to do. That is the impression I have retained on many subsequent visits to Pisa. The three buildings together seem somehow homely, welcoming, friendly, and yet also stupendous.

The Baptistery, begun in 1152, owes its present severe elegance to Nicola and Giovanni Pisano. The lower section of this vast marble building is still romanesque in style, modulating to Gothic at the second stage of the building. Elegant arcading is topped by richly ornamented gables, carrying busts and statues by Nicola and Giovanni. Above this stage, double windows are surmounted by uncomplicated gables, each with a little rose-window. Little dormer windows open out of the dome, which ends in a curious, satisfying truncated pyramid. Of the four doorways, the finest is the one facing the cathedral, decorated by an anonymous thirteenth-century sculptor with carvings of the apostles, David, the descent into hell, and the months of the year. The lintel is decorated in two parts, one depicting the life of St John the Baptist, the other showing Christ between the Baptist and the Virgin Mary. In the tympanum is a copy of Giovanni Pisano's *Madonna*.

The Baptistery at Pisa is 55 m high and over 35 m in diameter. The interior is tremendously impressive. From time immemorial guides have sung a note between the pillars to illustrate the remarkable echo. Here, for their better preservation, are kept the original busts that once decorated the outside walls. Corinthian pillars support the building, alternatively square and round, and detached from the walls. In the centre is the delicate and huge marble font, made by Guido da Como in the thirteenth century, with a slender statue of John the Baptist (by Italo Griselli) in the middle.

The masterpiece of the Pisan Baptistery is Nicola Pisano's amazing hexagonal pulpit, supported on seven marble columns, three of which are themselves supported by lions. This pulpit, the first major work carved by Nicola Pisano in Tuscany (it dates from 1260), created a new sculptural style in late-thirteenth-century Italy. Although it draws on classical motifs – derived from Roman remains, early Christian frescos, Guido da Como's pulpit at Pistoia, done nine years earlier – Nicola Pisano's pulpit at Pisa, marks the introduction of the gothic style to Italy. Its five reliefs represent the nativity and the message to the shepherds, the adoration of the Magi, the presentation of Jesus in the Temple, the crucifixion and the Last Judgement. Details from every one reveal Nicola's deep love for Roman and Etruscan art; but each one is also personally felt and realized in a fashion completely new to Tuscan sculpture.

The facade of Pisa cathedral has not changed since Rainaldo, who was also architect of the apse, completed it in the thirteenth century. He had taken over as architect from Buscheto, who began the work in 1063. The black and white marble which covers the cathedral inside and out achieves its effects with superb simplicity, almost entirely by use of lozenges and circles in its designs. But there are subtleties: see, for example, on the north side how the perspective of the second storey changes towards the west. The great central doors, made after a disastrous fire of 1595 destroyed the old ones, depict the life of the Virgin Mary. Some of the figures in the lower panels are highly polished by the touch of countless hands (including in the scene of the nativity not only the infant Jesus but also a little dog). The two side doors represent scenes from the life of Jesus.

Usually you enter the cathedral by the side of the south transept, through the bronze doors made by Bonnano da Pisa in 1180. (Note how King Herod evilly and placidly watches babies being executed, and how Christ at his baptism merges into the rippling water.) Inside the roof is glorious, redone after the fire of 1595. In the thirteenth century Cimabue covered the vault of the apse with a superb mosaic of Christ in Glory. Giambologna made the crucifix. Sodoma painted the *Sacrifice of Isaac* and the *Deposition* in the apse. The Luccan master Matteo Civitali made the lectern and its candelabra. In 1688 the munificence of Grand Duke Cosimo III of Tuscany paid for the great sarcophagus by Giovanni Battista Foggini in which lies the body of San Ranieri, the city's patron saint. On one of the entrance piers is a painting by Andrea del Sarto of St Agnes, meditatively holding a quill and stroking a little lamb. And the pulpit is by Nicola Pisano's son Giovanni.

He made it in the first decade of the fourteenth century. Curiously enough, it was dismantled in 1599 and not put together again until 1926. Its eleven columns rest on lions or on such powerful shoulders as St Michael and Hercules. No one today would claim that this pulpit is finer than the pulpit of Giovanni's father in the Baptistery (though the inscription in Latin running below the narrative reliefs does maintain that 'Giovanni is endowed above all others with command of the pure art of sculpture ... and would not know how to carve ugly or base things, even if he wished to do so'). Yet the carving is stunning. In the scene of the nativity, a servant pours water in a bowl, and Jesus's mother tests how hot it is before washing her baby. A celebrated caryatid on this pulpit feeds a child at each breast. Below her are two of the cardinal virtues. Fortitude nonchalantly holds a lion upside-down by its tail; Prudence modestly attempts to conceal nakedness.

Two other monuments make up this remarkable part of Pisa. One is small and charming: the cherub fountain created by G. Vacca in 1700. The other is massive and awesome: the Camposanto. This extraordinary cemetery dates from a decision of Archbishop Ubaldo da Lanfranchi in 1203 to bring earth here from Golgotha, where Jesus was crucified. Giovanni di Simone began building the rectangular cloister in 1278. Sarcophagi and ancient funerary sculptures and above all the frescos depicting the triumph of death contrast starkly in spirit with the delicate tracery and lawn. In the Second World War much here was almost irreparably damaged, including Benozzo Gozzoli's frescos depicting the adoration of the Magi and scenes from the Old Testament.

Charles Dickens judged the group of buildings clustered around the green carpet in this part of Pisa to be 'perhaps the most remarkable and beautiful in the whole world ... the architectural essence of a rich old city, with all its common life and common habitations pressed out, filtered away'. To visit the rest of this rich old city from here, walk down Via Santa Maria and left along Via dei Mille – passing the eleventh-century church of San Sisto on your right – as far as the Piazza dei Cavalieri ('Square of the Horsemen'). This piazza is both extraordinarily irregular and harmonious. The Cavalieri were an order of knights founded by Cosimo I in 1561, and their curved Palazzo, with its imposing steps, was modernized by Giorgio Vasari a year later. Pietro Francavilla (a Frenchman from Cambrai) sculpted the statue of Cosimo I in 1596. Next to the *palazzo*, the church of Santo Stefano dei Cavalieri, again by Vasari, displays the trophies taken by the knights as they battled against Islam. Don Giovanni de' Medici gave the church a marble facade in 1606 and the knights' emblem above the doorway. On the north side of the square is the delightful Palazzo dell'Orologio, pierced with an archway, bearing a clock and crowned with a single, slightly comical bell. The *palazzo* has a sinister history. When the Pisans were defeated at the battle of Meloria in 1284, the podestà of the time, Count Ugolino, suspected of treachery, was shut up in it, along with his sons and nephews, and starved to death.

To reach the River Arno from here follow Via Dini from the corner of this square and then take the narrow Via Notari as far as Piazza Garibaldi. This busy little square makes a splendid reference point for visiting the rest of the city. If you turn right from the piazza along the river bank, you reach the little Borgo Tretto. I very much enjoy the fruit, fish, meat, vegetable and clothes market, stretching into Via Domenico Cavalca, and based in Piazza delle Vettavoglie, which operates here each weekday morning from 9.30 till 12.30 (staying open on Saturdays till eight o'clock in the evening).

Turn left at Piazza Garibaldi and you can walk along the river past the fourteenth-century Palazzo Toscanelli and the thirteenth-century Palazzo Medici (enlarged two centuries later) as far as Piazzetta San Matteo, whose church was built in 1027 and restored in 1610 and whose former convent now houses the rich national museum of Pisa.

The picturesque, colonnaded Borgo Stretto leads north from Piazza Garibaldi and takes you to the church of San Michele in Borgo, built on a pagan temple dedicated to Mars in 990 and boasting a fine fourteenth-century facade. Walk on as far as Via San Francesco and then turn right to find the gothic church of San Francesco. This brick building is mostly by Giovanni di Simone, who worked on it in the late 1260s, but its facade dates from the fourteenth to the sixteenth centuries.

Retrace your steps and turn right along Via Fucini to cross Piazza Martiri della Libertà and reach the square and church of Santa Caterina. This Dominican church possesses a superb facade done in 1330. Inside is the early-fourteenth-century tomb of Archbishop Simone Saltarelli, the masterpiece of Nino Pisano. If you follow from here Via San Zeno you reach at the very end not only the ancient church of St Zeno (started at the very beginning of the tenth century) but also the gateway of the same name, with lovely views of the mid-twelfth-century ramparts of the city.

Finally cross Ponte di Mezzo from Piazza Garibaldi to explore Pisa south of the river. The town-hall is in Piazza XX Settembre. If you turn left here along Lungarno Galilei you come upon the octagonal eleventh-century church of San Sepolcro, and then the ruined Palazzo Scotto where Shelley lived between 1820 and 1822. If you turn right at Piazza XX Settembre along the left bank of the Arno you reach a famous gem: Santa Maria della Spina, a tiny oratory enlarged in 1323 by the Pisan Merchant Lupo Capo-maestro to house a spine from Christ's crown of thorns. (This alleged relic is now in the national museum of Pisa, as is a *Madonna and Child* by Nino Pisano, which was also formerly in the church.) The sculptures on the outside of Santa Maria della Spina are from the workshops of Nino and Giovanni Pisano. In 1871 this architectural treasure was raised three feet to save it from damage by flooding. (Devotees of the history of the Italian Risorgimento will turn left along Via Mazzini, before they reach Santa Maria della Spina, to visit no. 29, where Guiseppe Mazzini died on 8 March 1872. The house is now a museum and library of the Risorgimento, opening from 8 a.m. until 2 p.m., save for Saturdays when it closes at noon.)

Now walk on till you find on your left Piazza San Paolo a Ripa d'Arno, to see the splendid facade of the church of San Paolo and (if it is open, which in my experience it rarely is) its great Roman sarcophagus. Behind it is the romanesque chapel of Sant'Agata, a twelfth-century building with a pyramidical dome, attributed to Diotosalvi, the first architect of the Baptistery.

To return to the centre of the city, cross the river by Ponte della Cittadella. Lungarno Simonelli leads into Lungarno Pacinotti by the Palazzo Reale, behind which is the twelfth-century church of San Nicola, whose thirteenth-century bell-tower has a remarkable spiral staircase that is said to have greatly impressed the architect of the Vatican, Donato Bramante. Lungarno Pacinotti boasts two lovely palaces: Palazzo Upezzinghi (by Via XXIX Maggio) and a little further on the fifteenth-century Palazzo Agostini, with its lovely terracotta decoration.

The international airport Galileo Galilei is 3 km south of Pisa at San Giusto. (British Airways has an office here.) The central station (with an information office) is to the south of the city, along Via Corso Italia, across Piazza Vittorio Emanuele II and down Viale Gramsci.

Ente Provinciale per il Turismo (no. 42 Lungarno Mediceo and Piazza Arcivescovado near the cathedral) offers information about hotels and also about the many cultural and tourist events that take place in Pisa. These include a winter series of concerts, the annual Regatta di San Ranieri (17 June) and the annual Gioco del Ponte, a battle for Ponte di Mezzo with the contestants dressed in sixteenth-century costumes (28 June). Once every four years it is Pisa's turn to host the regatta of the four ancient maritime republics of Italy (Pisa, Amalfi, Genoa and Venice).

Five kilometres west of Pisa is the ancient church of San Pietro a Grado, where St Peter may well have stepped ashore on his journey from Antioch to Rome. Scenes from St Peter's life decorate the interior, above portraits of the popes (with Peter as the first). This early-eleventh-century basilica is remarkable for having apses at both ends (three at the east end), and incorporates Roman columns from previous buildings. Excavations left open reveal foundations and masonry from the former sixth-century basilica.

This site was once the old port of Pisa. A plaque over the entrance to San Pietro a Grado indicates the height of the waters when the River Arno flooded in February and March 1855.

PISTOIA, 37 km north-west of Florence, was founded by the Romans and is where Catiline was beaten and killed in 62 BC. It flourished in the early middle ages, became a free commune in the twelfth century and then fell under Florentine hegemony in 1306. Known for their fine ironwork, its citizens also developed a reputation for savagery, and the word 'pistol' (which initially referred to a dagger) derives from the name of this city. This reputation was perhaps unfair. Certainly its greatest poet, Cino da Pistoia (c. 1270–1337) could write heart-rendingly beautiful lyrics about the death of his beloved, lyrics that also reveal a deep love for the countryside surrounding his birthplace:

> . . . e quando l'aura move il bianco fiore,
> rimembro de' begli occhi il dolce bianco
> per cui lo mio desir mai non fie stanco . . .
>
> Quivi chiamai a questa guisa Amore:
> – Dolci mio iddio, fa che qui mi traggia
> la morte a sè, chè qui giace 'l mio core. –
> Ma poi che non m'intese 'l mio Signore,
> mi dipartii, pur chiamando Selvaggia:
> l'alpe passai con voce di dolore.
>
> [When the breeze moves the white flower,
> I recall the sweet whites of her lovely eyes
> for which my desire will never tire . . .
>
> There I called on Love thus:
> 'My sweet God, let me die here
> for here lies my heart.'
> But when my Lord heard me not,
> I departed, still calling on Selvaggia:
> I passed over the alp with the voice of grief.]

Today the citizens are neither so savage as their forefathers were reputed to be nor quite so romantic as their greatest poet. Their city is a prosperous industrial and agricultural centre, particularly noted for its huge market gardens and its trade in ornamental plants. And the old city remains entrancing.

Its artistic centre, the Piazza del Duomo, is an architectural feast: the cathedral, its bell-tower and baptistery, the Bishop's Palace (now a bank), the Palazzo del Comune and the Palazzo Pretorio. The cathedral of St Zeno, founded originally in the fifth century, now substantially dates from the twelfth. On to its severe and yet elegant romanesque facade with its slender pilasters was added a porch in 1311, decorated in marble in the Pisan style. Andrea della Robbia then beautifully embellished its central portal and its barrel vault in 1505. Cino da Pistoia lies inside, his tomb (in the south aisle) unchanged since Cellino di Nesi created it in the year of the poet's death. From this aisle you should certainly pay the entry fee for the Capella di San Jacopo, in order to examine the remarkable silver altar of St James. Fashioned between 1287 and 1456, it contains 628 figures by many different artists. Giulio da Pisa made the central statue of the saint in 1349; the two half figures on the left side are by Brunelleschi; Leonardo di Giovanni did the nine principal scenes from the saint's life; and so on.

In the choir of Pistoia cathedral are a couple of enormous statues, one of St James, the other of St Zeno, both by a pupil of Giambologna named Vincenzo. To the left of the high altar in the Chapel of the Blessed Sacrament is a *Madonna with John the Baptist and St Zeno* begun by Verrocchio and finished by his pupil Lorenzo di Credi in 1485. These two artists were also responsible for the powerful tomb of Cardinal Niccolò Forteguerra in the north aisle.

Directly opposite the cathedral is the splendid octagonal baptistery of Pistoia. Designed by Andrea Pisano and faced in green and white marble, this baptistery, begun in 1338, was twenty years in building. There's a pretty little open-air pulpit to the right of the entrance.

To complete the cathedral the Pistoians 'borrowed' another building for the bell-tower. Once a watchtower, three tiers of green and white marble arches were added in the fourteenth century to transform a military into an ecclesiastical building. The result is that the cathedral, baptistery and bell-tower together offer a

complex mix of colour – stone and marble – that somehow wonderfully succeeds in living in harmony. The whole is enhanced by the
colours of the stone used to build the three palaces in the piazza. The
Bishop's Palace is basically a twelfth-century building, partly redone
two hundred years later. The Palazzo Pretorio is a gothic building
of 1367, with a lovely courtyard. (Look for the coats of arms of the
city's former rulers displayed here.) The Palazzo del Comune is to
my mind the finest of the three, built by the Guelphs in 1294. Its
apparent simplicity is subtle: see how the arches become more
complex from the arcade upwards to the pointed windows of the
third floor. And one sinister feature of this palazzo must not be
missed: the black marble head in the wall – a bust of Filippo Tedici,
reviled for betraying the city to its enemies in 1315.

To visit all the churches of Pistoia during a holiday would require
some dedication, for they are many (though mostly masterpieces
too). Among their features are remarkable pulpits. The basilica of
San Bartolomeo in Pantano (in the Piazza San Bartolomeo in Pantano) is Pistoia's oldest, and the pulpit of 1250, built by Guido da
Como, has been painstakingly restored from pieces. The lions and
humans on whose backs its pillars rest are particularly sweet, patient
creatures. But the finest pulpit in Pistoia is undoubtedly that created
by Giovanni Pisano between 1298 and 1301 for the church of Sant'
Andrea (in the Via Sant'Andrea). Here he depicted with enormous
vigour scenes from the life of Jesus and the Last Judgement. He also
created the gilded wooden crucifix on the third altar on the north
side of the church.

There's another fine pulpit in the church of San Giovanni Fuor-
civitas (in the Via Cavour) with its splendid green and white marble
facing. This pulpit was created in 1270 by Fra Guglielmo da Pisa, a
pupil of Giovanni Pisano's father Nicola. Perhaps the best way to
enjoy these masterpieces of religious art in Pistoia is not to rush to
see them all at one go, but to visit one whenever the fancy takes
you as you wander through the bustling streets of this city.

What no one should miss in Pistoia is the Ospedale del Ceppo in
the Via F. Pacini. (A *ceppo* was a wooden box for collecting
offerings for the poor and needy.) The outside of this fourteenth-
century hospital is decorated with medallions in terracotta done by
Giovanni della Robbia in the first quarter of the sixteenth century,

above which is an appealing coloured terracotta frieze by the same artist depicting the virtues and the works of mercy.

Pistoia today is noted for its fashionable clothing. It has its own annual medieval joust (on 9 March) – the Giostro dell'Orso in the cathedral square. And just 4 km outside the city at La Verginina is a zoo.

The mountains around the city offer winter-sports facilities, especially at **Maresca**, which lies 1,200 m above sea-level; and the main town of the Pistoiese mountains, **San Marcello Pistoiese**, has established itself as a popular resort for summer holidays too. See Pistoia in the index.

PITEGLIO lies 700 m above sea-level in the Pistoiese mountains north of Marliana, looking across the River Lima. The road then descends to **Popiglio**, with its splendid romanesque church and a thirteenth-century bridge called the Castruccio.

PITIGLIANO, which lies level with Lago di Bolsena and 74 km south-east of Grosseto, is superbly, almost bizarrely sited on an escarpment of rock over three ravines. Etruscan in origin, the town became the seat of the Orsini family, who became masters of this region in 1293. Their *palazzo* (built from the fourteenth to the sixteenth centuries) is still here. There is also a baroque cathedral and an unspoilt medieval part to the town. Connoisseurs praise the wine of Pitigliano.

POGGIBONSI, due east of San Gimignano, boasts a fifteenth-century castle and (2 km to the south) a thirteenth-century gothic church, San Lucchese, with a Della Robbia altar and frescos by Bartolo di Fredi. Go south (taking the N2) for 7 km and you reach the village of **Staggia**, with its ruin of a mid-fifteenth-century Rocca and its fourteenth-century fortifications. (There's a painting by Antonio Pollaiuolo in the church, which is usually locked.)

POGGIO A CAIANO, 17 km west of Florence, is where Giuliano da Sangallo rebuilt an old villa for Lorenzo de' Medici between 1480 and 1485. For many years only the gardens have been open to the public, so that one is denied the pleasure of recognizing how consciously Cosimo il Vecchio and Lorenzo il Magnifico modelled themselves on the ancients. (There is, for example, a terracotta frieze by the house's architect and Sansovino, representing a Platonic myth; and Andrea del Sarto and his assistants painted scenes from

Roman history matched by events in the life of the two Medici.)
Six kilometres towards Florence lies **Perétola**. The church of
Santa Maria here contains a 1441 tabernacle by Luca della Robbia
– the Pietà and angels in marble, the frame in terracotta.

PONTASSIEVE, 18 km east of Florence, is the chief commercial centre
of the Chianti wine trade, and holds a great wine fair each May.
Here the River Sieve (crossed by the old Ponte Medicea) joins the
Arno. The Palazzo Sansoni is now the town-hall. The N69 towards
the south now follows the winding Arno and after 5 km reaches
Sant'Ellero with its medieval walls and thirteenth-century castle.

PONTEDERA stands on the N67 between Pisa and San Miniato, at
the confluence of the Rivers Arno and Era. Now a town devoted
chiefly to making motor scooters, it was the birthplace of Andrea
Pisano. The church of SS. Jacopo e Filippo dates from the twelfth century and contains some good fourteenth-century wooden sculptures.

PONTREMOLI, on the N62 north of La Spezia, surrounded by
mountains covered in chestnuts, is the chief city of the Lunigiana
valley. Its architecture is unusual for Tuscany: a baroque cathedral
(with a nineteenth-century classical façade); the oval-shaped
rococo church of Nostra Donna (or Madonna del Ponte), built in
1738; the church of Santissima Annunziata (1.5 km south of the
city) with its sixteenth-century interior. Only the church of San
Francesco, with its romanesque bell-tower and a fifteenth-century
polychrome bas-relief by Agostino di Duccio (on the second altar to
the north side) makes one feel truly in Tuscany.

The museum in the castle of the old town is equally unusual,
devoted principally to the pre-Etruscan archaeology of this ancient
region.

POPIGLIO, see under PITEGLIO.

POPPI, see under BIBBIENA.

POPULONIA, 15 km drive north from Piombino, is a port founded by
the Etruscans (their only one) where they smelted iron ore from
Elba and built a necropolis. You can visit the necropolis, which
served the Etruscans for six centuries. Populonia has a medieval
Rocca and a little Etruscan museum.

PORT'ERCOLE, see under MONTE ARGENTARIO.

PORTO AZZURRO, see under ELBA.

PORTOFERRAIO, see under ELBA.

PORTO SANTO STEFANO, see under MONTE ARGENTARIO.

PRATO, situated 19 km north-west of Florence, surrounded by green hills, is both an industrial and commercial centre and also a historic, artistic Tuscan city. The River Bisenzio became here a centre of the cloth trade in the early twelfth century. In the twentieth the same trade has made Prato rich. By the twelfth century it was also a free commune, but accepted the lordship of the Angevin rulers of Naples in 1313. They in turn sold the lordship to Florence in 1351.

Prato possesses a remarkable religious relic: the girdle of the Virgin Mary. It is said that Thomas the Apostle, who had found the resurrection of Jesus difficult to believe, held that the doctrine of the physical assumption of Mary into heaven was incredible. He insisted on opening her tomb, where he discovered not a corpse but roses and lilies. He looked up to heaven and saw the Blessed Virgin taking off her girdle to give him. This girdle reached Prato from the Holy Land in the twelfth century, and it now lies in the very fine late-fourteenth-century Chapel of the Holy Girdle in Prato cathedral. Agnolo Gaddi covered the walls of this chapel with frescos illustrating the legend, and Giovanni Pisano created the *Madonna and Child* for its altar. Then Donatello and Michelozzo created the lovely outdoor Pulpit of the Holy Girdle, from which it is displayed to the faithful on Easter Day, May Day, 15 August, 8 September and Christmas Day.

Prato cathedral is basically romanesque, with a facade in green and white striped marble by Guidetto da Como. The terracotta tympanum of 1489 is by Andrea della Robbia. And it is said that Giovanni Pisano designed the fourteenth-century apse and transepts.

The choir is decorated with outstandingly fine frescos, painted between 1452 and 1466 by a famous son of Prato, Fra Filippo Lippi. (You can put money into a slot in the chapel to the left to light them up.) Lippi's life was notably scandalous. Giorgio Vasari said that this monk 'was so lustful he would give anything to enjoy a woman he wanted', and the Salome whom he painted here dancing for the guests of King Herod is reputed to have been his mistress, the blonde nun Lucrezia Buti. Vasari adds that if he could not possess a desired woman, he would try to assuage his lust by using her as a model for his paintings. This happened with Lucrezia, who was a ward of the Carmelite convent at Prato. He was considered particularly wicked finally to have abducted Lucrezia on a day when she was going to see an exposition of the Virgin Mary's Holy Girdle. But much was forgiven such a brilliant artist; and Lucrezia eventually married Filippo, after his release from his vows, bearing him Filippino, a son as talented an artist as his father.

As Browning put it, this monk, who loved to

> play hot cockles,
> All the doors being shut,
> Till, wholly unexpected, in there pops
> The hothead husband,

also brought a new realism to his art:

> First, every sort of monk, the black and white,
> I drew them, fat and lean: then folks at church,
> From good old gossips waiting to confess
> Their cribs of barrel-droppings, candle-ends, –
> To the breathless fellow at the altar-foot
> Fresh from his murder . . .

That skill is supremely on display in the work which Lippi (and his friend and collaborator Fra Diamante) did at Prato. And there are other fine paintings in the cathedral, particularly some fifteenth-century frescos in the first chapel on the south side which show the hand of Paolo Uccello.

Art lovers should not fail to visit the Museo dell'Opera del Duomo (which does not open on Tuesdays). Here for instance, removed for safekeeping, are Donatello's original dancing putti from the outdoor pulpit of the cathedral; a portrait of St Lucy by Filippo Lippi; a reliquary for the Holy Girdle dated 1446 (with more dancing putti) by Maso di Bartolomeo.

Prato's other churches are fine, especially, I think, Santa Maria delle Carceri which Giuliano da Sangallo began in 1485 (and alas did not quite complete) to illustrate the new renaissance architecture as set out by the Florentines Alberti and Brunelleschi. The proportions of the interior are superbly harmonized in a fashion that then was obviously tremendously innovative and exciting. Secular architecture is also impressive at Prato, from the brutal, cube-like Palazzo Pretorio (thirteenth and fourteenth centuries) – built one part in brick, one part in stone, to the square Fortezza which Frederick II Hohenstaufen had built here in the first half of the thirteenth century. The former houses an important art collection, where you can judge whether Filippino Lippi was better than, or as good as his father. (Amongst Filippino's works here is a marvellous *Madonna*, and a frescoed tabernacle that once belonged to his mother Lucrezia.) The Fortezza (now known as the Castello dell'Imperatore) is unique in Tuscany, being modelled on the Norman castles of Apulia. Finally, as you cannot help noticing when you drive in, substantial sections of the powerful grey walls of Prato remain intact.

One of Prato's greatest citizens, Francesco di Marco Datini, the man who founded the city's riches on the wool trade in the fourteenth century, whose statue, in biretta and magnificent robes, now stands in the Palazzo Comunale, who built himself the Palazzo Datini (in the Via Rinaldesca) and lies buried in front of the altar steps in the romanesque church of San Francesco, may serve also as a reminder that Prato is gastronomically as well as architecturally rewarding. Iris Origo's enchanting book *The Merchant of Prato* records one of his most charming letters in which he insists on veal not from the tough grey cattle of the Maremma but from the smaller tender calves of his own region. 'Give me a good piece of veal like the one we had on Sunday,' he wrote to his carrier, '. . . and bid Margherita to put it on the fire in the saucepan in which I cooked it last time, and to take off the scum . . . and buy some melon and other fruit.'

Prato still offers the traveller tender veal and fine melons; and also a rich vegetable soup called *minestra di pane*, stuffed celery, biscuits with almonds, and Mantuan cake.

As if all this were not enough to attract the tourist to Prato, during the winter months the Metastasio Theatre (Via Benedetto Cairoli) mounts remarkably ambitious performances.

PRATOLINO, 15 km north of Florence, is the site of the Villa Demidoff, whose vast garden is now open to the public. Alas, it is no longer the garden that once roused Montaigne to raptures. Indeed Georgina Masson has described Pratolino as undoubtedly the 'greatest loss' of all the famous Tuscan gardens. Once it boasted – as she observes – 'surprise fountains and grottoes filled with automatons', as well as a 'superb central alley, fifty feet wide and flanked by fountains and watercourses, that led down the hill behind the house to Giambologna's colossal statue of the "Apennines"'. But this garden lacked the comprehensive planning and monumental treatment of terrain that distinguishes the Roman gardens. Sadly, Georgina Masson concludes, 'This fault rendered Pratolino particularly vulnerable to landscaping so that, except for Giambologna's colossus, practically the whole of the original garden has disappeared.'

PRATOVECCHIO in the upper valley of the Arno north of Poppi, lies 420 m above sea-level. Its castle was once the finest in this region (the Casentino), and known to Dante. The church of Pieve di Romena (like the castle, just outside the village) has a beautiful romanesque apse.

See Casentino in the index.

PUNTA ALA is a modern seaside resort at the opposite end of the Gulf of Follonica from Piombino (though the site is ancient). The sea here is perfect for underwater swimming. Hotels, villas, sports facilities abound. Just inland are lots of Etruscan remains and sites. And you look out to sea across to Elba.

QUERCIANELLA is a pretty little seaside resort, enhanced by its pine woods and lying 12 km south of Livorno.

QUINTO, see under SESTO FIORENTINO.

RADDA IN CHIANTI, a fortified medieval village 35 km north of Siena; became (incredibly it seems today, for the place is tiny) capital of this region and in 1415 chief seat of the Chianti League.

RADICOFANI, on the N478 27 km south-west from Chiusi, is remarkably situated on a hill of basalt 766 m above sea-level. Here the one English pope (Hadrian IV) built the now ruined castle. In Boccaccio's *Decameron* Ghino di Tacco imprisoned the Abbot of Cluny in it. There's an impressive Rocca. And the thirteenth-century church of San Pietro has a statue of St Catherine of the Della Robbia school.

In the mid nineteenth century Charles Dickens found this region to be 'as barren, as stony, and as wild, as Cornwall in England'. At Radicofani he was discomfited to stay at 'a ghostly, goblin inn', once a hunting seat, belonging to the Dukes of Tuscany. 'It is full of such rambling corridors, and gaunt rooms,' he reported, that all the murdering and phantom tales that ever were written might have originated in that one house. There are some horrible old *palazzi* in Genoa: one in particular, not unlike it outside: but there is a winding, creaking, wormy, rustling, door-opening, foot-on-stair-case-falling character about this Radicofani Hotel, such as I never saw anywhere else.

As for the inhabitants of Radicofani, Dickens declared that they were all beggars, 'and as soon as they see a carriage coming, they swoop upon it, like so many birds of prey'.

Happily, times do change.

ROCCA D'ORCIA, see under CASTIGLIONE D'ORCIA.

ROSELLE, see under GROSSETO.

SAN ALBINO, see under MONTEPULCIANO.

SAN CASCIANO IN VAL DI PESA lies 17 km south of Florence, not far (3 km north, by secondary roads) from **Sant'Andrea in Percussina**, where the exiled Machiavelli wrote his greatest works (and where the house in which he lived still stands).

SAN GALGANO, see under MASSA MARITTIMA.

SAN GIMIGNANO, once known as San Gimignano of the Fine Towers, stands amidst three rings of walls 324 m above sea-level on a hill 55 km south-west of Florence. The approach to the town is superb, through cypresses and vineyards, as the thirteen famous medieval towers (out of seventy-six that were once built here) dominate the distant skyline.

Yet however charming the present aspect of San Gimignano, these walls and towers hint at a far savager past. The Etruscan vestiges around the town, and the early Roman foundations, were under continual attack by barbarians until Bishop Gimignano drove them away for good and the town gratefully took his name.

San Gimignano flourished as a crossroads and pilgrim route from Lombardy to Rome. The Templars and the Knights of Malta set up hostels for travellers. At the end of the eleventh century the Templars built their church of San Jacopo (near the Porta San Jacopo), and in the nearby woods was founded the monastery of San Vittore. But internal rivalries between great families plagued the town. These were the years when the sullen, brooding towers were built – often in pairs, joined together at the top by wooden bridges – expressly to wage war whenever a rival great family hidden inside a neighbouring tower ventured out.

Plunder and fighting became the rule outside the walls of San Gimignano too, and her second ring of walls was almost certainly built as much to protect refugees from the surrounding countryside as the old inhabitants of the town. In the thirteenth century San Gimignano fought bitterly against Poggibonsi, Volterra, Colle Val d'Elsa and her other neighbours. The conflict between Guelph and Ghibelline brought factions to the town. From 1240 to 1269 San Gimignano supported the Ghibellines; from 1269 she was a Guelph stronghold, and was still supporting the Guelphs in 1300 when Dante arrived from Florence to make his impassioned plea for the unity of all the Tuscan Guelph cities.

Soon San Gimignano would become a client town of Florence. But the early years of the fourteenth century brought an era of comparative calm here. San Gimignano's trade prospered. In 1315 Ubaldo Palmieri endowed the foundling hospital (Spedale degli Innocenti). Five religious houses were set up in the town: Santa Caterina, Santa Maria Maddalena, San Girolamo for women; San Domenico and the Olivetans for men. The cathedral, the churches of Santa Fina, San Francesco, Santa Chiara, Sant'Agostino and the rest, most of them founded in the previous century, were painted and adorned.

These were the years of San Gimignano's finest poet, Giacomo da Michele, who is always known as Folgòre, since his poetry was so dazzling as to seem like lightning. Folgòre writes entrancingly of a time of luxury and intense joy – a luxury dependent in part on a rich international trade that was soon to disappear:

> *I' doto voi nel mese de gennaio*
> *corte con fochi di salette accese,*
> *camere e leta d'ogni bello arnese,*
> *lenzuo de seta e copertoi di vaio;*
> *tregèa, confetti e mescere arazzaio,*
> *vestiti di doagio e rascese . . .*
>
> *D'april vi dono la gentil campagna*
> *tutta fiorita di bell'erba fresca,*
> *fontane d'acqua che non vi rincresca,*
> *donne e donzelle per vostra compagna;*
> *ambianti palafren, destrier di Spagna*

e gente costumata a la francesca,
cantar danzar a la provenzalesca
con istrumenti novi d'Alemagna.

[I give you for January a courtyard
of straw-kindled fires; I give you
rooms and beds with every lovely furnishing,
silk sheets and fur coverlets. I give you
sugared nuts, sweets and sparkling wine.
I give you clothes from Douai and Rascia . . .

For April I give you the gentle *campagna*,
all flowering with beautiful, fresh grass,
fountains of water that shall not disappoint you,
women and girls for company,
nimble horses, chargers from Spain,
and persons dressed in the modes of the French,
singing and dancing like people of Provence
to the sound of new instruments from Germany.]

In 1348 nearly everything changed. The Black Death of that year
was devastating; San Gimignano was desperately impoverished; in
1353 (by a majority of one) the town council voted for complete
submission to Florence. From that time the city went into decline.
One of its two main squares is today known as the Piazza della
Cisterna. Formerly it was called the Piazza delle Taverne, since it
contained a multitude of inns for travellers and pilgrims who broke
their journey here. But Europe as well as San Gimignano was also
broken by the plague, and for a long time the medieval religious
and commercial tourist trade that had brought so much wealth to
this town came virtually to an end.

Worse, San Gimignano continued to suffer because of further
terrible plagues in 1464 and 1631. Yet all was not lamentable.
Perhaps its very poverty meant that San Gimignano has preserved
so much of its medieval past (for many other Tuscan cities built
such towers in the middle ages – Siena and Florence among them –
only to destroy them as better times arrived). Moreover, the religious foundations of San Gimignano managed to preserve their
wealth and continued to receive legacies, even when times were

bad, with the result that the churches of the town continued to be embellished and restored.

The citizens of San Gimignano nowadays concentrate on making and selling their wines (particularly the lovely white Vernaccia), with a second trade in locally made furniture. They create an almond-sweet speciality (known as 'Mandolata delle Torri') that Folgòre would have loved, and a powerful, heavy cake called *panforte*.

The best way to visit the town is certainly on foot, entering from the south through the Porta San Giovanni which stands today substantially as it was built over seven hundred years ago. You pass on the left the Biblioteca Comunale, the town library housed in the Pratellesi Palace. As well as its superb collection of ancient books, the library has fine wooden beams holding up the baked brick roof, and a seventeenth-century wall-painting depicting saints flagellating themselves before the Blessed Virgin Mary. The Via degli Innocenti up which we have been walking leads directly to the superbly satisfying Piazza della Cisterna – basically a triangle, paved with brick, centring in a thirteenth-century well. The buildings around it are entrancingly varied and, like most fine houses here, of stone in the lower storeys with brick above.

They are varied because of an unusually welcoming attitude shown by the medieval citizens of San Gimignano to anyone else who wished to live there. This once belligerent town had the good sense to decree that any immigrant who had behaved well for a decade could build within its walls. As a result Florentine, Sienese, Lucchese, Pisan, even Arabian styles contribute to this vastly varied architecture, as people built in the fashion they were most familiar with. We have records of the great families whose architects created the present Piazza della Cisterna. The finest house, for example, the fourteenth-century Palazzo Tortoli, was built by the Cetti family in the style then fashionable in Siena.

Religious San Gimignano is just around the corner in the Piazza del Duomo. Even so, the secular world intrudes here too. Opposite the cathedral is the twin-towered Palazzo Salvucci, once owned by the Ghibelline Palatoni family. Opposite the Palazzo Salvucci is the Palazzo dei Chigi-Useppi, which is half Florentine, half Pisan in its inspiration. Here too is the Palazzo del Podestà, built by the Gregorio family in the thirteenth century. It supports the Torre Rognosa, 51 m high (the legal limit for a long time in San Gimignano), and was once a medieval prison.

The cathedral is marvellous (but, since San Gimignano no longer has a bishop, this church is now called the Collegiata). Barna da Siena painted scenes from the New Testament as frescos in the south aisle (till he died after falling from his scaffolding, and the work had to be finished by his pupil Giovanni d'Ascanio). Simultaneously Bartolo di Fredi was covering the opposite wall with frescos of the Old Testament, including the exquisite scene of Eve being created from the rib of Adam.

All this leads to the most gracious masterpiece in Tuscany. In the open-air baptistery adjoining the south side of the Collegiata the Florentine painter Domenico Ghirlandaio in 1482 painted a fresco of the Annunciation. If Mary seems a young girl, the angel is yet younger. She kneels before a pot of flowers, separated from the angel by an hour-glass and a cupboard containing some books. And through the window Ghirlandaio has painted the cypresses of the Tuscan countryside.

From here you step into the Palazzo Comunale of San Gimignano, the town-hall where Dante made his impassioned speech. Built for the most part in the decade beginning 1288, it now houses the civic art gallery and its tower looks out on a terrific panorama of this especially fine region of the Tuscan countryside. And here, once again, San Gimignano offers a remarkable artistic surprise. The second floor of the town-hall is decorated with most unusual fourteenth-century frescos by Memmo di Filipuccio on what are called 'profane themes', in which, for example, lovers bathe together and a man creeps into bed with a naked woman. I think that many of the artists of San Gimignano were both extremely talented and also a rum lot. Taddeo di Bartolo certainly depicts the torment of the damned with great brilliance in his Collegiata frescos; but his scenes are also decidedly savage. Again, in the romanesque church of Sant'Agostino, Benozzo Gozzoli was in one sense doing no more than represent an important religious event in the life of this town when he painted Jesus and the Virgin Mary desperately kneeling to beg God the Father not to let his angels shoot poisoned arrows at the town; but the scene is still macabre. And perhaps our suspicions about Gozzoli's sadism are confirmed in the same church when, in a painting of St Augustine's schooldays, he depicts a young boy's bare bottom being birched.

Perhaps those plague years affected the psyche of San Gimignano. None the less today the aspect of this town is peaceful. Walk down the Via Folgòre past the Templars' church of San Jacopo through the Porta alle Fonti. Here are arcades where for the past eight hundred years or so men and women have washed not only themselves but also the wool they sheared from their sheep.

SAN GIOVANNI VALDARNO, on the N69 45 km south-east of Florence, possesses a medieval Palazzo Podestà with a fifteenth-century porch. The fifteenth, century church of Santa Maria delle Grazie has an eighteenth-century facade, and under its arcade a terracotta relief by Giovanni della Robbia (as well as numerous Tuscan paintings inside). Here in 1401 was born the painter Masaccio.

SAN MARCELLO PISTOIESE, see under ABETONE and PISTOIA.

SAN MINIATO. Although its hill site on the N67 almost exactly halfway between Pisa and Florence is no more than 156 m above sealevel, it dominates the Arno valley. In the twelfth century Frederick Barbarossa rebuilt its Rocca, though only two towers remain. The smaller one (known as the 'Torre di Matilde', after Countess Matilda who was born here in 1046) has been cannily utilized as the cathedral bell-tower. From the other tower Piero della Vigna leapt and killed himself. (Dante, in the seventh circle of hell, discovered that as a punishment Piero had been turned into a rough, knotted tree in which the harpies were building their nests.) From high up the hillside there are excellent panoramic views. The romanesque cathedral has been much altered over the centuries, but its brick facade with majolica roundels seems to me more or less original. Some foolishly deplore the richly decorated interior.

To the left of the cathedral of San Miniato stands the thirteenth-century Bishop's Palace and diocesan museum of sacred art (closed on Mondays). Here is an unexpected plethora of treasures: works by Filippo Lippi, Nero di Bicci and Andrea Verrocchio, and so on, many of them brought here from the churches of the neighbourhood.

You descend not too steep steps from the cathedral square to the finest square in San Miniato – the Piazza della Repubblica – to discover the monumental Seminario with its (excellently restored) fourteenth-century shops.

San Miniato offers many other architectural treats: the church of San Francesco, rebuilt in 1276 on the site of an even older church (namely that built in 783 for the relics of the town's patron saint); the Sanctuary of the Crucifix, built in the shape of a Greek cross between 1706 and 1712 and housing within its frescoed walls a twelfth-century wooden crucifix; the fourteenth-century Chiesa del Lorentino, with its frescos of the school of Giotto; and the fourteenth-century church of San Domenico. This last (situated in the Piazza del Popolo) shelters a lovely tomb designed by Donatello and executed by Bernardo Rossellino in the mid fifteenth century. Other noteworthy churches are Santa Caterina, dating from the thirteenth century though much altered in the seventeenth, and SS. Michele e Stefano, again dating from the thirteenth century but later transformed into a baroque church. As for great palaces, don't miss the fourteenth-century Palazzo Comunale (down the steps opposite the Sanctuary of the Crucifix) with its contemporary frescos in the Council Chamber, or the Palazzo Grifoni built by the Medicis in the first half of the sixteenth century.

The Germans brought here the body of the saint after whom this town is now named. (Before then, as a Roman military station, San Miniato was known as Quarto.) The envoys of the emperors used to live in the twelfth-century Palazzo Pretura-Miravalle. So great was this German connection that San Miniato was at one time dubbed 'San Miniato dei Tedeschi' – of the Germans. Curiously enough, however, the place also fascinated Napoleon, who believed his ancestors came from here and visited San Miniato in 1796 to meet the last survivors.

As far as food is concerned, San Miniato is neither German nor French in its cuisine but quintessentially Tuscan, specializing in bread soup (peasant style, with red cabbage and beans), newly born eels with sage, stockfish with tomatoes, eels in *ginocchioni*, and other such marvels.

I do, however, sometimes wonder whether the mystery plays put on by the San Miniato Istituto del Dramma Popolare each summer (culminating in a great festival on 25 August) betray an interesting German influence.

Ten kilometres towards Pisa lies **San Romano,** where in 1432 the Florentines fought against the Sienese. Paolo Uccello did a famous painting of this battle (with virtuoso perspective effects) which is now in three parts in three European capitals: one part in the Louvre, another in the Uffizi, and a third in the National Gallery, London.

SAN PIETRO A GRADO, see the index.

SAN PIETRO A SIEVE, see under MONTE SENARIO.

SAN QUIRICO D'ORCIA, 43 km south-east of Siena, is blessed with an ancient church that in its present form dates substantially from the twelfth and thirteenth centuries. Some of its finest features, though ravaged by shell-fire in the Second World War, are still extremely beautiful, namely the south portal, for which a disciple of Giovanni Pisano sculpted caryatids and lions, and the gothic doorway to the transept, which dates from 1298. Fortunately the sculpted romanesque portal of the west facade, which dates from the last decades of the eleventh century, escaped unharmed. The fifteenth-century Sienese painter Sano di Pietro made a triptych that would be the pride of this Collegiata were it not surpassed by the marquetry of the stalls which the Sienese architect and woodworker Antonio Barili made in 1500 for the San Giovanni chapel of Siena cathedral and which were brought here in 1502.

In the twelfth century San Quirico d'Orcia was a stronghold of Emperor Frederick Barbarossa, and each June the Festa del Barbarossa, a costumed procession and other festivities, recall this era.

SAN ROMANO, see under SAN MINIATO.

SANSEPOLCRO, 39 km north-east of Arezzo is famed above all because here, some time in the second decade of the fifteenth century, Piero della Francesca was born. Most visitors as soon as they arrive will thus feel rightly drawn to the Museo Civico in the Palazzo Comunale, hoping to find a masterpiece. Piero trained as an artist in Florence, but he was back in Sansepolcro (as a councillor) in 1452. He thereafter travelled afar in Italy, to Urbino, to Rome. But his native town displays today a picture that embodies (as Kenneth Clark put it) 'values for which no rational statement is adequate', quite simply because before it 'we are struck with a feeling of awe older and less reasonable than that inspired by the Blessed Angelico'.

Kenneth Clark was referring to Piero della Francesca's famous *Resurrection*, commissioned for the Palazzo Comunale, though it has been moved from its intended position and the sides partly shaved. (It also once was even covered in whitewash!) Lord Clark frequently emphasized what he called the 'earthy, peasant quality' of Piero's greatest work, and he perceived this quality especially in this painting, expressed in Piero's vision of the risen Jesus who is depicted – again in Kenneth Clark's words – as the 'country God, who rises in the grey light while humanity is asleep', the God who 'has been worshipped ever since man first knew that the seed is not dead in the winter earth, but will force its way upwards through an iron crust'. Kenneth Clark's interpretation may not be yours; but to my mind he was completely right to speak of a feeling of awe before the eyes of this Christ who steps from his tomb here while the soldiers lie asleep and the Tuscan landscape stretches out behind.

In the same museum is the *Madonna of the Misericordia* which Piero painted for the church of the Misericordia, Sansepolcro. There are also fine works by, for example, Luca Signorelli, Jacopo Pontormo and Giovanni della Robbia (or one of his pupils: a lovely terracotta *Nativity*). There's a *Birth of the Virgin* by Santi di Tito – another native artist of this city (b. 1253).

A visit to Sansepolcro cathedral is also rewarding. Built in the first half of the eleventh century and extensively renovated in the fourteenth, it contains a remarkable number of works of art, including a great wooden crucifix known as the 'Volto Santo' dating (in part at least) from the tenth century, and a *Resurrection* by Raffaelino del Colle, who was also a native of Sansepolcro (b. 1490). Amongst the fifteenth-century frescos in the cathedral, seek out the crucifixion by Piero's Florentine disciple Bartolomeo della Gatta.

There are other fine churches in Sansepolcro – particularly San Lorenzo and San Francesco. And on the second Sunday in September you can enjoy the annual Palio della Balestra, when the citizens of Sansepolcro dress in medieval costumes to shoot crossbows.

SANTO STEFANO, see under MONTE ARGENTARIO.

SANT'ANDREA IN PERCUSSINA, see under SAN CASCIANO.

SANT'ANTIMO, see under MONTALCINO.

SANT'ELLERO, see under PONTASSIEVE.

SAN VINCENZO, on the coastline some 20 km north of Piombino, is powerfully geared to tourism, with not only a fine sandy beach (and a view of Elba) but also tennis courts, a swimming-pool, mini-golf, roller-skating courts, horse-riding, night spots, dancing and extensive parks. It is also very convenient for visiting the increasingly well-excavated and extensive Etruscan remains in this area.

San Vincenzo's fine tower – dating from the time of the Emperor Maximilian – can also be seen in a fresco by Vasari in the Palazzo Vecchio, Florence.

The cuisine here is typical of the Livorno region, with such specialities as mullet and cuttlefish served with black rice.

SARTEANO is a medieval village lying 573 m above sea-level a dozen kilometres south of Chiusi, and well worth visiting to see its *palazzo* and its fifteenth- and sixteenth-century castle. Giacomo di Mino painted *Madonna*s for both its churches.

In Etruscan times its mineral waters were prized. There are modern sports facilities and swimming-pools. And 6 km to the south is **Cetona**, with another medieval castle and *palazzo* (containing some exhibits of Etruscan origin).

SATURNIA, see under MAGLIANO IN TOSCANA.

SCARPERIA, 30 km north of Florence, has a Palazzo Pretorio of 1306, prettily decorated with coats of arms. Its oratory of the Madonna di Piazza boasts fourteenth-century frescos and a *Madonna and Child* by the fifteenth-century Florentine sculptor Benedetto da Maiano.

The town is famous for its cutlery and wrought iron. Close by Scarperia is the Franciscan convent of **Bosco ai Frati**, with fine fifteenth-century buildings and a little-known crucifix by the greatest sculptor of the fifteenth-century, Donatello.

SESTO FIORENTINO, 4 km west of Florence, is where the Marchese Carlo Ginori founded the celebrated Doccia porcelain factory in 1737, bringing here some of the finest Viennese porcelain painters of his generation. The firm is still here, and the Museo delle Porcellane di Doccia (closed on Mondays) displays an entrancing historical collection of its work. The Palazzo Pretorio at Sesto Fiorentino dates from the fifteenth century.

Close by Sesto Fiorentino is the tiny village of **Quinto**. At no. 95 Via Fratelli Rosselli you find the custodian of the extremely impressive Etruscan tumulus, with its domed burial chambers.

SETTIGNANO, 8 km east of Florence, is beautifully set among cypresses and olives. The art historian Bernard Berenson (1865–1959) who lived in the town, watching oxen slowly dragging a plough between olives and grapevines, recorded 'a feeling that I was looking at what has been going on here ever since civilization began'. He bequeathed the villa in which he lived (I Tatti) to Harvard University, to be used for Italian renaissance studies.

In the fifteenth century Settignano's sculpture workshop nurtured such artists as the brothers Bernardo and Antonio Rossellino and Desiderio da Settignano. Michelangelo spent his youth in the Villa Buonarroti. The writer Niccolò Tommaseo chose to die here in 1874 (his statue is in the main piazza, opposite the church of Santa Maria). During their celebrated love affair, Gabriele D'Annunzio and Eleonora Duse lived in the Villa Capponcina. And Mark Twain wrote his *Pudd'nhead Wilson* here.

The town's churches are richly endowed. Santa Maria, built in the early sixteenth century, rebuilt in the late eighteenth and restored in the twentieth, possesses a sixteenth-century pulpit by Bernardo Buontalenti, a white terracotta group of the Madonna, Child and two angels that is by Andrea della Robbia or one of his pupils, and a sixteenth-century organ (in excellent repair and voice). Close by the town on the road to Florence is the Benedictine church of San Martino a Mensola, founded by the ninth-century Scottish St Andrew (his body lies inside the church, marked by a stone slab). The interior is now fifteenth century (as is the bell-tower), with many fine works of religious art; and the loggia outside dates from the seventeenth century.

Settignano is where the Florentines built many renaissance villas and gardens. Many of their original gardens have been obliterated – either by neglect or by later alterations – but one, that of Villa Gamberaia, is in superb condition, still following the traditional renaissance pattern of four parterres with a circular open space and fountain at the crossing. The garden is so superb because the villa is in private hands and the owner saw to its extensive restoration. Georgina Masson has described it as 'at once the loveliest

217

and most typically Tuscan that the writer has seen. In it the light and air and breeze-swept site, advocated by all the garden authors from Varro to Alberti, is exploited to perfection.' The garden of Villa Gamberaia also perfectly illustrates the influence of antiquity on the Florentine renaissance, for (as Georgina Masson notes) from the grassy terrace in front of the villa 'the domes and spires of Florence are seen in the distance across the olive groves and vineyards that, as in Pliny's Tuscan villa, come close up to the house'. But the spirit is also partly baroque, with mosaics and rustic stonework, with stucco reliefs of nymphs and a huntsman out with his dog.

SIENA, 68 km south of Florence, retains that remarkable shape which Fynes Moryson described in 1617 as 'not unlike to an earthen vessell, broad in the bottom, and narrow at the mouth, which narrow part lies towards the West'. He added: 'In the center of the City lies a most faire Marketplace, in the forme of an Oyster.'

This is the famous Campo of Siena, sloping, semicircular, where the three hills on which she is built meet. Another Englishman in our own century has praised the enlightened civic authorities for their policy towards this square, observing that this 'outpost of medieval civilization became a model for urban planning when it banned motor traffic from its historic centre. It is a profound satisfaction,' Harold Acton continued, 'even when one is far away, to know that the unique shell-shaped Campo is not used as a parking lot.'

An Etruscan settlement which later became the Roman Sena Julia, the city virtually disappeared in the early middle ages, rising again under the Lombard kings and reaching the acme of its power when the Sienese defeated the Florentines at the battle of Monteaperti in 1260. (See Siena in the index.) Duccio painted his remarkable *Maestà* in the cathedral to celebrate this victory. The Black Death ravaged the city – and seems to have promoted a powerful sense of religion, for Siena bred two notable saints at this time: Catherine and Bernardino, whose influence is still much in evidence in the art and architecture of the city today.

Siena managed to remain independent, despite economic decline, until 1487, when the dictator Pandolfo Petrucci seized power. His dynasty continued to rule the city until 1524. Her fortunes continued to decline, and when the Spaniards ceded her to Florence in 1557, for sixty years she was forbidden even to operate public banks.

Yet this decline partly accounts for the unique fascination of this Tuscan city, which is a treasure-house of medieval gothic monuments and art, unspoiled by later alterations or 'improvements'. Siena thrives on tourism, and her seventy hoteliers and restaurateurs have set up a Cooperativa Siena Hotels Promotion, in Piazza San Domenico, to foster this. There is also an active Azienda Autonoma di Turismo at no. 20 Banchi di Sotto. Ente Provinciale per il Turismo is at no. 5, Via di Città. Other addresses are:

Automobile Club, no. 47 Viale Vittorio Veneto;

Casa della Studentessa, no. 96 Via San Marco;

Casa dello Studente, no. 43a Viale XXIV Maggio, and no. 31 Via delle Sperandie;

Mense Universitarie (i.e. students' eating places), Via Santa Agata and Via Santi Bandini;

Ufficio Informazioni, no. 55 Piazza del Campo.

Any tour around Siena ought to start at its historic centre, the Campo. In 1347 this square was divided into its present nine segments, paved with brick and divided by long stone strips, signifying the beneficent government of the Nine (see the history of Siena, under Siena in the index). In the past factions have fought against each other here, and the people waited anxiously praying for news of the great battle of Monteaperti. These days the chief rivalry is that provided each year by the famous Palio. This horse race in medieval costumes takes place on 2 July and on 16 August. The first date refers to a miraculous appearance of the Virgin Mary in Siena, in whose honour the first Palio was raced in 1656. Each district of the city draws lots to decide which of the seventeen shall race (there is room only for ten). The festivities today occupy four days in all, culminating in the two traditional Palio festivals. Siena is naturally packed for the occasion. Tickets are not cheap. The Palio race is not the only cultural event of Siena's year. The Musical Academy organizes concerts and master-classes in summer.

A walk around the Campo should begin with the mighty Palazzo Pubblico, built between 1297 and 1310 and later enlarged. The ground floor with its rows of simple impressive gothic arches is made of stone. Two more storeys are of brick, with slender pillars dividing the gothic windows into three lights. Topping this is a squat storey, dwarfed by the slender Torre del Mangia, 102 m high. The nickname of this tower derives from the first city watchman, Mangiaguadagni, whose job was to strike the hours. Minuccio and Francesco Rinaldi built this tower between 1338 and 1348, the whole of brick save for the stone bell-chamber and battlements. The great bell – which the Sienese dub 'Sunta', from Maria Assunta – weighs 6,764 kg and was placed here in 1666. It is rung only on great civic occasions.

The art inside the Palazzo Pubblico is astounding. Guido da Siena's *Maestà*, with the Infant Jesus's green robe tied with an orange sash; a lovely *Maestà* by Simone Martini, in which some of the myriad attendant saints hold up the canopy over the heads of the Madonna and Child (who is actually standing up, to bless us); Ambrogio Lorenzetti's *Allegory of Good and Bad Government* (see Lorenzetti in the index); a *Madonna and Child* by Sodoma, in which Mary seems to be giving Jesus away; another lovely Sodoma of the Resurrection; these are only a few of the treasures of the Palazzo Pubblico.

One famous fresco has recently become the subject of much debate. It depicts Guidoriccio da Fogliano riding to the siege of Montemassi, and is said to have been painted by Simone Martini in 1328. Behind the knight are pitched tents. In the distance is a walled city, and he rides towards another hill-top town ahead.

In the 1980s American scholars began to argue that the fortifications depicted are renaissance, not gothic in style. Some insisted that this fresco actually covers one done by Sodoma in 1530. Guidoriccio, they argue, was not a knight in 1328. If they are right, one of the first recognizable portraits painted since Roman times and one of the first recognizable pictures of a landscape happens to be a romantic fake. Understandably, the Sienese authorities have been reluctant to allow the necessary tests to show whether these doubters are correct.

At the foot of the slender tower of their Palazzo Pubblico the Sienese built the Cappella di Piazza as a thanksgiving for the ending of the great plague of 1348. In the shape of a loggia with three arches, the chapel's first architect was Domenico di Agostino and the work was completed in 1376 by Giovanni di Cecco. Statues of

Saints James the Great and James the Less, of John the Baptist, Thomas and Bartholomew adorn this chapel. The fine ironwork gates were added in the fifteenth century. Over the altar Sodoma painted a fresco of *God the Father with his Saints*.

Beyond this chapel is the courtyard of the Podestà, created in 1325 and bearing the coats of arms of the medieval magistrates of Siena. The courtyard is the way into the former Council Chamber of the Republic which was begun in 1352. A little doorway here lets you into the vestibule from which you may climb to the top of Torre del Mangia.

The highest point of the Campo at Siena is the setting for the Fonte Gaia ('Gay Fountain'), placed here in the early fifteenth century and decorated with reliefs by Jacopo della Quercia. Alas these have now been removed to the safekeeping of the Palazzo Pubblico, and replaced by reproductions made by Tito Sarrochi in the late nineteenth century.

One other palace in the Campo should not be missed. Palazzo Sansedoni, with its dark reddish bricks and three-fold windows, stands to the north-east of the square. It was built in 1216 and enlarged over a hundred years later by Agostino del Rosso and Cecco di Casino. For the rest the Campo at Siena is a satisfying blend of shops, restaurants and bars, where one should sit and drink in architectural bliss.

Siena can be explored endlessly without the help of abstruse, detailed information about every quiddity of architecture. In spite of its massive palaces, it remains a homely city, symbolized for me in the plaque at no. 17 Via Banchi di Sotto (which leaves the Campo at the extreme right-hand side, when you are facing the Palazzo Pubblico) proudly proclaiming that here was born Giovanni Caselle, inventor of the humble pantograph.

My favourite walk winds from the Campo as far as Via della Cerchia. (It would be quite perfect if only it also took in the splendid church of San Domenico.) Before tackling its superb architectural and artistic treasures, it is wise to take a reasonable refreshment in one of the bars of the Campo.

Once refreshed, walk through Vicolo di San Pietro, in the centre of the paved semicircle, out into Croce del Travaglio, where three streets meet. One of them – Via di Città on the left – contains more entrancing palaces than any self-respecting street has any right to. At the beginning of Via di Città is the Loggia della Mercanzia, with its powerful arches, built as the tribune of the merchants in the early fifteenth century. Although this is essentially a renaissance building, note how the niches with the saints are still gothic in style. The vaults are finely ornamented with sixteenth-century frescos and stucco work. This marvellous street of medieval and renaissance secular architecture now becomes narrower until (at no. 75) Palazzo Patrizi appears, and then (at no. 82) the superb Palazzo Chigi-Saracini, a thirteenth-century palace (much restored) with a curved facade. In the delightful fashion of this city, Palazzo Chigi-Saracini is part brick, part stone. Today it is the home of the Chigiana Academy of Music, which sponsors both concerts and international music studies. The works of art housed here include a marble relief of the *Madonna and Child* by Donatello, a *Madonna Adoring Her Son* by Lorenzo di Credi, and a superb *Madonna and Child between Two Angels* by Botticelli.

Even if you have not time to explore all the art galleries of this enchanting city, always look into the courtyards of Sienese palaces. The fine statue inside the entrance of Palazzo Chigi-Saracini is of Pope Julius II, sculpted by Fulvio Signorini in 1609. Commemorative inscriptions and coats of arms adorn the walls, and the relief is dedicated to a famous Sienese gentlewoman called Sapia di Salvani. Living in exile at Colle Val d'Elsa, she was overjoyed when the Sienese were defeated near by, declaring that she wanted nothing more to make her content. Dante met her in Purgatory because, as she told him, she was 'gladder far of others' hurt than any good that befell me'.

Opposite is a bank which occupies the lovely Palazzo Piccolomini, designed by Bernardo Rossellino in the 1460s for the sister of Pope Pius II (so that this building, with its rusticated bosses in the lower storey and its double windows above, is often called the Palazzo delle Papesse). The beautiful brick Palazzo Marsili on the corner of Via del Castro was built in 1444 by Luca di Bartolo da Bagnacavallo. And then you come upon the graceful fifteenth-century column bearing the she-wolf of the city. To its right is the late-sixteenth century Palazzo Chigi. Turn right into Via del Capitano and you confront the thirteenth-century Palazzo del Capitano, with its row of nine Sienese arches, its coats of arms of the great ones who once lived here, and (again) a superb courtyard. And then we walk into the cathedral square.

If ever a cathedral divided the opinions of the British it is Siena's. 'There is nothing in this city so extraordinary as the cathedral, which a man may view with pleasure after he has seen St Peter's [Rome], though it is of quite another make, and can only be looked upon as one of the master-pieces of Gothic architecture,' wrote Joseph Addison early in the eighteenth century. Ruskin expressed a different opinion (though admittedly he had a terrible headache at Siena): 'the cathedral seemed to me every way absurd – over-cut, over-striped, over-crocketed, over-gabled, a piece of costly confectionery, and faithless vanity'.

I find it superb. The lower part is romanesque, for Siena cathedral was begun in 1196 and the whole structure was essentially finished by 1215. But what gives this building its thrill is that its spirit is pure gothic. At the end of the thirteenth century work was begun on the outrageously ambitious polychrome marble facade designed by Giovanni Pisano. He and his pupils created the statues of prophets, patriarchs and philosophers which embellish it. Then the upper half, with its magnificent rose-window, was added in the second half of the next century. And the Venetian mosaics in the three gables were not completed till the nineteenth century. The black and white marble bell-tower rises dramatically, its windows starting humbly as single openings, rising to no fewer than six at the top. In the lunette of the door of mercy at the foot of the bell-tower is a *Madonna and Child* by Donatello.

The interior of the cathedral is equally outrageous and equally successful. Black and white marble bands decorate the walls and columns. Fifty-six remarkable designs (dating from 1369 to 1547) decorate the pavement. Over forty artists in all contributed to this great pavement. For my part I always seek out two sections by Domenico Beccafumi: Moses striking water from a rock (between the two central pillars of the crossing) and the sacrifice of Isaac (before the high altar).

To the east is Nicola Pisano's fantastic pulpit, created between 1265 and 1268 after he had already designed a pulpit at Pisa brilliant enough to make him immortal. Underneath the one at Siena a lioness feeds her cubs; another seeks her prey. Above are seven narrative reliefs, depicting scenes from the life of Jesus and the Last Judgement. These panels are masterpieces of gothic art – even though classical elements are still to be seen, for example in some of the nudes of the Last Judgement. The whole rests on ten columns of granite, porphyry and marble. Nicola Pisano was helped on this, his last great pulpit, by his son Giovanni and the Florentine Arnolfo di Cambio. But the impulse to move from classical to gothic – in part inspired by French ivories that were now circulating in Tuscany – must surely be his.

When Siena cathedral was built this city was at its richest and most powerful. Nothing seemed beyond the reach of her citizens. And all the energy that created her wealth and power seems to have been poured into the masterpieces that run riot inside this amazing house of God.

The Sienese wanted more. The citizens planned what is now called the New Cathedral, using the original church merely as its transept. The Black Death of 1348 and the city's waning fortunes destroyed these ambitious hopes. The cathedral museum now occupies what was built of this unfinished nave. It houses the original statues which Giovanni Pisano sculpted for the facade. Here is the lovely *Madonna with the Large Eyes*. But my own favourite painting in this museum is an apparently simple thirteenth-century picture of the *Madonna and Child* by Duccio di Buoninsegna, in which the chubby infant, a lock of brown hair falling over his forehead, reaches up to pinch his mother's cheek. It is, however, by no means his most famous painting in this museum, for that is surely the *Maestà* which depicts on its reverse the story of the subsequent sufferings awaiting the infant Jesus.

Opposite the cathedral of Siena is the hospice of Santa Maria della Scala, founded – legend has it – in the year 832 by a cobbler, but in its present form dating from the thirteenth century. Next to it is the fifteenth-century church of Santissima Annunziata, with its lovely wooden chancel stalls and choir galleries. The cathedral square houses the Palazzo Granducale, built in the sixteenth century by the Medici conquerors of Siena to designs by Buontalenti, and the seventeenth-century archbishop's palace, set against the cathedral and decently faced in black and white marble. At the corner of the square is the Palazzo del Magnifico, built for arrogant Pandolfo Petrucci in 1508.

The baptistery of Siena's cathedral is not reached from the cathedral square at all. To reach it you walk behind the cathedral to Piazza San Giovanni and descend a steep flight of steps. The late-fourteenth-century facade (alas, unfinished) is by Jacopo di Mino del Pellicciao. Inside is a superb renaissance font, with sculptures by such masters as Jacopo della Quercia, Lorenzo Ghiberti and Donatello.

Walk back into the cathedral square and take Via del Capitano on the left corner opposite the cathedral facade. It crosses Piazza di Posteria to join Via San Pietro, where you come upon one of Siena's finest buildings, the fourteenth-century Palazzo Buonsignori. Again the charm of this building derives in part from its mixture of brick and stone, as well as its battlements adorned with sculptured busts. Today it is the main art gallery of Siena. Apart from the works of Simone Martini (which are mostly to be found elsewhere), the collection offers the finest opportunity to see exactly why Sienese painting is such a rare achievement. A thirteenth-century Christ, his eyes closed (in death?) blesses us. St Clare, painted by Guido da Siena, miraculously drives back the Saracens, who tumble like idiots from the city walls. In a strange altarpiece by Jacopo di Mino del Pelliciaio the infant Jesus leans from his mother's arms to crown St Catherine of Alexandria. In an extraordinarily magical picture, Giovanni di Paolo paints a beaten Jesus, the blood draining from his white body, alongside a Christ in triumph, his pierced side still bleeding. Taddeo di Bartolo depicts the adoration of the shepherds, one in a green robe, the baby Jesus wrapped round and round in his swaddling clothes like a snail in its shell. Lorenzo Vecchieta paints St Bernardino, carrying the IHS symbol so pervasive in this city because of his own powerful preaching. Domenico Beccafumi presents us with that other great saint of Siena, Catherine, ecstatically receiving the stigmata, as well as a picture of Jesus in limbo meeting up with the good thief who was to be taken that day to paradise. And Sodoma depicts an all-too-human Jesus bound to the column, bleeding.

No. 31 Via San Pietro is reputedly the house of a Sienese lady who, having married a jealous husband named Nello Pannochieschi, was kept a prisoner in the Maremma until she died. (Dante succinctly summed up her unproductive life: 'Siena made me, Maremma destroyed me.') Here is a little square, and at the top of a flight of steps the church of San Pietro alle Scale, first built in the thirteenth century but completely rebuilt in the eighteenth. Then the street winds into Piazza Sant'Agostino. This basilica, too, was rebuilt in the eighteenth century, though it originates in the thirteenth. Luigi Vanvitelli, who shaped it as a Latin cross in 1755, was no incompetent architect, and he created a handsome home for the many fine works of religious art (by Perugino, Lorenzetti, Sodoma and others) inside.

South-west of the square is Via della Cerchia, which leads to the early-sixteenth-century church of Santa Maria del Carmine. Baldassare Peruzzi, who was responsible for the present form of this church, also designed the simple, extremely impressive Palazzo Pollini which stands at the other side of the street.

As I have said, the tour just outlined would be perfect if only it somehow included the church of San Domenico, which, however, lies further to the north of the city in its own piazza. The building is severe and imposing, a brick gothic church begun in 1225 by Dominican monks. The crypt alone would suffice for a normal church. No one bothered to finish the facade. The cloister to the south makes some concessions to gentleness by giving shelter to lovely late-fourteenth-century frescos by Lippo Memmi and Andrea Vanni. The stern interior is rendered almost bizarre (save in the eyes of the faithful) by the head of St Catherine, displayed in her chapel, which was built in 1488. This visionary, mystic and adviser of popes died of a paralytic stroke in Rome in 1380, and her confessor and biographer, Raymond of Capua, brought the saint's head back to Siena four years later. He must also have brought a finger, for that is preserved in a niche in the outside wall, as well as the chain with which Catherine flagellated herself.

Sodoma seized the opportunity to decorate this chapel with brilliant frescos. His masterpiece is the painting of the swooning saint to the left of the altar. She appears as you look almost to be breathing. The scenes from her life show her casting out demons and include a painting of the execution of a young man who has just been brought to a state of grace by St Catherine.

Siena is by no means exhausted by these two itineraries. St
Catherine's own home in Via Benincasa is well worth visiting. So
are the gothic basilica of San Francesco, well restored in the nine-
teenth century, and the late-sixteenth-century Santa Maria di
Provenzano, which houses a famous terracotta of the Blessed
Virgin Mary. The fifteenth-century oratory on the spot where St
Bernardino preached his great mission (close by the church of San
Francesco) is filled with works of art celebrating his piety and
vigour.

Siena has an ambience all of its own, though many have tried to
encapsulate it by comparing the city with other gems. For Dickens
it was 'like a bit of Venice, without the water'. Elizabeth Barrett
Browning found its air 'as fresh as English air, without English
dampness'. Perhaps John Evelyn, of all visitors, summed it up best,
since he remarked, not only on its architecture but also on the
charm of its inhabitants. 'The Citty,' he wrote, 'at a little distance
presents the Traveller with an incomparable Prospect, occasion'd
by the manyplayne brick Towers.' He added that the air was incomparable, the inhabitants courteous and provisions cheap.

See also Siena in the index.

SORANO, see under SOVANA.

SOVANA, a seemingly neglected and half-tumbledown village 8 km
north-east of Pitigliano, is – on a second look – an extremely
interesting spot. Here was born Pope Gregory VII (and his family
built the thirteenth-century Rocca). A street of medieval houses
leads to the Piazza del Pretorio, with its Palazzo Pretorio (built
between the thirteenth and fifteenth centuries) and the sixteenth-
century renaissance Palazzo Bourbon, as well as the romanesque
church of Santa Maria (which houses a ciborium that may even
date from as early as the eighth century). Almost outside the village
one is amazed to discover a former cathedral, built between the
twelfth and fourteenth centuries, with a dome, a fine portal and
lovely capitals.

One and a half kilometres south of Sovana is an Etruscan necropolis, with the fine facades of the tombs carved out of the rock.
And 10 km to the east is the medieval village of **Sorano**, which was
evacuated in 1929 owing to the danger from landslides, and possesses a fifteenth-century castle and Palazzo Orsini.

STAGGIA, see under POGGIBONSI.

STIA lies 26 km north-east of Vallombrosa, 440 m above sea-level at the foot of Monte Falterona. The Piazza Tanucci contains its romanesque church of Santa Maria, among whose treasures is a *Madonna* by Andrea della Robbia. Just outside the town is the castle of Porciano, still looking extremely threatening, which once belonged to the Ghibelline Guidi family. This is good skiing and walking country.

TALAMONE is a haunt of fishermen, on a headland north of Orbetello, with the wooded Monti dell'Uccellina behind (now a national park) and a view of Monte Argentario across the waters. Its name derives from that of the Argonaut Telamon, its legendary founder. Other sailors to embark from or arrive at Talamone were Marius on returning from Africa in 87 BC, and Garibaldi and his Thousand in 1860.

Close by is the ruined Torre della Bella Marsilia, from which Barbarossa the Corsair abducted the daughter of the house, Margherita (taking her to the harem of Suleiman the Magnificent), after murdering everyone else.

See also under ORBETELLO.

TIRRENIA is an extremely well-ordered seaside resort with lovely pine woods, just south of Marina di Pisa, where no building has been allowed on the coast.

TORRE DEL LAGO PUCCINI is 7 km from Viareggio. Here is the villa by Lake Massaciuccoli that the composer Giacomo Puccini (1858–1924) made his home, now open to the public mornings and afternoons in summer, in the afternoons in winter. Here Puccini wrote all his operas (save for *Turandot*) and also shot many wild birds and animals. 'Second only to the piano,' he used to say, 'my favourite instrument is the rifle.' On display in the villa are both musical mementoes and also his armoury. Each August Torre del Lago hosts a festival of his operas.

The composer's memory was phenomenal. Even in his later years he could sing *Cavalleria Rusticana* faultlessly. At the end of his life the conductor Toscanini visited him. Puccini, mortally ill, played *Turandot* on the piano for his distinguished visitor. He sipped black coffee and his son lit him a cigarette. Perceiving that Toscanini was crying, Puccini jested, 'My music must be good if it makes *testa piccina* weep.' His last words to the conductor were, 'Arturo, whatever happens to me, do not neglect my sweet, lovely princess *Turandot*.'

Puccini and his wife, along with their son Tonio, are buried in the nearby chapel. He once wrote:

> ... *anche la musica*
> *triste mi fa.*
> *Quando la morte*
> *verrà a trovarmi*
> *sarò felice di riposarmi.*

> [... even music
> saddens me.
> When death finds me
> I shall be happy to rest.]

VALDICASTELLO, see under PIETRASANTA.

VESPIGNANO, see under MONTE SENARIO.

VETULONIA, see under GROSSETO.

VIAREGGIO lies 17 km west of Lucca, with a tremendous flat golden beach, gentle pine woods, and a view of the Apuan Alps. In 1822 the drowned corpse of Percy Bysshe Shelley was washed ashore here, hence the Piazza Shelley in Viareggio with its 1894 bust of the poet by Urbano Lucchese.

The municipal authorities fill the streets with flowers during the summer season. The promenade is as safe as can possibly be for children, with pedestrians separated from road traffic. There are fine hotels, parks, boats, tennis, and bathing huts and very well organized, properly patrolled bathing and sunbathing on the beach. Small wonder this is the most popular seaside resort on the west coast of Italy.

The inner port is dominated (if that isn't too strong a word) by a sixteenth-century tower. And in the Piazza Mazzini the former Palazzo Comunale is now a museum.

As a further attraction, in the month preceding Lent a colossal carnival is organized here, with football tournaments, a procession of floats, masked balls and fireworks.

VICCHIO, see under MONTE SENARIO.

VICOPISANO, situated 8 km north-west of Pontedera at the foot of Monte Pisano, still possesses the romantic towers of its former fortress and fortifications (which no less an architect than Brunelleschi once restored). Its Pisan-romanesque church, built in the eleventh century, houses a fine fourteenth-century statue of John the Baptist.

VINCI, 11 km north of Empoli, as the alleged birthplace of Leonardo da Vinci (1452–1519), has made part of its restored thirteenth-century castle into the Museo Vinciano (containing, for example, some fascinating models of the machines he designed). Here too is the Biblioteca Leonardiana, devoted to documenting his life and work. Next to it is the church of Santa Croce where he was baptized.

VOLTERRA is one of the strangest, severest and most exciting cities in Tuscany, with an atmosphere quite different, quite apart from anywhere else in this part of Italy. Situated 550 m above sea-level on the highest peaks of a mountain ridge that separates the valleys of the rivers Cécina and Era (57 km north-west of Siena), this ancient Etruscan city was built as a powerful stronghold, commanding magnificent views. D. H. Lawrence, who adored the vigour of the Etruscans, described it as grim, an epithet that leaves aside the peculiar charm of Volterra, but has a certain force (especially when you are looking at its fearful north-eastern aspect where the cliff long ago fell away, taking part of the Etruscan city with it). And a city with two great defensive walls (one Etruscan, one medieval) bespeaks an often savage past.

Volterra has perhaps imbibed its brooding character from this dark, savage side of its history. Known in Etruscan times as Velathri and one of the most powerful cities in the Etruscan Federation, the city was able to dominate an enormous region of present-day Tuscany. As the most important strategic base in the lower Arno valley, Volterra was rarely at peace, and around the mid third century BC finally surrendered to Rome. In 82 BC Sulla laid siege to its inhabitants, who were supporters of his rival Marius in the civil war. They suffered for two terrible years before capitulating.

In the middle ages Volterra was for some time the seat of the Lombard kings. It had become an episcopal see – and its bishops

were often at this time ambitious men whose territorial designs
provoked bitter struggles. Soon a weakened Volterra was the object
of rivalry between the three expansionist powers, Florence, Siena
and Pisa. Although the city continued to claim a nominal independence, by the mid fourteenth century Volterra was essentially a client
of the Florentines. Its people loathed their subjection. A Volterran
tried to assassinate Lorenzo il Magnifico; there was an abortive
revolt in 1429; and in 1530 the whole city rebelled against its masters
– a rebellion that had no chance of success.

In the Albergo Nazionale, in the Piazza Martiri della Libertà,
Gabriele D'Annunzio was inspired in 1909 to compose his 'Forse
che si, forse che no' ('Perhaps yes; perhaps no'). Inscribed on the
wall of that hotel are some powerful verses he wrote summing up
the character of this city. Translated they read:

> On your Etruscan walls, secluded Volterra,
> Built on the rocks at your silent doors,
> I saw dead people from your buried city.
>
> The scourge of plague and war
> Had bent and destroyed your destiny;
> And others from the past in your virile fort
> Filled the shadows that no one can disperse.
>
> In the distance I saw the industrious Maremma,
> The gloomy mountains, the whitish sea,
> Elba, and the wild archipelago,
>
> Then my idle flesh composed itself
> In the sculpted alabaster coffin,
> Where are Circe and her mortal beverage.

Alabaster has been worked at Volterra since Etruscan times.
Alabaster is a mineral (calcium hydrosulphate) derived from
gypsum and here extracted from the ground either in mines or in
open-air quarries. The 'purest' kind is ivory-white, slightly transparent, sometimes very delicately striped. But other alabaster
(and, in truth, the sort I like best) is beautifully coloured: yellow
(varying from pale lemon to orange), or else grey-black, reddish,
or even green.

The Etruscans themselves used only the purest kind, painting the surface, sometimes decorating it with a thin layer of gold leaf. Then, incredibly, the fashion for alabaster disappeared, to be virtually recreated anew at the time of the renaissance and coming into its own only in the 1830s. Under an unsung genius named Marcello Inghirami Fei, the precious subterranean deposits at Castellini, as well as those in the hilly Volterran region with their many different varieties of alabaster, were at last properly exploited.

The alabaster work in the Museo Guarnicci at Volterra offers an artistic experience that has never left my memory. Etruscan work from the centuries before the birth of Jesus depict ancient myths with great subtlety and astonishing vigour. In the *palazzi* of the city, and in the cathedral museum, are elaborate and superb works of alabaster art – chalices, ciboria, candelabra – dating from the renaissance to the present. And in countless workshops today Volterran alabaster modellers are still at work. By contrast with the cost of alabaster elsewhere, their products are amazingly cheap. Certainly elaborate, gorgeous and expensive works are on sale too. But however tight one's budget, anyone who comes away from Volterra without buying, say a simple and beautiful chess set and pieces is wasting a marvellous opportunity.

The Museo Guarnicci contains, of course, far more than superb works of alabaster art. It is the home of a remarkable collection of Etruscan remains that was begun in 1732, including seven hundred or so cinerary urns dating from the fourth to the fifth century B C, often depicting on their sides fascinating pictures from everyday life over two thousand years ago with sculpted representations on their lids of the deceased. Among the most moving of these is the famous terracotta lid known as 'Degli Sposi' ('of a married couple'): the husband, half reclining, looks apprehensively yet stoically beyond the grave, while his wife clings to him lovingly, hopefully, perhaps despairingly.

Having read D'Annunzio's eulogy of Volterra on the hotel wall turn left from the Piazza Martiri della Libertà along the Via Marchese and you reach, in the centre of Volterra, the enormously appealing Piazza dei Priori, one of the most beautiful squares in the whole of Tuscany (with setts as a pavement). Here is the thirteenth-century Palazzo del Podestà (or Palazzo Pretorio, as it is also called), with its golden stone, its lovely arcades, its crenellated tower; and next to it, the Bishop's Palace which (according to the tourist information office in this square) was once the city's granary! Opposite is the oldest civic building in Tuscany, the Palazzo dei Priori, built in the first half of the thirteenth century. On its facade are coats of arms carved in terracotta and stone. Spot the wild boar carved on its crenellated tower (hence the tower's nickname: Torre del Porcellino). This *palazzo* houses the city art gallery, and a superb collection it is (Ghirlandaio's *Christ* and an *Annunciation* by Luca Signorelli are among its masterpieces).

Next to the Palazzo dei Priori is a charming building, faced in green and white marble, three-storeyed, with a lovely, two-storeyed asymmetrical tower.

Close by is the cathedral itself (take the Via Giusto Turezza to reach it). First built in the twelfth century and rebuilt in the next, only its doorway and pillars are in marble with simple and very effective geometric patterns. Its bell-tower, built in 1493, is yards away, at the end of a long wall on the other side of the square.

A Volterran architect, Leonardo Ricciarelli, re-did the interior in 1584. The great pink marble pillars (with sixteenth-century capitals) turn out to be not marble at all, but painted. The sixteenth-century coffered roof is deliciously decorated in gold and blue and green. On the high altar is Mino da Fiesole's celebrated ciborium, made in 1471 and flanked by two angels he sculpted to stand on the twisted twelfth-century columns. Here are beautiful early-fifteenth-century gothic stalls, and (in the second chapel to the right of the high altar) a marvellous wooden *Deposition*, carved in 1228 and painted in blue and pink and white, with gold leaf for the garments. In the second chapel to the left of the high altar is a Madonna by the Sienese sculptor Jacopo della Quercia (1374–1438).

The cathedral at Volterra is in truth a treasure-house of exquisite religious art. Find the light to examine its frescos. Marvel at its terracottas – the prettiest (I think) by Zuccaria Zucchi (1473–1544) of Joseph, Mary and the infant Jesus scratching his chin. (Joseph is thinking, puzzled and amazed at the wonder he has been permitted to have had such a part in; the Virgin is praying.) Behind it is a fresco by Benozzo Gozzoli (1420–97) showing the Magi on their way to adore him, one black, one with a turban, one with a crown. In the oratory (to the left as you enter the cathedral) is a sixteenth-century *Ecce Homo* where Jesus has been given a beard as red as his blood and wears a real crown of thorns. Near the oratory door is a *Martyrdom of Saint Sebastian* that surely gave the artist a chance to exult in depicting a superb nude male. Under the twelfth-century pulpit a lion eats a man and another fearsome beast has caught another human being. On the pulpit itself Jesus presides over the Last Supper, giving a morsel to Judas who is about to be taken by the Devil. On other panels are sculpted the Annunciation, Mary greeting Elizabeth, and Abraham and Isaac. Find the unbelievably agile yet still stylized Deposition. (One man takes out a huge nail from the dead Christ with equally huge pincers.) Our own century has contributed an organ to Volterra cathedral, built in 1934 behind the high altar.

Behind the cathedral is the baptistery, an octagonal masterpiece built by Giroldo di Jacopo in 1283, with green and white stripes of marble and a lovely romanesque portal. Inside is another master-piece, Andrea Sansovino's font, dated 1502. Its reliefs depict the baptism of Jesus and the four greatest virtues.

Walk back up the Via Roma where (at no. 1) the former Bishop's Palace now houses the museum of sacred art. (It is closed on Mondays.) Its treasures include a bust of St Linus (the second Pope, born in Volterra) by Andrea della Robbia, a crucifix by Giam-bologna, and a marble polychrome statue of the Virgin and Child by Nicola Pisano. As a plaque at no. 6 Via Roma records, Giordano Bruno once lived here. (Another famous resident of Volterra was the Danish geologist Niels Stenson, who did his most important work here.)

The Via Roma leads you into the Via Buonparenti and then right into the Via Sarti. Here (no. 1) is the Palazzo Solaini, attributed to Antonio da Sangallo the elder, and (nos. 37–39) the fifteenth-century Palazzo Viti, with a lovely mannerist facade by the Flo-rentine architect Bartolommeo Ammannati. At the junction of this street with the Via Guarnicci stands the romanesque church of San Michele (with a Pisan facade, and inside a *Madonna and Child* from the workshop of the Della Robbias).

We turn left along the Via Guarnicci through the Porta Fiorentina to come upon the excavated Roman theatre and baths. A lovely walk west, outside the city walls along the Viale Francesco Ferucci, leads to the Porta San Francesco, where we enter the city again to find the Piazza Inghirami and the church of San Francesco. San Francesco was built in the thirteenth century and many times restored. It boasts a fine fourteenth-century *Madonna* and a terracotta *Pietà* by Zuccaria Zucchi. Steps to the right lead to the gothic chapel of Santa Croce. This delightful church was built in 1315, and a hundred years later Cenni di Francesco Cenni filled it with frescos – depicting the legend of the True Cross (recognizing the value even of its splinters, people are cannily cutting it up), the slaughter of the Innocents (everyone in medieval dress, with an executioner nonchalantly sheathing his sword) and a picture of St Francis receiving the stigmata.

Walk on past the church of San Lino on the left (built between 1480 and 1513) and turn left into the Via Ricciarelli. The painter Daniele Ricciarelli (known as Daniele da Volterra) was born at no. 12 here in the first decade of the sixteenth century. His house, the Casa Ricciarelli, is famous for its unusual windows, set low enough for little children to peep out.

Shortly we arrive back in the Piazza dei Priori and must walk on down the Via Marchesi. If we turn right down the Via Porta all'Arco we reach the Arco Etrusco, with its three huge Etruscan heads. The views from here are splendid, and a little further on at the bottom of the hill stands the romanesque church of Sant'Alessandro. If we continue along the Via Marchese instead of turning right to the Arco Etrusco, we reach the Parco Archeologico Enrico Fiumi – an excellent spot for a picnic – and beyond it the great Fortezza of Volterra. This powerful fortress, dominating the highest hill of the city, is in two parts: the 'old' Rocca to the east was built in 1343 and rebuilt by Lorenzo il Magnifico. The 'new' Rocca to the west, with its five towers, was also built by Lorenzo, in 1472. (The Volterrans call the middle tower of this Rocca 'il Maschio' and the middle tower of the 'old' Rocca 'la Femmina'.)

I and my friends have eaten extremely well in Volterra. (I can recommend, for example, the Ristorante La Grotta, at no. 13 Via Giusta Turazza.) Today the cuisine in this city includes most Tuscan specialities; but if you want to try traditional Volterran dishes –

which are many and delicious – look out for newly hatched eels with sage, eels in *ginocchioni*, mullet or bream from the Arno, pheasant *alla carovana*, and the cheese made from the milk of the local sheep.

9

Some Tuscan Recipes

Cacciucco veloce

olive oil
2 cloves of garlic, finely chopped
2 tablespoons of finely chopped parsley
salt and pepper
1.5 kg (3 lb) sole, hake, swordfish, squid and
cuttlefish (at least 5 different kinds)
two thirds of a cup of dry white wine
4 Italian tomatoes, peeled and chopped
one small hot chilli pepper, seeded
4 tablespoons tomato sauce
slices of fried brown bread

1. Put oil, garlic and parsley into a saucepan, simmer gently. Add salt and pepper to taste.
2. Add the fish, beginning with the larger, tougher varieties. Cook gently for about 8 minutes, then add the wine, tomatoes, chilli pepper and tomato sauce. Simmer until all the fish is thoroughly cooked.
3. Put a slice of fried bread into each bowl and pour over the hot soup, making sure that the different varieties of fish are well mixed.

Ribollita: Tuscan bean and cabbage soup

225 g (8 oz) small haricot beans
a small head of celery, chopped
225 g (8 oz) peeled tomatoes, chopped
2 chopped leeks
olive oil
2 tablespoons of parsley
2 cloves of finely chopped garlic
2.3 l (4 pt) stock
salt and pepper
340 g (12 oz) green cabbage
6 slices of white bread

1. Put the beans in plenty of cold water and bring to the boil; boil for one hour. Drain well.
2. Gently cook the chopped vegetables (but not the cabbage) in the oil for about 10 minutes. Add the garlic. Cook for another 5 minutes.
3. Pour in the hot stock and drained beans; season.
4. Simmer the soup for 1 hour.
5. Cook the cabbage and chop it after having drained it well.
6. Put a slice of bread into each bowl and pile the chopped cabbage on top. Ladle on to this the hot soup. Garnish with the parsley.

Trippa alla Fiorentina

herbs
2 pig's trotters
0.9 kg (2 lb) tripe
0.6 l (1 pt) tomato sauce
Parmesan cheese for garnish

1. In a large pot boil the herbs and pig's trotters with plenty of water.
2. Simmer until the meat is almost done, and then put in the tripe and cook for about another 45 minutes.
3. When the tripe is cooked, cut it quickly into strips, together with the pig's meat.
4. Mix with the hot tomato sauce and divide between the soup bowls. Sprinkle on top the Parmesan cheese.

Crostini di fegatini

340 g (12 oz) chicken livers
flour; a slice of ham
butter; stock; ½ glass white wine
lemon juice; salt and pepper
8 slices of French bread
parsley

1. Clean the chicken livers and chop. Dredge in flour.
2. Cut the ham into small pieces and brown it in the butter.
3. Put in the chicken livers and cook them very gently.
4. After 5 minutes add a little stock, the wine, a squeeze of lemon juice, some parsley and salt and pepper to taste.
5. Cover the pan and cook gently for about 12 minutes.
6. Remove the crusts from the French bread and fry gently in butter. (It should be soft inside.)
7. Arrange the bread on a dish and pour the chicken mixture over it.

Trote al vino bianco

4 medium-sized trout
3 tablespoons flour
salt and pepper
olive oil
3 cloves of garlic, crushed
2 tablespoons chopped parsley
1 glass dry white wine

1. Clean and wash the trout; mix the flour with two teaspoons salt and plenty of pepper. Turn the trout in the mixture.
2. Heat the oil in a frying-pan big enough to hold the four trout; add the garlic and parsley and cook gently for 3 minutes. Add the trout and fry for 4 minutes on each side.
3. When the trout are browned, pour in the wine and cook gently until most of it has evaporated. Remove the fish to a warmed serving dish.
4. Stir the remaining ingredients in the pan and if necessary add a little more wine, to make a creamy sauce. Pour this over the fish.

Fegato di vitello alla toscana

3 tablespoons butter
2 tablespoons olive oil
3 cloves of garlic
1 teaspoon of sage
455 g (1 lb) veal liver, sliced
flour
salt and freshly ground black pepper

1. Melt the butter in a frying-pan; add the oil, garlic and sage. When the garlic darkens, remove it from the pan.
2. Toss the liver in the flour and place it in the hot fat. It should be fried rapidly on both sides, just so that it is cooked through. Season and serve at once.

Petti di pollo alla fiorentina

2 small roasting chickens
salt and pepper
flour
butter

1. Remove the skin from the chickens and cut each side of the breast away from the bone. The meat divides easily into two fillets. Season them and coat with flour.
2. Heat the butter in a large frying-pan and add the fillets.
3. Cook them quite quickly at first until one side is brown, and then turn them over. Reduce the heat and cover the pan.
4. Leave to cook for about 25 minutes.
5. When cooked, place in a serving dish and pour over the remaining fat from the pan.

Further Reading

Burton Anderson, *Vino: the Wines and Winemakers of Italy*, Macmillan, 1980.

William Beckford, *Italy with Sketches of Spain and Portugal* (2 vols.), 2nd ed., 1834.

Hilaire Belloc, *The Path to Rome* (1902), Penguin Books, 1985.

Antony Bertram, *Michelangelo*, Dutton Vista, 1964.

Raymond Bloch, *Etruscan Art*, Barrie & Rockliff, 1966.

Edmund Blunden, *Shelley: A Life Story*, Collins, 1946.

Giovanni Boccaccio, *The Decameron*, trans. G. H. McWilliam, Penguin Books, 1972.

Jacob Burckhardt, *The Architecture of the Italian Renaissance*, trans. James Palmes, Secker, 1984.

Enzo Carli, *Sienese Painting*, Summerfield Press, 1983.

Benvenuto Cellini, *The Life of Benvenuto Cellini, Written by Himself* (1558–62), Phaidon Press, 1949.

Kenneth Clark, *Piero della Francesca*, Phaidon Press, 1951.

Robert Coughlan, *The World of Michelangelo, 1475–1564*, revised edition, Time-Life International, 1972.

Mario Cristofani, *The Etruscans. A New Investigation*, trans. Brian Phillips, Orbis Publishing, 1979.

Charles Dickens, *Pictures from Italy*, John Murray, 1848.

E. M. Forster, *A Room with a View* (1908), Penguin Books, 1955.

E. M. Forster, *Where Angels Fear to Tread* (1905), Penguin Books, 1959.

Stephen Gwynn, *The Life of Horace Walpole*, Thornton Butterworth, 1932.

J. R. Hale, *Renaissance*, Time-Life International, 1966.

Sheila Hale, *The American Express Pocket Guide to Florence and Tuscany*, Mitchell Beazley, 1983.

Denys Hay (ed.), *The Age of the Renaissance*, Thames & Hudson, 1967.

Dorothy Hewlett, *Elizabeth Barrett Browning*, Cassell, 1953.

Elizabeth Jennings (trans.), *The Sonnets of Michelangelo*, The Folio Society, 1961.

D. H. Lawrence, 'Flowery Tuscany', in *Selected Essays*, Penguin Books, 1960.

Eric Linklater, *The Campaign in Italy* (1951), HMSO, 1977.

Christopher Lloyd, *Fra Angelico*, Phaidon Press, 1979.

Alta Macadam, *Florence*, 3rd ed., Ernest Benn, 1984.

Alta Macadam, *Northern Italy from the Alps to Rome*, 8th ed., Ernest Benn, 1984.

Niccolò Machiavelli, *Mandragola*, trans. J. R. Hale, Fantasy Press, Eynsham, Oxford, 1966.

Robert B. Martin, *Tennyson. The Unquiet Heart*, Oxford University Press, 1983.

Andrew Martindale and Edi Baccheschi, *The Complete Paintings of Giotto*, Weidenfeld & Nicolson, 1969.

Georgina Masson, *Italian Gardens*, Thames & Hudson, 1961.

Georgina Masson, *Italian Villas and Palaces*, Thames & Hudson, 1959.

Franz N. Mehring (ed.), *Italy: a Phaidon Cultural Guide*, Phaidon Press, 1985.

John Pope-Hennessy, *Fra Angelico*, Phaidon Press, 1952.

John Pope-Hennessy, *Italian Gothic Sculpture*, Phaidon Press, 1955.

John Pope-Hennessy, *Italian High Renaissance and Baroque Sculpture*, 2nd ed., Phaidon Press, 1970.

Giuseppe Prezzolini, *Machiavelli*, Robert Hale, 1968.

Laura Raison, *Tuscany. An Anthology*, Cadogan Books, 1983.

Cyril Ray, *The New Book of Italian Wines*, Sidgwick & Jackson, 1982.

Elizabeth Romer, *The Tuscan Year. Life and Food in an Italian Valley*, Weidenfeld & Nicolson, 1984.

Francis Russell, 'A means to devotion: Italian art and the clerical connoisseur', in *Country Life*, 5 December 1985.

Victor Selwyn, Dan Davin, Erik de Mauny and Ian Fletcher (eds.), *Poems of the Second World War: the Oasis Selection*, Dent, 1985.

Claire Tomalin, *Shelley and his World*, Thames & Hudson, 1980.

Mark Twain, *Innocents Abroad* (1882), New American Library, 1966.

Nicholas Wadley, *Michelangelo*, Paul Hamlyn, 1969.

Horace Walpole, *Private Correspondence* (4 vols.), Rodwell & Martin, 1820.

Index

INDEX

INDEX